Understanding Developmental Disorders

For G and Pooch, with love

Understanding Developmental Disorders

A Causal Modelling Approach

John Morton

 **Blackwell**
Publishing

BLACKWELL PUBLISHING
350 Main Street, Malden, MA 02148-5020, USA
9600 Garsington Road, Oxford OX4 2DQ, UK
550 Swanston Street, Carlton, Victoria 3053, Australia

First published 2004 by Blackwell Publishing Ltd

4   2008

Library of Congress Cataloging-in-Publication Data

Morton, John, 1933–
   Understanding developmental disorders : a causal modelling
approach / John Morton.
        p. ; cm.
   Includes bibliographical references and index.
   ISBN 978-0-631-18757-8 (hardback : alk. paper) — ISBN 978-0-631-18758-5
(pbk. : alk. paper)
1. Developmental disabilities—Etiology.   2. Child development
deviations—Etiology.   3. Conduct disorders in children—Etiology.
4. Cognition disorders in children—Etiology.   5. Mental retardation—
Etiology.   6. Parent and child.   7. Cognition.   8. Causation.
   [DNLM: 1. Developmental Disabilities—physiopathology—Child.
2. Developmental Disabilities—psychology—Child.   3. Models,
Theoretical.   WS 350.6 M889 2005]   I. Title.

RJ506.D47M67 2004
616.85′88071—dc22

1005701322

2004009013

ı0057O ı32ᒎ
ISBN: 978-0-631-18757-8 (hardback : alk. paper)
ISBN: 978-0-631-18758-5 (paperback : alk. paper)

A catalogue record for this title is available from the British Library.

Set in 10/12.5pt Baskerville
by Graphicraft Limited, Hong Kong
Printed and bound in Singapore
by C.O.S. Printers Pte Ltd

For further information on
Blackwell Publishing, visit our website:
www.blackwellpublishing.com

CONTENTS

Preface and Acknowledgements

Human development can be seen as the unfolding of a particular pattern. Genes are responsible for producing proteins that lead to structures of various kinds – legs and hands and hearts and tongues and, the bit that concerns us, brains. Within the brain there is structure, and this is formed under the influence of the genes in complex ways, together with the influence of the environment, both internal and external. There is a lot of variation in the genes, and a lot of variation in the environment, but the result is a human being. The variations in the genes and the variations in the environment give rise to individual differences – in eye colour, height, temperament and intelligence – within the range of what is often termed normality. This is a difficult term, however, since what is normal is often confused with what is acceptable. A man who is seven foot tall is acceptable in the context of a professional basketball team, but not in the context of an airline seat, particularly next to me!

Things can go wrong with early brain development: there might an unfortunate combination of allelic variants of genes; one of the critical genes might be damaged; the environment might be unsuitable – for example, the intra-uterine environment provided by a drug-taking mother. As result of one of these misfortunes, the child develops outside the normal range – the problem may be a general one or may be specific, but in either case some health or education professional is going to want to describe the condition and relate that child to other children who are similar. The reason for doing this may be to help with prognosis – to predict what the future may be like for that child. The description will be of use in helping to understand the nature of the condition, predicting other kinds of problems, and giving a hint as to what might happen in various situations or in the future. It will also be help to guide any treatment plan.

Later on, the interaction of the child with his or her environment may make things better or worse. In some cases, the environment may be so aversive that children with physically normal brains may develop in a way that leads them to be termed abnormal in some way. Such children will also attract labels.

Sometimes, the labels that are used relate only to the child's behaviour – conduct disorder is a good example. Sometimes the labels refer to a specifiable genetic problem – William's syndrome is an example here. In other cases the labels have deeper significance, with the defining features being more complex – autism is a good example here. One of the problems with the labels is that different people mean different things by the same label. Take 'dyslexia', for example. For some people, this is simply a term applied to children whose reading age is significantly below their mental age (usually by two years). For others, it means people with a deficiency in their magnocellular cortex. For yet others, it means people with a particular deficiency in phonological processing (and who, curiously, may have no observable problem in reading!). How can we discuss such different types of theories in the same breath?

I have felt for many years that understanding developmental disorders requires us to think about biological, cognitive, behavioural and environmental factors, and to discover the causal relationships among these elements. This is a way of thinking about developmental disorders which grew from my time at the Medical Research Council's Cognitive Development Unit (CDU) in London. My colleague Uta Frith and I felt the need for clarity in theorizing about this process and developed a methodology for enabling that clarity. We called the method 'causal modelling', and wrote a very long chapter about it (Morton & Frith 1995). This book is an extension of that work. This book is about the nature of causal theories.

The actual theories that I use are partially chosen for illustrative reasons, as I will repeatedly remind you. What I cannot do here is to list all the most up-to-date theories of each of the developmental disorders. To give a complete up-to-date account of any one of autism, dyslexia, conduct disorder or ADHD would take a book of the length of this one. So I have taken the theories I am most familiar with, and those that illustrate the range of theories that exist. I don't think that use of the causal modelling method makes any of these theories more correct.

Instead, it helps to identify weak spots in the theories, and also helps us to see the relationships between different theories. This makes it easier to set up ways of testing the theories against each other. This is what the book is about. At the CDU, we did develop our own beliefs about autism and dyslexia, for example, and, although I have tried to be dispassionate I may seem to favour those beliefs here. However, these beliefs are not fixed, and it is important for the reader to realize that what I want to communicate in this book is a way of thinking about different theories of developmental disorder. I am proposing a tool. This tool has been found useful by students and by practitioners, as well as by fellow scientists. It is offered as a way to help you formulate your own theory of any developmental disorder as well as a way of understanding other people's theories.

Of course, you cannot just pick up a complex tool and use it; you need to think about the problem appropriately. Using causal modelling encourages you to think about development in a particular way. Specifically, you have to learn to work productively with cognitive concepts, and clarify in your own mind the distinction between cognition and behaviour. It was the application of these principles to the problems of developmental disorders that I learned from Uta Frith. In a sense, causal modelling was my attempt to formalize the way in which Uta thought about autism and dyslexia. Her voice will be heard often through the book, and the only reason she is not co-authoring it is that she is too busy moving on our understanding of these disorders. I hope that she endorses much of what I have written, but I excuse her from endorsing it all.

The book has chapters of two kinds, those concerned with setting up and explaining what causal modelling is and how to do it, and those chapters illustrating how causal modelling can help us to understand and compare different theories of particular developmental disorders. Since this is a book on causal modelling, I will rarely refer to any theory that does not make causal claims about the syndrome. The major exception is in the chapter on conduct disorder (chapter 9), where, following Krol et al. (2004), I look at the structure of the main theories of conduct disorder, which are not causal in nature.

It is worth noting briefly the contrast between causal modelling as I have been describing it here and structural equation modelling, which is also sometimes called causal modelling (for an overview, see Fife-Shaw 2000). Structural equation modelling is an analytical technique that is applied to data. Roughly speaking, you look for *latent variables* that mediate between measured variables. There may be an *a priori* theory connecting the variables, but the techniques do not depend on this. All you need know is that this is not what I am going to talk about.

In chapter 1, I introduce the notion of cause, comparing the everyday use of the term with a more scientific use. This discussion leads us to appreciate that when we are trying to account for a developmental disorder we have to distinguish between internal and external factors and, within the internal factors, we have to distinguish between biology, cognition and behaviour. I then discuss the need for a scientific tool, a tool to aid thinking, a tool which uses diagrams instead of words. Here I point out for the first time, as I will point out repeatedly, that use of the tool does not commit one to any particular theoretical position.

In chapter 2, I spend some time explaining why the study of developmental disorders requires us to consider cognition. This is the only theoretical point that I argue for in the whole book. If you don't believe that cognition has any role to play in the study of developmental disorders, and if I fail to convince you in this chapter, then you had better stop reading and I will give you your money back. But your reasoning had better be good!

The elements of causal modelling are introduced in chapter 3. The fundamental principle is that the verbal expression of your theory gets converted into a diagram. The notation is very simple, and I work through three examples of different types to give you a feel for what I am trying to do.

Chapter 4 is of the second kind. In it I take you through some of the history of the development of causal modelling – the evolution of the 'mentalizing deficit' account of autism.

In chapter 4, a number of issues raise themselves about the causal modelling technique. In chapter 5 I bring these issues together in the form of a number of maxims. These maxims go towards helping to establish good practice in formulating theories of developmental disorder and representing them in a causal model.

In chapter 6, I go through most of the current alternative theories of the origin of autism and frame them using the principles of causal modelling. This exercise helps us to see the relationships among the various theories, and pinpoints which theories are insufficiently explicit or are ambiguous in expression.

One of the major issues which becomes evident in chapter 4 is that of diagnosis. Thus, if we do not know what autism is we cannot have any theory about its development, nor can we properly diagnose it.

In chapter 6, we face these issues and show how causal modelling can help us to reconcile different approaches to diagnosis.

Chapter 7 takes up some of the general points raised in the previous chapter, concerning the notation of causal modelling and the ways that are available for elaborating our causal theories.

In chapter 8, I apply the lessons we have just learned to a discussion of the various current theories of dyslexia. In particular, the causal modelling method enables us to show clearly how some theories can be embedded in other theories, rather than being directly opposed. In this way, the debate about dyslexia can be focused on specific questions rather than involving major confrontations.

In chapter 9, I look at theories of ADHD. More properly, this is a set of disorders that are usually defined in terms of behaviour, without regard to the origins of the behaviour. This has led to much confusion over the years and it is only recently that decent cognitive theories have emerged.

Chapter 10 is devoted to a detailed analysis of conduct disorder. This work, based on a collaboration with Nicole Krol and Eric de Bruyn of Nijmegen, focuses on a disorder to which there is thought to be a major contribution of environmental and developmental factors. In this respect, the disorder is different from autism and dyslexia, for which there is a dominant well established biological/cognitive base. In this chapter I also compare causal modelling with other ways of talking about developmental disorders, particularly psychosocial pathways.

In chapter 11, I look at some of the more general issues of the relationships among the three levels of description; in particular, the relation between brain and cognition. The use of causal modelling has sharpened my own view of this relation.

Now let me say two words concerning what this book is not about. To start with, it is not about the nature of cognitive mechanisms. I do not address the question: How does cognition cause behaviour? This is not my concern here. I will say more about this in chapter 2. Nor will I say much on the topic of the relationship between a developmental disorder and an acquired disorder, although I will touch on that topic in chapter 8.

Developmental psychology is difficult, more difficult, I think, than constructing theories of adult cognitive function. I never managed to become a competent developmentalist, but managed in the CDU environment by being able to bring theoretical methods from the world of cognitive psychology, and by having support and continual interaction from a number of outstanding developmental scientists. Their influence pervades this book. I have already mentioned Uta Frith, and I should add Annette Karmiloff-Smith, the late Rick Cromer, Alan Leslie, Mike Anderson and Mark Johnson. Of the many friends, visitors and short-term staff that we had at the CDU, Sue Carey, Anne Christophe, Mike Cole, Francesca Happé, Lila Gleitman, Mani das Gupta, Geoff Hall, Kang Lee, Jean Mandler, David Olson, P. Prakash and Prentice Starkey all played a role in my education.

In relation to the manuscript of the book, thanks are particularly due to Sarah-Jayne Blakemore, Elisabeth Hill, Franck Ramus and Essi Viding, who I have encouraged to be remorseless and detailed in criticism and who have repaid me handsomely! I have not always taken their advice, and no doubt will regret it. Mike Anderson, James Blair, Nichole Krol and Edmund Sonuga-Barke have also made invaluable suggestions. Sarah White has helped in many ways, particularly organizational.

Most of all I am indebted to my wife, Guinevere Tufnell, who has not only tolerated the five-year incubation of the book but has added invaluable clinical insight throughout.

The figures were drawn using CHARTIST™.

John Morton

1 ■ Introducing Cause

Cause and public issues ■

'Working Mums Blamed for Children's Failures' is a typical newspaper headline of today. As government and other organizations vie to shed responsibility, the supposed reasons for undesirable states of society are tossed around with abandon. These issues are so imbued with political, social and moral values that rational discussion seems impossible and not much changed over the past 20 years. How could working mothers be the cause of their children's failure? And what might one do about it if they were?

For the layman, there is a fairly obvious relationship between cause and remedy. So, if there is supposed to be a particular cause for an unwanted outcome, you can undo the outcome by removing the cause. It is obvious, isn't it? If the tap drips, fit a new washer. Although many government policies seem to be based on this principle, human problems are rarely that simple.[1]

Let us look more at working mums. The headline, quoted from *The Guardian*, was a very clear causal statement concerning the relationship between mothers working full time (as opposed to part time) and the school achievement of their children. This could be illustrated as in figure 1.1, where the arrow is intended to indicate a causal relationship, and the boxes are only there to package the text.

---

[1] A notable example is the logic that says that the way to stop an individual from committing another crime is to lock him up (this, of course, is a politician's logic, not a scientist's). Could it be, here, that it is the individual's liberty that is the causal factor? Take away the liberty and you take away the crime?

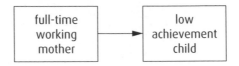

Figure 1.1

The remedy is clear. Use everyday reasoning: if A causes B, then if A is prevented, B will not occur. So, mothers with school-age children should be forbidden from working full time and this will result in increased school achievement! In these ways, strong government can be effective! Expressed like this, the conclusion is clearly monstrous. But why? The issue is not one of individual liberty. Suppose, instead of *compelling* mothers to work part time, that the state *rewarded* them for doing so. Would this be any better? This is one case in which common sense and other methods of data acquisition will be in agreement: it would depend. Without understanding the mechanism underlying the relation between mothers working and their children's school achievement, we cannot begin a rational approach to the solution. What is missing? One assumption is that mothers who move from full-time to part-time working will spend the surplus in the home and would thus be profitably available to the children.

Already, then, we see that the notion of full-time working as a cause is insufficient. We will return to the mother in a moment, but there are factors to do with the child which have to be addressed first. First of all, it must be apparent that, within the group of children in the study, there must be a vast number of individual factors that contribute to their performance. Let us for the moment include them all under the heading of the *child's state of mind* and represent that this is a factor in determining

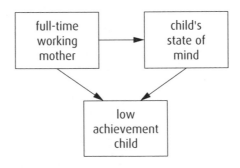

Figure 1.2

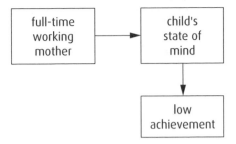

Figure 1.3

the level of achievement (behaviour) of the child. I diagram this in figure 1.2. This is not meant to be a profound thought, but we will see that it makes a difference to the way in which we think about the problem.

The next stage is to see that it is inappropriate to represent mothers working full time as having a direct effect on achievement. This is because the achievement referred to is a piece of behaviour – performance on school tests – which has an immediate cause, as it were, in terms of the intellectual capability of the child (plus other internal factors, such as motivation). The state of the child, then, has rather to be inserted into the chain of reasoning between the mother's behaviour and the child's achievement, as in figure 1.3.

In line with this, the causal diagram in figure 1.4 suggests that mothers who work full time are crucially not available to the children in certain ways. In other words, the absence of the mother causes something. What might that be? One suggestion is that if the children just returning home from school have nobody to talk to, they become

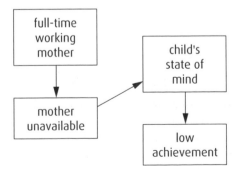

Figure 1.4

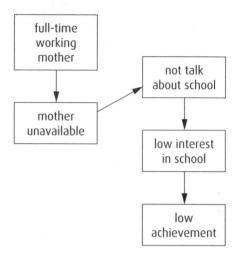

Figure 1.5

uninterested in school and this results in lower performance. This is diagrammed in figure 1.5. Such a statement would require some elaboration before it could be considered serious, and it might be interesting to consider the reverse relationship – that if the mother was home when the child finished school, the child would be able to talk to her and interest in school would be maintained. In other words, it seems that we still have a question about which way round the cause is; whether absent mothers depress performance or present mothers increase performance, or both. Before we can find a remedy, we have to discover which way round it is. If we were to go with the lack of interest in school as a cause, then we could correct it by finding some other way of increasing interest which did not involve the mother. But if it is the absence of the mother herself that is important, the lack of interest in school may be a symptom, and attempting to correct that (without the mother) would be pointless. Note that the data remain the same on all these interpretations, although the solutions differ.

Even with these moves, there are two obvious problems. The first is that there seem to be too many classes of exception, groups of mother/child pairs for whom the postulated relationship is manifestly incorrect. Examples would be children of depressed mothers, and those of mothers working full time at home. There is some research showing that the children of depressed mothers have low school achievement whether the mothers are at home or not. I leave it to you to imagine the complications involved with mothers who are working full time at home. Note that *individual* exceptions in the level of performance are of no interest to this line of thinking. The thrust of the research is that certain effects obtain in general over the population as a whole. There will be both high and low performers wherever the mother is. For any individual, then, the question is not whether or not the child has done well or badly by some absolute measure, but whether he or she would have done better or worse if the mother had behaved differently. In general, such things are unknowable.

The second problem, already referred to, is that the mother, simply by being in the home, cannot be the *direct* cause of any change in intellectual capacity or motivation. We have to determine a *mechanism* to connect the two. Remember we are trying to understand the relationship between the mother's presence in the home and the child's educational achievements. *Being available* may be a useful concept, but is scarcely a mechanism. More specifically, one might argue that the mother's mere presence in the house at critical moments is not sufficient to produce the effects. Rather, the mother has to behave in particular ways, to be specified, in order to influence the child.[2] Even more likely would be an indirect effect, where the mother was fulfilling a pedagogical function, actually increasing the teaching time and the child's intellectual capacity. Such a proposition would be testable by looking at the mother's educational level, which would be expected to be closely related to her ability to teach the child. There are other possibilities, however, most obvious of which is that some mothers, perhaps by their presence in the house with the child and the interest that they show, have an effect on the child's motivation, which, in turn, increases the capacity to learn.

This extended, but still rather shallow, analysis illustrates how populist attempts to assign cause, blame and responsibility with the aim of correcting a problem are doomed to fail through their lack of subtlety. There are so many other factors, some of which could be major – for example, the effect of the absent father. In general, the scientific focus is missing. For a developmental scientist, the first trick is to define the problem properly. 'Children's Failures' is too broad a category to be subject to proper analysis. As we will see, the identification of the cause

---

[2] One mother I know of, expressing her concern over her 15-year-old son's tribulations, was told by him 'Why don't you find another interest?'

of a disorder is very much tied up with issues of diagnosis, treatment and management. But we will also see that classical development disorders, such as autism and dyslexia, although these are the terms used in diagnosis, turn out to be very complex when examined under the spotlight of causal analysis.

Cause and individual events: 'Why did Romeo die?' ▪

Is the problem with working mothers that there are too many exceptions? Would we gain more understanding by looking at individual cases? To test this, I asked a number of friends why Romeo died. The responses were quite varied, but the general impression was that it was not a good question.

'OK, what *caused* Romeo's death?'

This was a little better. 'Love' was the most usual initial answer, but the question invariably provoked a lot of argument and successfully diverted people away from the war in the Balkans – the news topic of the day.

The kinds of answers that my friends came up with were varied and often strongly held. Was Romeo's death caused by Juliet's apparent death? By an underlying depressive state that ran in his family? By the drug Juliet took earlier, that persuaded Romeo that she was dead? By the feud between their families? Or by the parlous state of the postal service between Verona and Mantua?[3]

What we want to find are more or less proximal steps in the chain – cause and effect in a disciplined and systematic way. The most obvious answer is:

'Romeo was killed by the poison that he took.'

This is a scientifically acceptable answer. There is a gap in the causal chain – Did the poison lead to heart failure or brain failure? – but that doesn't matter if you know where the gap is and how to go about filling it. So, we might not know how that particular poison works

---

[3]   In fact, Friar John, who had been entrusted with an explanatory letter from Juliet to Romeo, got caught up in a health scare and never managed to leave town.

other than that it acts quickly[4] and, with most actors, painlessly. But the kind of information that we would need to fill the gap in the chain will be clear. However, there is something rather pedantic about this answer.

Let us now take another answer that aspires to scientific status. Suppose it were the case that suicidal tendencies were heritable and we had evidence that the Montague family had some long history of assorted suicides, associated, say, with depression. We would still not be at all happy with a claim such as

'Romeo's genes caused him to commit suicide.'

Even if we accept that Romeo was depressive, it would have taken a remarkable conflation of circumstances to make him take the poison. A stronger personality would have said 'Mother was right. You can't trust those Capulets', but Romeo's genetic weakness showed up at that instant. Clearly, the jump from gene to behaviour in one go is too much. The gaps in the causal chain are chasms. One reason for being particularly unhappy with this explanation in the current scientific climate is that gene-to-behaviour statements give the illusion of having settled an issue, of having explained something, in spite of the explanatory chasm. On the contrary, I would claim that such statements only sketch one of the many jobs that have to be done. It should be clear that committing suicide is not one of things that genes code for.[5] So the job that has to be done will involve bridging the gap in some degree of detail. I insist on this for two reasons. The first is because it is becoming clear that almost every ability, trait or behavioural tendency is at least slightly heritable. In such a world, the claim of partial heritability for something, without some significant support to the causal chain, adds absolutely nothing. By a parallel argument, the bald claim that the environment exerts an influence on something is equally uninteresting. We have to be more specific.

The second reason for insisting on some kind of detail in the specification of genetic influence is that the probability of the outcome given the gene is so low, depending as it does on a multitude of environmental circumstances as well as on the presence of other genes.

[4]   (For the benefit of all those people who believe that Romeo stabbed himself:) 'O true apothecary! Thy drugs are quick. Thus with a kiss I die.' *Dies.*
[5]   Freudian notions concerning the universality of the death wish notwithstanding.

However, the specification of the environmental contribution to Romeo's death is equally shaky:

'Romeo committed suicide because he was brought up in a violent culture (where life was valued little and the means of killing easy to come by).'

Again, the gaps left by this sort of explanation are simply too great to allow the feeling of a satisfying answer. This is as vague an answer as the genetic explanation; the supposed cause here is much too ill-defined. Consider the intuitive psychological explanation:

'Romeo committed suicide because he thought that Juliet was dead.'

At first glance, this familiar phrasing in everyday language may look acceptable, but at second glance, it scarcely approaches the issue. This explanation, too, leaves enormous gaps. It implies that he did not want to live without her. However, if Romeo had thought that Juliet had died in a traffic accident, for example, on her way to see him, we could imagine that his response might have been different.

The drama, of course, does not use a single cause. Many factors conspire together to bring about the conclusion, which is all the more dramatic and poignant for having been multiply avoidable. Indeed, one might say that the whole play is a causal model for the finalé.

Everyday transactions provide a number of reasons for looking at cause. The most common, perhaps, is as a means of establishing responsibility for a particular event. In this way, we can establish blame (and our own innocence). Alternatively, we might want to know why something happened in order to find out what to do about the situation right now, or how to prevent the same thing happening again in the future. Such uses are not relevant to our current aims. Notions of responsibility or of cause of individual events are well suited to courts of law or detective novels. They are not usually suited to scientific questioning.

We are left, then, with some clues as to what is needed for a scientifically valid causal explanation. The example showed that cause and effect must neither be broad nor be too far removed from each other in conceptual space. In addition, it is clear that when we try to examine the individual case, it's easy to become overwhelmed with detail. There are a variety of individual factors that are central to the story and that have claims for a role in determining the outcome in this individual case. Some of these factors are unique to this particular case, and knowing them would not help at all in understanding other cases or preventing future accidents. For other factors, there might be generalizations that could be formulated, such as *don't mess around with poisons* or *don't get involved with someone whose mother disapproves of you murderously.*[6] In the end, however, science has to deal with aggregates and probabilities – not with individuals and certainties – and a more appropriate framework for Romeo would be that of psychosocial pathways, where the primary concept is one of risk (of suicide) rather than cause (of death). Psychosocial pathways are touched on in chapter 3.

Some more reasons for not looking at individual cases ■

Suppose we were asked whether a particular eight-year-old would become delinquent in the future. We would need a variety of information, some to do with the child and some with the current environment. Perhaps we would ask first whether the eight-year-old was a boy. Knowing the sex of the child will get us a long way – we have information that violence is much more common in males – though it would be strange to attribute maleness as a *causal* factor.[7] Instead, being male is what we would call a *risk factor,* following Rutter (1989). Certain personality characteristics will also be important. Furthermore, we would want to obtain information on the child's parents: their past history, their employment, social class and marital status, the degree of marital discord and their current income. In this information, the contribution of social and genetic factors is unknown, and the interaction between them is extremely complex. Strictly speaking, in order to start to disentangle the variables, we would have to randomly assign people to live in large housing estates or lush penthouses. There might be opposition to such a trial. In any case, as scientists we would not be able to make a prediction for a particular child. We may, of course, use population statistics, as insurance companies do, in order to quote the *probability* of a child becoming a future delinquent, given certain genetic and

---

[6] Lady Capulet said that she was going to contact a hit-man in Mantua to deal with Romeo – but that message didn't get through in time either.
[7] The y-chromosome or testosterone might, however, be arguable.

environmental conditions. This is not the same as understanding the *causes* of delinquency.[8]

Is it possible that understanding the causes of delinquency can be achieved by careful longitudinal studies of many specially selected families? The issues are complex, and I am not an expert in the technical job of examining longitudinal data. I am wary of this approach, however, because longitudinal data is only data about a selection of behaviours, and in an area such as delinquency, different behaviours are found at different ages and in different contexts. Tracing something like an underlying propensity to violence would need many preparatory studies just to define and validate suitable measures. From time to time I will review the work on psychosocial pathways, which seems to lead to an interpretation of *disadvantage* that is different from *cause*.

The need for a framework for thinking in ▨

The analysis in the previous two sections has given some hints as to where we are going. The cause of an individual suicide may be impossible to establish definitively, even though we might be able to say more about the contributions of genes and environment to patterns of individual differences in the risk of suicide more generally. But, as the brief analysis of delinquency indicated, we must be careful to distinguish contingency from cause. We have also seen that broad claims about genes or about the role of particular aspects of the environment – the kinds of account beloved of politicians – require more circumspection. Of course, science does not always provide the circumspection required. Newspapers may be quick to produce headlines assigning responsibility for promiscuity, homosexuality and so on to particular genes, but behind a lot of these stories is a scientist who has made a similar claim on the basis of inadequate evidence, and with the underlying message that no other account need be given.

To protect us from error, we need a scientific framework which is suited to the task that we have set ourselves. I explain what I mean by the term 'framework', and how it differs from 'model' and 'theory', in box 1.1.

---

[8] Of course, such an actuarial exercise may be the appropriate thing to do in some contexts. For example, it would be the appropriate way of estimating the future needs for social services in a particular region. The question of *cause*, in any of its senses, would not be relevant here unless there were a massive break with tradition, with a multi-agency, long-term attack on the problem.

Box 1.1 A note on models and related things

In my thinking, I make distinctions between *models, theories* and *frameworks*. Other people may use these terms differently, so, to avoid unnecessary confusion, I will introduce my own distinctions. The reason why I am stressing this is that you can use the causal modelling *framework* that I am proposing without believing our particular *theory* about, say, autism or dyslexia. Indeed, it seems to be the case that my colleagues and I become more convinced of the potential of alternative causal theories after we have expressed them in a causal modelling notation.

Framework

A framework is a set of ground rules that a community agree on to enable them to express and discuss ideas in a commonly understood fashion. This agreement is usually tacit. These rules would include the types of data that are allowed to influence or test a theory. When people who are operating within different frameworks disagree, it is often because they do not understand each other or because they have conflicting priorities, not because they disagree about the facts or their interpretation. In fact, both people could be correct.* Note that a part-icular framework may not allow the expression of certain kinds of data. Thus, the framework within which most linguistic theory is expressed does not allow discussion of the time course of speech. This is because linguistic theory is concerned with the underlying structure of language, not with language behaviour. Such facts put a systematic restriction on the range of an individual framework, and, it might also turn out, put restrictions on the scope of the causal modelling framework.

Theory

A theory is an expression of a hypothesized relation among data. Since there is always a choice of data to include in theories, they will always be systematically incomplete. Theories must always be more general in their form of expression than the data that they attempt to encompass. Hence, a theory will always make a prediction about new data. Note that a particular theory can usually be expressed in different frame-works. Thus, two superficially different theories may cover the same data set and make exactly the same predictions about new data. An analogy for this, which might be useful, is the alternative expressions of a circle as $x^2 + y^2 = c^2$ and $r = c$ (for all $\emptyset$). Such alternatives can also be known as *notational variants*. One worked out example of this is the relation among associative nets, schema frameworks and the Headed Records framework in accounting for memory phenomena such as context-sensitive recall (Morton et al. 1985; Morton & Bekerian 1986).

Model

A **model** is a way of presenting a theory. The modelling *method* (such as the one I am going to present) is ideally free of both framework and theory assumptions. The model is often a means of generating predictions from the underlying theory. In practice, the modelling itself reveals assumptions that have been made, so that models often look different from the originating theory. From my own work, an example of this is in the way in which the **logogen model** (Morton 1969) handles the interaction between stimulus and contextual information in the recognition of words in context. The underlying theory merely specified that this interaction took place. The mathematical model required a specification of the nature of the interaction (in fact, the addition of activation).

It is important not to confuse the form of a model with its content. For example, the form of expression of much information processing theory has been that of labelled boxes joined by arrows. The underlying theories are sometimes dismissed as 'mere boxes and arrows models', as though the boxes or the arrows themselves had inherent content that could be true or false. I use boxes and arrows throughout this book, but usually they have a different meaning from that in an information processing model or an information flow model (as in figure 10.3). Of course, anything expressed by boxes and arrows can also be expressed in other ways – including, if you have that particular pathology, words.

---

*Note that I am not saying that any story is as good as any other story. I happen to believe that one particular story is the correct one. However, that story could be told in a number of different ways, and it would still be the same story. What is told is the science. Where things go wrong is when the limitations of a framework go unnoticed. For example, interpreting the concept of intelligence within a social framework is fine and might help in the formulation of egalitarian policies. However, the inability to represent biologically given individual differences in intelligence within such a framework should not – but, regrettably, sometimes does – lead one to deny the possibility of such individual differences.

What we need is a framework within which *causal* theories can be expressed. What properties would be good to have in this framework? Here are a few:

1 The framework would allow us to represent complex claims about the cause of a disorder in an easily understood manner.
2 It would require us to explicitly distinguish causal relationships from merely contingent ones.
3 It would allow both genetic and environmental factors to enter into any claims.
4 It would distinguish clearly between cognitive and behavioural factors (I will say more about this in the next chapter).
5 It would enable us to represent alternative theories in an easily comparable form – essentially, the framework would be theoretically neutral.

Unfortunately, there does not seem to be such a framework. The nearest are the kinds of representations that have been developed for behavioural genetics and psychosocial pathways. These are both ways of representing the outcome of certain kinds of statistical analyses on population data, and so do not enable us to make explicit distinctions between association (contingency) and cause. So, Uta Frith and I set out to develop a new framework that would help us to think about cause in developmental disorders. We have called this the **causal modelling** framework (Morton & Frith 1995). It is important to note that a framework, of itself, makes no empirical claims about any pathological condition, nor does it commit the user to any particular theory about anything (see box 1.1). This feature makes a framework a neutral forum for the comparison of alternative, or even contradictory, theories. Our aim is that any coherent theory about developmental psychopathology should be expressible within the framework. From this point of view, it doesn't matter if you consider a particular theory to be wrong, or incomplete. If it is coherent, and it is supposed to do with cause, then it will still be expressible within the framework. For example, suppose that there are two claims about a particular condition, one that it has a single genetic cause and the other that there are multiple genetic causes. The consequences of these two alternative claims can be mapped out over biological, cognitive and behavioural levels in ways that enable them to be compared. When the two competing theories are represented in a directly comparable fashion in this way, empirical data can then be brought to bear on those points that emerge as critical in deciding between alternative theories. If a theory is unclear, however, or inconsistent or simply confused, then our aim is that the framework can be used to isolate the problem, and help to discover possible coherent theories behind the confusion. Put more bluntly, you can use the causal modelling framework to talk about any developmental disorder, even if you disagree with everything that my colleagues have written about that disorder. Indeed, if you want to persuade us that we are wrong in our views about autism or dyslexia, for example, you are more likely to do so within the framework than outside it, since, inside the framework, you can be more certain that we will understand your ideas and accept that your causal arguments are coherent. But let me stress again that my aim in this book is not to debate theories but to examine ways of representing (modelling) theories.

Creating a tool: the problem of notation ■

In the course of establishing diagnostic categories, and in the course of attempts to explain developmental psychopathology, a variety of claims are made that touch on the principles I have mentioned above. The debate between proponents of opposing views is often confused. There is a lack of clarity of expression, as well as much unresolved conflict. There is sometimes even more conflict between people whose ideas turn out to be minor variations on each other. There is a sociological account of some of this – to do with the fury of competition for the same piece of turf – but much of it, I believe, is because the only tool that most people have for communicating their ideas is language. Purely verbal expression of immensely complex ideas is difficult to achieve. I find that such expression of ideas is even more difficult to comprehend. This is because language is predominantly linear, while ideas are multidimensional in their relationships. I propose that some of the problems of understanding what is going on can be relieved by use of a graphical notation within which the underlying ideas can be expressed. A graphical representation of ideas can reveal structure that was previously obscured.

This is really a very simple idea. Take the following problem:

> Jim was sitting on Helga's left. Helga was opposite Mary, who was between Pierre and Lorraine. Pierre was on Jim's left. Who was opposite Lorraine?

Such a problem is difficult to solve without constructing a diagram of the seating plan:

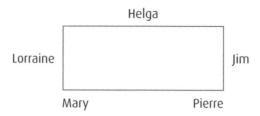

With such a plan, much more difficult problems become child's play.

An example of the limits of language – be careful when you read this ▪

Let me begin to illustrate the limitations of language with an example from our own work. In Morton and Frith (1993a), we comment on some of the implications of a paper by Cossu et al. (1993). These authors showed that Italian children with Down's syndrome could read non-words and yet failed on certain phoneme segmentation tasks. These are tasks in which the children are asked to play games with sounds. For example, they might be asked to delete the first sound in the word 'table' – in which case the correct answer is 'able'. These two facts, it was claimed, contradicted certain theories about reading acquisition. In commenting on this paper, Uta and I found that we needed to specify some of the cognitive abilities that were necessary if the children were going to carry out particular tasks successfully. To start with, what ability was necessary for the child to be able to succeed on typical phoneme segmentation tasks? Let's say that successful performance on such tasks requires both the development of a **grapheme–phoneme** (**GP**) correspondence system and a competence in relation to phonemes, which could be called **implicit phoneme awareness** (**iPA**). The GP system would also be a prerequisite for non-word reading tasks and the iPA system would be needed for the understanding of rhyme. Both GP and iPA depend on a common underlying phonological system, P. The factor M, which underlies meta-representational skills, is a prerequisite for iPA (but not GP). We continue:

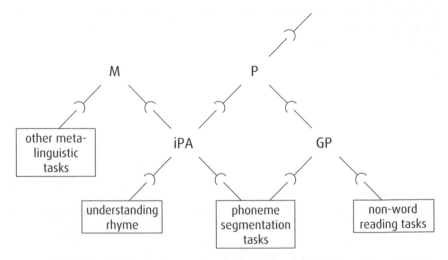

Figure 1.6 A developmental contingency model (Morton 1986) to account for the data in Cossu et al. (1993). The horseshoe shape between two elements is to be understood in the following way: the former is necessary for the normal development of the latter. The detail of the diagram might be intelligible in conjunction with the text (from Morton & Frith 1993a).

> it can be seen that failure in phoneme segmentation tasks would result from lack of development of iPA. This could be due to an absence of P (which would also cause a lack of GP) or from absence of M. We assume that this is the case for the Down Syndrome children and predict that they fail both on iPA dependent tasks and on other metalinguistic tasks. (Morton & Frith 1993a, p. 295)

I predict that most of you will not have too easy a time with the above passage. In fact, in the journal article, the prediction was accompanied by five diagrams, the last of which is reproduced in figure 1.6. The diagrams make the descriptions seem self-evident, even if you are unclear about the nature of the components.

For a second example, take the following passage from Russell (1996). This is a little unfair, since the passage in question was preceded by 250 pages of closely argued text concerning the nature of the cognitive deficit in autism.

> If agency plays the role in the development of self awareness – or 'ego development' – that I have claimed it does, then human beings with congenital impairments in agency will undergo deviant ego-development;

and if ego-development is impaired so too will be the acquisition of a theory of mind. My concern here is with what I called 'mind$_o$' – the individual's immediate knowledge of being a centre of responsibility for his or her action-generated experiences, of having the power to determine what is experienced and thus of being the 'owner' of a mental life. If there is an early impairment in the ability to determine what one does and how one's attention is directed then there will develop an inadequate sense of oneself... (Russell 1996, p. 253)

I think that this causal model would be considerably easier to appreciate with a diagram. One of the problems is that Russell uses different words to refer to the same conceptual entity. Thus, we have

the individual's immediate knowledge of being a centre of responsibility for his or her action-generated experiences

meaning the same as (having the same reference in the argument as)

the ability to determine what one does

and

the power to determine what is experienced

referring to the same idea as

the ability to determine how one's attention is directed

This is an interesting literary convention, not to fatigue the reader with repetition of word or phrase, but for certain kinds of modelling and deductive thinking one needs to be sure that the referent has not changed in the smallest way. We are all familiar with the kind of creeping referent that can occur in political settings, where the argument starts with, say, children with mothers who work, moves to children who play in the street, thence to juvenile delinquents and finally to psychopathic murderers.

Words can be sharp and precise: they convey nuances in a way that a newly invented visual notation cannot possibly offer. I wonder, however, whether in scientific debates the sharpness of verbal definitions sometimes exceeds the refinement of the underlying thought. For this reason, we often hear the cry that somebody's new theory is 'just words'. I propose that a notation that has not yet gathered bad habits, sloppy practice or ossified schemas is useful to check out the soundness of verbally formulated theories. In no way do I claim that a theory can or should *only* be visually represented, but we have to beware of purely rhetorical science.

There are other reasons too for opting for a visual instead of verbal notation. Words have a short shelf life. They change with use, and many a discussion ends with the realization that the discussants have used the same words with entirely different meanings. The use of a suitable framework will enable us to anchor such terms in relation to particular kinds of behaviour, tasks or experiments.

An invitation to consider diagrams as a tool ■

We have come to believe that there are wide individual differences in the way in which people use words or diagrams in scientific texts. Doubtless, there are a number of reasons for this. Some of the individual differences might be related to individual differences in people's abilities to use maps, or differences in skill with verbal reasoning. Certainly, I have difficulty in fully comprehending any complex scientific argument unless I have pencil and paper in hand to help convert it into diagrammatic form. In addition, however, there will be factors such as familiarity or simple prejudice. Clearly, it also depends on training. It's hard to imagine mathematics, physics, anatomy, physiology or biochemistry without diagrams, although one could use a thousand words instead for each ('the hip bone's connected to the thigh bone . . .'). It is certainly the case that behavioural scientists are used to mere words, and many a textbook on psychology can be found without a single diagram, apart from graphs. But I regard this as a pathology in itself, as a symptom of something even worse – such as behaviourism or reductionism.[9]

A tool for representing causal relationships ■

Cause is a complex issue in any domain. An additional complication is that, as I will stress, the set of causal elements (the terms used in tracing causal chains) come from different types of thing – from genes, through brains and cognitive entities to socio-economic factors. So we will need to

[9] The reasons for this leap are complex and based on experience. I leave it to historians and philosophers of science to spell out the inferential links.

be able to express competing claims that some problem has been inherited, caused by brain damage at birth, by pollution in the environment, by lack of learning, by bad parenting or by peer pressure, or through the interaction of genes with the environment. We may also want to refer to different time scales. Some developmental disorders have their roots in the genes, and we may want to refer to elements in the causal chain whose existence is brief, because they play only a transitional but crucial role in neural development. On the other hand, we will want to refer to the immediate cause of some current behaviour as based on a combination of some aspect of the environment in interaction with an abnormal or deficient process that is specified at the cognitive level.

What I am presenting in this book is a method of helping to express causal statements that include any and every kind of element. In the method itself, there is nothing to believe or disbelieve – it is simply a tool. I believe that this tool, which we call *causal modelling*, is more than useful. I believe that it can help to raise standards in evaluating different ways of looking at etiology, and in diagnosis. However, it will not change the basis of your thinking. As a tool, it has the properties of a tool. You do not live by tools. You pick them up and use them when you need to. Physical tools help you to do things that you could not do by yourself. Conceptual tools serve exactly the same function, but because they are conceptual they help you mentally – remind you; suggest ways to do things; start you off; help you to know when the job is finished or characterize what is left still to do; and tell you what other tools or equipment (such as facts or experiments) are needed. There are a number of features to watch out for in the causal modelling framework:

- it is a tool that helps you to clarify your ideas
- it is a memory tool – it enables you to represent all the complexity you want to represent in an easy-to-understand form
- some checks for inconsistency are built in
- it enables you to establish both common ground and incompatibility with others with a degree of precision
- it allows the formulation of more precise tests of alternative ideas
- it reveals what you could know but don't yet know.[10]

I also hope that the book will help you think about development and developmental disorders in a new and more productive way.

[10] For instance, the gap between a chromosomal abnormality such as trisomy 21 and the anatomical condition of mongoloid eye folds in Down's syndrome.

2 ■ Introducing Cognition

In chapter 1, I introduced various notions of 'cause' in development and prepared you for a framework within which we would be able to explore the topic. I will introduce you to the framework seriously in the next chapter. Before doing that, however, I need to make sure that you understand what I mean by **cognition** and why I feel that cognition is an essential part of any theory of development. Cognition refers to the functions of the brain. It contrasts with other brain sciences in the terms that it uses. Words such as *perception, memory* and *language* are everyday terms for cognitive functions. They are not words used as part of the vocabulary within other biological sciences, such as neurophysiology or neuroanatomy. One may ask questions such as 'What parts of the brain are involved in word perception?' but the terms used to describe what is involved in word perception – terms such as *grapheme, lexicon* and *semantics* – are not brain words; they are words that refer to the cognitive level of description.

One thing I do want you to believe ■

In the area of human development, most of the explicit scientific search is for direct relationships between biology and behaviour. I believe that this search will have only limited success so far as human beings are concerned. The reason for this is that there are cognitive factors that mediate between biology and much of behaviour. For some of you, this claim will be obvious; for others, it will be difficult. Let us say briefly what I do not mean. I do not mean that there are non-biological systems at work: I do believe that the human mind is entirely contained within the human brain. But the language of biology does not allow us to describe what the higher functions of the brain are, any more than the language of neurochemistry allows us to say what the function of a neuron is. As I will illustrate, it is the higher brain functions that control behaviour.[1] These higher brain functions correspond to cognitive functions. The language of function is the language of psychology.[2]

Let me illustrate with a simple example. For my PhD, many years ago, I worked on word recognition. My initial concern was to understand the nature of the interaction between contextual information and stimulus information in the recognition of words. It was known that words were easier to recognize in context but it was not clear why. Information Theory, one of the dominant (mathematical) frameworks at the time, specified that the perception of a stimulus was influenced by the probability of that stimulus occurring. This statement had a lot of mileage predictively, and served to link together a variety of observations. However, it was descriptive rather than explanatory, since there was no mechanism postulated to effect that influence. What I did was postulate a cognitive unit, later called a **logogen**, in which the interaction between stimulus and contextual information could take place (Morton 1961, 1964a,b, 1969). The operation of the logogen system was much more than a redescription of the behaviour from which the idea sprang, and gave rise to specific predictions and a way of thinking about the mental operations involved in word recognition. The specification of the function of this system did not depend on the underlying physiology. Indeed, so far as the theory was concerned, the function of a single logogen (a unit corresponding to a word) could either be implemented by a single neuron or be distributed over a network of neurons. Indeed, the function could also be implemented in a digital computer, or in an analogue computer. It could be thought of as a set of rules or as a

---

[1] We will want to make a distinction between brain functions that can be established as a result of direct observation and those that require inference. Examples of the former are that particular neurons serve to inhibit the activity of other neurons; and that area V4 serves to create a topographic representation of colour. Examples of the latter are what I mean by cognition.

[2] If anyone wishes to assert that the language of higher brain function is the language of biological function and is still biology, then they are at liberty to do so without loss. All they need grant is that the language is different from that used for simple brain function (and that the discovery methods are different as well). Certainly, in most of what I do, I would think of myself as a biological scientist rather than a social scientist.

connectionist network, or as some combination of the two. Whichever of these options one chooses, the function is a cognitive function.

In our discussions of developmental disorders, I will usually refer to three levels of description – biological, cognitive and behavioural. We could envisage more complex configurations, but three is simpler and the limit doesn't seem to constrain us unduly. Within the framework, the biological includes the genetic; the cognitive includes the emotional. The one substantive assumption in the framework that I will present to you is that what I call the **cognitive level** has a major role to play in the causal chains of interest to us. This is implicit in many of the diagnostic descriptions that we see. In the framework, the cognitive is made explicit. The reality of cognition makes it clear why people get so confused when they try to map biology straight on to behaviour.

Reductionism ■

Why should we use cognitive entities in our causal accounts? Why cannot we just use brain and behaviour as the basis for the model? Cannot the real explanation of behavioural developmental phenomena be found through biological research?

Absolutely not. There will be neither causal adequacy nor descriptive adequacy at the biological level. With behaviour and no cognition, one cannot get a proper story. With biology alone, there will be no story at all.

Just as in our earlier example of what caused Romeo's death, there is too big a gap between a suggested biological cause and most events of interest to us. I claim, then, that the cognitive level is a necessity if one is to have a complete account of human development and of developmental psychopathology. This is the only strong theoretical claim that I am making. In the rest of the book, I will, *en passant*, illustrate the justification of this principle both from our own work and from the practice of others.

It may be remarked that while the biology and the behaviour can be observed, there is nothing to observe directly at the cognitive level. However, in espousing cognition, I would also like to make it clear that I am not putting myself above the ordinary principles of objective and replicable observation. It may not be possible to observe cognitive entities directly, but one can predict their effects quite systematically. Let us explore an example of this from the world of artefacts.

You believe that your electronic calculator is capable of doing multiplication using ordinary decimal numbers, and you perhaps believe that it knows such facts as $4 \times 7 = 28$. After all, you key in '4×7' and up on the display comes '28'. That is multiplication as we were taught it in school. It turns out that the claim about multiplication is a cognitive interpretation of the behaviour of the calculator. In fact, if you look at the 'biology' by probing around in the innards of the calculator, you will see that it actually does addition in binary arithmetic. It is only *as if* it does multiplication.

'That is good enough for me', you may say, when dealing with a calculator. 'It is supposed to behave as if it is doing multiplication, and as long as it continues to do so I will be very happy.'

But suppose that you didn't know what this machine was supposed to do, and that you wanted to figure out what it was up to. Suppose that the buttons were not labelled in a way that you were familiar with and that you had to probe the innards as well as exploring the relationship between the keys and the display. You might readily discover that the innermost part of the machine was doing addition in binary arithmetic. However, you would still characterize that particular use of addition in binary arithmetic as *multiplication*. The reason for characterizing it in this way is because 'multiplication' best describes what the machine is doing when you use the '$\times$' key; what the input–output relations are; what the machine is *designed* to do; and the principle by which the machine interacts with the user. Furthermore, you would back your claim that the machine was doing multiplication by predicting the outcome of 'multiplying' any two numbers together. And, in the absence of special instruments, the imaginary function of multiplication is more observable than the underlying function of binary addition.

Note, by the way, that the machine doesn't even have to behave completely accurately. It could say that 102×103 equalled 1.05×10^4, rather than 10,506. We would understand that the display was limited to three decimal places, but still claim that we were seeing decimal multiplication. What I mean, here, is that *multiplication* is equivalent to a cognitive description of the calculator.

A serious problem that follows from the unobservability of cognitive processes is that the rules for postulating cognitive entities are neither clear nor agreed, although Morton (1981) and Shallice (1981, 1988) have made some preliminary statements. What is clear is that we should not postulate cognitive processes (that is, brain function) simply as a redescription of some aspect of data. Examples of such violations of good practice vary from Gall's 'Love of grandeur and infinitude'[3] to Posner and Carr's (1992) 'the generation of semantic associations that are relatively novel but strongly consistent with past processing experience'. We must of course guard ourselves against such abuse. In general, in our own theorizing, my colleagues and I have taken the view that any cognitive entity that we postulate must have a number of independent manifestations in behaviour. This is the property that allows predictions to be made about behaviour in significantly different circumstances.

The central role of cognitive elements in prediction is related to their central role in accounting for the cause of disorders. One tailor-made tool for linking cognitive and behavioural phenomena will be presented in chapter 3, when I talk about the notion of developmental contingency in normal development.

Can we rely on behaviour? ▪

When we are thinking about developmental disorders, there are three kinds of reason for not relying on behaviour. The first reason is that the same deviant behaviour can arise from more than one different underlying cause. The second reason is that the same underlying cause can give rise to quite different patterns of behaviour. The third class of example is where the pathological behaviour vanishes if the circumstances change, even though there is no reason to suppose that the underlying state has changed. None of these arguments are surprising, but they are easily forgotten.

First, I will discuss whether or not we can adequately describe developmental disorders on the basis of behaviour alone. Doctors talk in terms of signs and symptoms. Symptoms are things described by patients when they report how they are feeling. Signs are observations made by the clinicians. Symptoms are essentially cognitive, since they are reports on internal states; signs usually reflect underlying problems, rather than being the problem themselves. The reason for this, quite simply, is that the same behaviour can manifest itself for a wide variety of reasons. I will spend some time in elaborating on this point, because it is central to the whole approach. I will take a variety of well known clinical signs of developmental disorder and sketch alternative underlying causes at the cognitive level. I do not expect that you will find any of these to be

[3] From Fowler (1895).

surprising. However, the accumulation of obvious individual points may help to establish the general principle most firmly:

- We find that a child has a very poor performance on an intelligence test. The superficial interpretation is that the child is retarded – that is, has generalized brain damage. Obvious alternatives are that the child has specific language impairment, due to localized brain damage or (partial) deafness. I will make the point frequently that performance in any test, particularly intelligence tests, has to be seen as behaviour. The underlying cognitive factors have to be established carefully.

- Take the case of a nine-year-old boy with a reading age of six. The tempting interpretation, which is inadmissible without further evidence, is that of specific learning difficulty (i.e. specific brain abnormality leading to dyslexia). The alternative explanations are that the boy has undiagnosed visual problems (correctable by glasses); that the child has undiagnosed hearing impairment, which led to delay in language acquisition; that he is trying to read in a second language; or that he has not attended school regularly. To clarify the diagnosis and establish the state of his cognitive processes, systematic investigations are required.

- A child presents with the symptom of over-activity. The alternative diagnoses are anxiety, lack of parental control – for example, a depressed mother – food allergy, a drug-related phenomenon or hyperkinetic disorder (a diagnostic category that contrasts with over-activity, the behaviour).

- A 12-year-old girl with autism succeeds on the standard false belief task, which, according to the standard pattern of autism, she ought to fail. The inadmissible interpretation without further evidence would be that she is no longer autistic and is a competent mind-reader. The alternatives are that she might have learned the test, or that she might have built up enough experience in the world to be able to reason by analogy. To clarify the true extent of her disability/ability, systematic investigations are required so that the state of her cognitive processes can be established.

- A 12-year-old-girl is not eating. This could be a manifestation of anorexia nervosa or of depression. The treatment patterns required in the two cases would be vastly different.

Let me repeat: it is often assumed that a pattern of abnormal/ deviant behaviour of a child reflects directly the underlying pathology. The examples that I have just listed are clear-cut illustrations of the fallacy of such an assumption. Note that in all of the cases I have used there is also the possibility that there are multiple problems that have led to the observed behaviour.

Another example of the same apparent behaviour arising for different cognitive reasons has been highlighted by Annette Karmiloff-Smith, one of my former colleagues at the Cognitive Development Unit at University College, London. When she started working with children with Williams syndrome, the received wisdom was that while, in addition to physical abnormalities and a general intellectual deficit, these children had a number of specific deficits, particularly with spatial abilities and number, their language and face recognition abilities were untouched. Undoubtedly, they did relatively well on standard tests of verbal abilities and with face processing, but Karmiloff-Smith and her colleagues discovered that there were a number of peculiarities in their performance. She has concluded that, rather than having an intact face processing module, children with Williams syndrome may use a general object processor to recognize faces (Donnai & Karmiloff-Smith 2000). With language, the conclusion is much the same. Rather than learning their native language in the normal way, the data suggest that the language acquisition of children with Williams syndrome might turn out to be more like second language learning (Karmiloff-Smith et al. 1998). The implication is that there is a neural mechanism that normally ends up being specialized for syntax. With Williams syndrome, this mechanism is damaged and language is learned by more general mechanisms. Such a position would be incoherent without a clear distinction between behaviour and cognition.

The second method of illustrating the need for the cognitive level over and above the behavioural level lies in the way in which a particular underlying condition manifests itself differently in different individuals. We would normally want to say that these individuals are similar in important ways, and so give them the same label:

- one individual hearing voices; one catatonic; another with delusions about people broadcasting their thoughts to him – all classified as schizophrenic
- one person not eating; another manifesting acute irritability – both suffering from depression
- one child being highly disruptive in class; another listless but failing to engage and respond to stimulation – both suffering from attentional disorder.

There is something of a paradox about this last set of examples. I talked about 'a particular underlying condition' and equated that with a diagnostic 'label', such as 'schizophrenic'. But the point of the examples is to show not what the individuals have in common, but how they differ. There seem to be two choices. One option is that we count the similarities as greater than the differences. We claim that all three patients are the same in some important way, which we will label as schizophrenia. Then we have to express the essence of schizophrenia in cognitive (or, possibly, biological) form since, by virtue of the examples, we cannot categorize them on the basis of their behaviour. The second option is that we focus on the differences, saying that there are three kinds of disorder previously labelled as schizophrenia. This term will then have to be dropped, because it would not refer to anything at the behavioural, cognitive or biological levels. This theme will recur through the book.

A related set of examples may be drawn from cases in which the behaviour of an individual may differ greatly as a function of the circumstances:

- An English–Italian bilingual child who is dyslexic in English but has no apparent problems with reading Italian. Since the condition has genetic origins, it would seem odd to claim that the dyslexia (the diagnostic category) came and went as the child put one book down and picked up another.
- An eight-year-old boy who is restless at school, does not seem to be able to learn, lacks concentration, and is diagnosed as having ADHD (see chapter 10) and prescribed Ritalin. At home, he concentrates ferociously as he surfs the Internet.

Again, I wish to emphasize that none of this material is at all unusual, surprising or controversial. Indeed, most of these examples have been contributed by my clinical consultants, as everyday cases encountered in clinical practice.

The IQ example: a note of caution ▌

The above examples illustrate the dangers of taking behaviour or test performance as directly representing an underlying condition. It is also important to understand what I am not saying here. I am not saying

Box 2.1 IQ and intelligence

The confusion between IQ and intelligence is just one example of how test results are to be interpreted. The process of confusion often runs along the following lines:

- The nature of an individual difference – or *trait* – is hypothesized. This may spring from everyday language, as with *intelligence*, or from clinical observation of extreme cases.
- The trait is given a name if it doesn't have one and there is debate as to the meaning of the term.
- The name is taken to refer to a real entity and debate focuses on its true nature (as in 'Can computers be intelligent?').
- Tests are based on intuitive analyses of the trait in question, to produce a number for each individual who takes the test.
- Tests are validated with respect to performance for the normal population or with respect to a clinical population defined by the trait.
- The test is taken as equivalent to the trait within the design population ('the WISC measures intelligence').
- Another test is designed that correlates highly with the first test for a sub-population (e.g. the Peabody vocabulary test for children).
- This test is taken as equivalent to the trait within the design population (e.g. 'the Peabody measures intelligence').
- This test is taken as equivalent to the trait within some other population (e.g. the intelligence of autistic children is 'measured' using the Peabody).

The problem with this progression, as we shall see in a number of contexts, is that all tests are tasks, they are behaviour, and all tasks call

that it is wrong to study behaviour or that it is inappropriate to apply tests. Observations of behaviour and the application of well understood tests are essential to the study of normal and abnormal development. As I have already pointed out, cognitive processes cannot be studied directly. The state of cognitive processes can only be inferred from their manifestations. The error is to assume that the relation between the manifestations and the underlying cognitive state has to be transparent. The clearest, most venerable and most understandable confusion of this kind is to equate performance on an 'IQ test' with intelligence, where intelligence is to be seen as an irreducible and possibly genetically determined property of the child. My point is that intelligence, if it is anything,

on a number of cognitive elements in their performance. The reasonable assumption is that one can regard the normal population as being equi-valent with respect to all these cognitive elements except for the one being measured. More precisely, the assumption is that the limit on performance can be attributed to the cognitive element being measured. The unreasonable assumption is that performance limitations in other populations (e.g. autistics) can be attributed to the same cognitive element.

A similar progression with related problems arises when the test is supposed to indicate developmental progression. A good example is the use of a **picture–word matching test** (**PWMT**) as an index of verbal mental age. Note that the scope of the term **verbal mental age** is much more general than mere receptive vocabulary, both in the way in which it is measured in tests such as the WISC and in the way in which it is generally understood by psychologists and other professionals. This doesn't matter, since, with normal children, syntax and vocabulary would develop at the same rate (this is by definition – a normal four-year-old performs like a four-year-old no matter what is being tested) in a normal environment. A test that is easy to administer, such as the PWMT, will be a perfectly good index of the rate of development of all aspects of language – in the normal population – and it has the advantage of being fast and friendly. But, while the PWMT is a perfectly good index of verbal intelligence, it is not *equivalent* to verbal intelligence. And with abnormal populations, it cannot even be assumed that the PWMT is an index of general linguistic development, whether the cause of the deviation is biological or environmental. To demonstrate this to the doubting, imagine administering such a test to a blind child or to a child who does not speak the language of the test.

is a cognitive property of the mind. Measuring IQ is a way of estimating intelligence from behaviour. The behaviour is what happens when you are doing the test. But there are other cognitive factors that can influence this behaviour in ways that make equating IQ with intelligence highly unreliable, under certain circumstances. This topic is explored in box 2.1.

Why cause needs cognition ▌

Recall that what I am doing at the moment is emphasizing the case for considering cognition as a necessary intermediary between brain and behaviour. I have already rehearsed some reasons for believing that invariants in behaviour are only captured by the cognitive level. We also have to contend with the effects of knowledge or belief on behaviour. Not wanting to go to school because of bullying is one example. More dramatic is anorexia nervosa, which – according to one, dominant view – can only be understood in terms of the girl's belief system. That is, according to this view, anorexia nervosa is entirely cognitive in origin, but without any *structural* abnormality at the cognitive level. In other words, on this view, the cognitive *processes* are normal and the girl's reasoning is impeccable; it is just that her beliefs lead her to strange (though logical) conclusions and so lead her to behave in a particular way.

A further point is that the contingencies of abnormality are only fully revealed when the cognitive level is included. Why, for example, should the behavioural problem be so much less in some autistic people than in others? One answer has to do with the way in which cognitive processes interact with each other. Thus, two autistic children could have the identical central deficit. However, they might differ widely, although within the normal range, in general cognitive abilities. This normal variation, in combination with the autistic deficit, could lead to quite dramatic differences in behaviour. This is an example of the general problem of variability, and co-morbidity, that is found all over diagnosis (see chapter 7).

Some of the answers to these problems will be found at the neural, biochemical or genetic levels. For example, a child with a particular cognitive deficit will usually be able to compensate more adequately if he or she has higher intelligence. Now, suppose that we were able to equate higher intelligence with a lower synaptic transmission time. In the cases of interest to us, however, it would be insufficient simply to say that the synaptic transmission time was faster. The reason for this is that the low synaptic transmission time is only necessary – it is not sufficient. The critical factor in compensation would be that particular kinds of knowledge had been accumulated, knowledge that the child was able to use in the compensatory process. Thus, if it were the case that the synaptic transmission time was low but the knowledge had not accumulated, there would be no amelioration. If it were the case that the synaptic transmission time was high but – for environmental reasons and over an extended period of time – the necessary knowledge was accumulated, there would be amelioration in the condition in the respect of interest. Biological factors play a limiting role here, but with respect to the condition of interest – compensatory activity – it is the cognitive factors, such as the underlying autism (see chapter 4), that are definitional.

Suppose that the enterprise was to look at the effects of variability in development. How might we go about this? One approach would be to go into the cell and discover sources of variance in concentrations of enzymes, pH values, synaptic transmission time and so on. Perhaps you select a number of individuals with high values on one of these variables and then see if high values on the other variables can be predicted. Suppose that they could be. What then? You might go to a higher level and check whether the properties of specific neural circuits are different. What in particular might you check at the higher level? Surely you wouldn't check things at random, relying on who happens to be in the next laboratory, or a comment by a total stranger over dinner. No, rather, there will a hypothesis that relates the two. But why go to the higher level in the first place? Because the lower level by itself is not the natural place to look when thinking about implications. Remember that we are thinking about the effects of variability, not the variability itself. Variability of any particular kind is only interesting if there are consequences.

In medicine, there has been a strong focus on severe consequences, such as the premature death of the organism.[4] In development, the interest in the past has been solely in behavioural consequences. For child psychiatrists this was seen as being the non-controversial thing to do, but at the cost of moving towards the abandonment of scientific diagnosis in favour of description: 'These descriptions and guidelines carry no theoretical implications. They are simply a set of symptoms and comments that have been agreed . . . to be a reasonable basis for defining the limits of categories in the classifica-tion of mental disorders' (World Health Organisation 1992, p. 2). Diagnosis through cognitive criteria would, to be sure, be impossible to agree universally, but I am certain that it is the only route to understanding.

How does cognition cause behaviour? While any complete account of a developmental disorder will include details of the relevant cognitive

[4] Back pain, chronic indigestion, PMT, migraine, freckles and hair loss have attracted relatively little investment of time or money in spite of what looks like an enormous market demand. The common cold is a notable exception, and was a notable failure.

processes, I will not be concerned particularly with such details. There are many theories in different areas of cognition, which explicate how a particular set of inputs are transformed by cognitive-level computations into a particular behavioural output. However, they are usually limited in scope. Let me take a specific example. The set of inputs could be a printed non-word; that is, each of the inputs is a letter. The behavioural output could be a lexicalization error made by a dyslexic reader. Theories of this process (e.g. Thomas & Karmiloff-Smith 2003) mostly focus on grapheme–phoneme translations, and say nothing about the meta-phonological problems. I don't know of any computational models that actually explicate the dyslexic syndrome (for more details of the syndrome, see chapter 8). Equally, none of the theories about the syndrome have any computational detail. In the book by Jackson and Coltheart (2001), you will find both (and some causal modelling to boot!), but the computational model is only applied to the grapheme–phoneme relationship.

Does this matter? Is it actually possible to talk about the cause of a syndrome without having a detailed computational model of the underlying cognitive processes? I think that it is. The structure of an explanation in cognitive psychology takes the form:

■   *C* enables *B*

where *C* is a cognitive mechanism and *B* is a pattern of behaviour. *C* may be specified more or less completely, and this specification is a task for cognitive science. I have spent much of my working life doing this sort of thing, mostly using information processing models, occasionally computationally or mathematically specified. On the other hand, the kinds of statement that I am dealing with in this book with respect to behaviour take the form:

■   a problem with *C* causes a problem with *B*

Statements of this form can be made irrespective of the degree to which *C* has been specified, although the ease of testing the theory will be improved as the theory becomes more specific. In the following chapters, you will meet a number of claims of this form, where *B* refers to one or more of the major symptoms of a classic developmental disorder. Occasionally, I will point out that the specification of *C* in someone's causal theory is in need of some expansion before it can be taken seriously (e.g. the ubiquitous 'frontal deficit' or 'executive deficit'), but for the most part I will not be concerned to evaluate different ways of doing C (e.g. the phonological problem in developmental dyslexia) but, rather, with the problem of how to evaluate different C's (e.g. the phonological hypothesis versus the magnocellular hypothesis of dyslexia).

Finally, it will be obvious to most people that the framework within which the theory of cognitive function is located is irrelevant from a causal point of view. If cognitive mechanism C is specified as a production system, as a connectionist network or as a series of rewrite rules, the causal claim

▮ a problem with C causes a problem with B

remains the same. Equally, if a theory of the origins of a developmental disorder postulates a problem with a cognitive mechanism, the causal theory will finger the environment, the brain or some combination of the two as the immediate cause of this cognitive problem. Someone will need to explicate the cognitive mechanism using one of the methods that cognitive science has developed over the past 50 years, using experimental and computational techniques. But so far as the causal model is concerned, the claim

▮ the problem with C is caused by a deviant environment E

will be the same irrespective of the particular framework within which the mechanism is described. It should also be clear that there are many models of psychological mechanisms related to developmental disorders that have no causal content whatsoever. This is the case with connectionist and other kinds of models. [I have already mentioned Thomas and Karmiloff-Smith (2003) and Jackson and Coltheart (2001) in a related issue.] While such models are of great interest in the goal of explicating the nature of the cognitive mechanisms, their detail seems of little relevance with regard to the causal issues. These matters will hopefully become clearer as you progress through the book. Let me say again, this time with emphasis:

▮ *this is not a textbook on developmental disorders.*

It is a book on how to *think about* developmental disorders.

3 REPRESENTING CAUSAL RELATIONSHIPS: TECHNICAL AND FORMAL CONSIDERATIONS

In this chapter, I will introduce the conventions of causal modelling. To create a causal model, all you need is an idea about a developmental disorder, a blank sheet of paper and a pencil. What I hope to enable you to do is to sort out your thoughts, make a distinction between facts and theories, separate out biological, cognitive and behavioural elements, and enable you to put the most complex and extended idea on to paper in such a way that it can all be seen at the same time, in just the way you think about it.

Categorizing facts

Take the sheet of paper and draw two lines across it to create three spaces. These spaces correspond to the three levels of description – biological, cognitive and behavioural – that I discussed in chapter 2. If you first review the facts that you know about a particular developmental disorder, you can sort them into the appropriate category, biological, cognitive or behavioural, and write them into the appropriate space. To illustrate how this works, let us suppose that you have been to an introductory lecture on autism. You want to construct a model along the lines I have discussed, and you have noted down a few facts about autistics and autism in general from this lecture:

- some autistics have outstanding drawing ability and memory
- they tend to have low IQ
- they are slow to learn language
- the question of whether they are missing 'Theory of Mind' or 'executive functions' is disputed

- they are socially strange
- they have no imagination
- they are very good at hidden figures (see box 4.5 on p. 92)
- if autism occurs in one identical twin, it tends to occur in the other
- it occurs more in boys than in girls
- it starts very early (how early?).

The major problem that you face in sorting these facts according to the framework is to keep behavioural facts separate from cognitive ones. The problem, if we are actually interested in explaining the behaviour, is the tendency to think of the behavioural facts as though they directly represent traits or abilities or propensities. This has to be avoided at all costs. What we have to remember is that a fact that concerns a test or experimental score is a behavioural fact. Thus, performance on an IQ test has to be regarded, initially at any rate, solely as a piece of behaviour, which may or may not relate directly to any underlying ability. This is not a doctrinaire step, by the way, but mere prudence. If you want to claim that IQ tests measure directly and simply some single human quality called intelligence, then you actually commit yourself, unwittingly, to a very complex theory. What treating the IQ test as a piece of behaviour buys for the moment is flexibility. Thus, for example, we have the possibility of thinking about an idiot savant as being, by some definition and measure, really very intelligent, but that this intelligence is masked in the usual IQ tests.

In general, when we consider poor performance on any task, we want to be able to represent either of two possible reasons: a specific deficit and a general one. Thus, for the slow language learning of autistics, we might want to say there is something specifically the matter with their language learning system (assuming that we believe that there is a special device for this), or that language learning is slow because autistics have low IQ (a belief that used to be widespread), or because of some other cause such as poor social interactions. Our notation must be able to express such alternatives.

Taking these points into account, we would classify as *behavioural* the following facts:

- some autistics have outstanding drawing ability and memory – idiot savants
- they tend to have low IQ (i.e. poor performance in IQ tests)
- they are slow to learn language

- they are socially strange
- they are very good at hidden figures.

Looking at the other facts, there is no problem in classifying the statements:

- if autism occurs in one identical twin, it tends to occur in the other
- it occurs more in boys than in girls

as biological. But what about:

- it starts very early (how early?)

Is this biological, cognitive or behavioural? We might even consider that this early start refers to the fact that autistic infants only point at things if they want them; they never point at things simply because they find them of interest and wish to share this interest. This piece of information is behavioural, but contaminated with cognitive language such as 'want' and 'interest'. On the other hand, there might be a temptation to say that the autistic signs starting early are evidence for a biological basis. We would need a lot more analysis to be happy with such a conclusion So, for the moment, rather than going into all the arguments, we will not attempt to classify *starts early*.[1]

For the remaining facts,

- the question of whether they are missing 'Theory of Mind' or 'executive functions' is disputed

clearly belongs to the cognitive space, and refers to alternative cognitive theories. The fact

- they have no imagination

is more problematical. It appears to be a convenient summary of some observations, such as their difficulty in understanding pretend play, and impressions, such as the problem in understanding the plots of stories. Since it would be tedious to list all the contributing behaviours,

[1] On the other hand, there is nothing to stop you from thinking about the alternatives right now.

• more boys • twin effects	biological
• 'theory of mind' vs. 'executive functions' • no imagination	cognitive
• drawing good • low IQ • socially strange	behavioural

Figure 3.1

we might decide that, for the moment, a lack of imagination should be thought of as a cognitive hypothesis. Of course, in the future, the term may turn out to be too vague and have to be rethought.

The piece of paper now looks like figure 3.1. This piece of paper is a representation, at the three different levels, of what we have been told about the autistic individual. We have managed to distinguish between biological, cognitive and behavioural factors in all cases, apart from the fact that autism starts early. So far we have focused on the individual. But what about the influence of the environment? Let us take a look at a couple of theories that have been popular in the past decade or so.

External influences

Suppose that we now wished to include the possibility that maternal viral infections in the first trimester also give rise to autism. This would be an example of an external agent at a biological level. Then there is the idea that bad bonding between the mother and the infant just after birth could lead to serious abnormalities of development in the infant, in relation to social development, which look very much like autism. Suitable therapy is supposed to reverse these effects. As a matter of fact, I don't actually believe this theory, but this does not stop me from being able to represent it. Indeed, I would argue that being able to represent alternative theories in exactly the same format is the most productive way of viewing and comparing them.

Where might such pieces of information be placed in the diagram? Within the framework, the virus would have to interact with the individual at the biological level. On the other hand, faulty attachment

virus?	• more boys • twin effects	**biological**
faulty attachment?	• 'theory of mind' vs. 'executive functions' • no imagination	**cognitive**
	• drawing good • low IQ • socially strange • slow language learning • hidden figures	**behavioural**

Figure 3.2

would be caused through interaction with the environment (specifically, the parents), leading to problems at the cognitive level. What I have done is to create a space that functions at all levels of description and allows the representation of any outside agent relevant to the disorder. It is shown in figure 3.2.

Let us summarize where we have got to at the moment. The basic layout of the framework is clear. To start with, we would include these four spaces – biological, cognitive and behavioural (which represent the individual) and environmental – whether or not we had anything to go in them. The spaces are a reminder that new things might arrive to further complicate the picture. At the moment, I do not think that any more spaces are needed than those already depicted. It would be easy to add on more levels (e.g. a social level, an emotion sub-component of the cognitive level, or subdivisions inside the biological level), but I prefer the minimum that we can get away with for our purposes.

The causal notation ▮

Having first sorted out the available information, the next thing to do is to try to make sense of it. This involves setting out the causal connections among the available facts. The simplest symbol that I could think of is an arrow. For the purposes of this exercise, we will use a particular arrow, a hollow one, to indicate cause. This will help us to distinguish arrows denoting cause from arrows denoting other relationships, such as temporal sequence or the passage of information.

Figure 3.3

Before returning to the problem of representation, we can review some of the alternative causal connections that we might want to talk about in a developmental theory. First of all, we might want to say that there is a direct causal relation between biological and behavioural levels, without any cognitive mediation. This would be represented as in figure 3.3. An example of this kind of connection would be the effects of damage to the basal ganglia on movement. Another example is deafness.

For most development disorders, at least some of the causal account will involve the cognitive level. What we will want to say is that observed behavioural abnormalities are caused by abnormalities at the cognitive level; these, in turn, have biological precursors. This pattern of relationships is shown generically in figure 3.4. An example of this would be the genetic effects on intellectual ability in Down's syndrome. The phrase *intellectual ability* is meant to refer to the constellation of relevant cognitive problems found in these children. These, in turn, will lead to reduced performance on IQ tests. We will see many more causal chains of this kind. It is important to note here that it is not satisfactory to conclude simply that the genetic abnormality is responsible for the poor IQ performance. Eventually, we will need some other intervening biological factors if we are to have a useful account of the relationship.

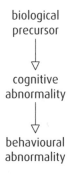

Figure 3.4

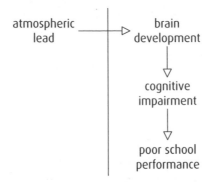

Figure 3.5

The statement of the gene–cognition relationship is the start of a causal tree, not the end.

Now we can look at ways of representing theories that include the effects of the environment. An example of this kind of theory, shown in figure 3.5, is the one relating the presence of lead in the atmosphere to poor school achievement. The theory is that the lead affects brain development in such a way that it creates a general impairment in cognitive ability. This could lead to a variety of behavioural impairments. The one that I depict is poor performance at school.

Next, we have the possibility of the environment acting simply at the cognitive level, without there being any causal involvement at the biological level. An example would be the simplest theory concerning the effects of bullying on school performance, shown in figure 3.6. With this formulation, it is being claimed that there is no biological causal factor. Note the stress on *causal* here. Of course there is biological (physiological, hormonal) involvement in factors such as motivation,

Figure 3.6

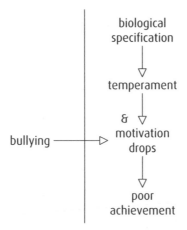

Figure 3.7

but in the scenario in figure 3.6 the biological component adds nothing to the causal chain.

The notation actually prompts us to think about whether the biological level might be involved causally in this case, and if so, how. One possibility is that the children who are bullied are those with a particular temperament and that such temperamental factors are genetically conditioned. Temperament, as well as motivation, are cognitive factors, and in this case I might want to show the environment and the biological factors interacting at the cognitive level, as in figure 3.7. In the figure, I have signalled the interaction between the two factors by inserting the '&' sign. Note, however, that such a move is not neutral with respect to the term 'cause'. The implication is that if the child was not bullied, then the temperament would not matter. Equally, however, it could be argued that if the child did not have the particular temperament, then the bullying would not matter with respect to school performance. This puts the bullying and the temperament as equivalent factors in causing the poor school performance.

Starting a causal model for autism ▓

With the benefit of the examples given in the previous section, we can begin to work on the data relating to autism. We start with the biological level. First, we can ask whether

Figure 3.8

- it occurs more in boys than in girls

should be considered a part of the causal chain. Clearly not. This fact is, rather, good evidence for there being a genetic contribution to autism, whether it takes the form of risk or protection. It is the genetic aspect that needs to be stressed. So, *genetic factor* is the first item to be inserted in the causal model. Clearly, the genetic factor does not cause a cognitive abnormality directly. That is too big a jump for a reasonable explanation. What we can state is that the genetic factor causes some abnormality in the brain. This connection is indicated in figure 3.8.

Another factor we have mentioned that could be seen as acting on the (unborn infant) brain is a maternal viral infection, which is sometimes proposed as a cause for autism. We include this in figure 3.9. The diagram indicates that the brain abnormality could be caused by *either* the genetic factor *or* a virus. There is a contrast here with figure 3.7, in which both of the factors are required in the causal chain. Figure 3.9 further implies that the brain abnormality created by rubella is the same as that caused by genetic conditions. If we wanted to propose the theory that the two kinds of brain abnormality were different, one way of indicating this is shown in figure 3.10. There are other possible relationships between the two kinds of abnormality, which could be equally easily diagrammed. If we did not wish to commit ourselves, we

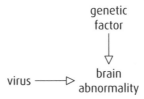

Figure 3.9

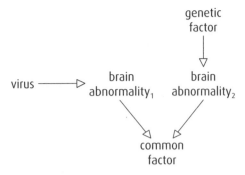

Figure 3.10

would annotate one diagram or the other with a question mark, or present both kinds of brain abnormality as alternative causes of the same or different cognitive malfunction(s). These are left as exercises.

Next, we can move on to the cognitive level. Theory of Mind (ToM) and executive functions are often presented as different causal theories of autism (see chapters 4 and 6). We can start with Theory of Mind. We might believe that the Theory of Mind problem was separate from the lack of imagination, but that both might have a common cognitive cause. This is shown in figure 3.11. Deficits in Theory of Mind tasks, such as the false belief task (see chapter 4), would be shown separately at the behavioural level.

This arrangement would not be possible if we were considering the executive function deficit theory. In the latter case, in the way in which it is usually expressed, the lack of imagination would be seen as a separate problem. These problems could be derived from the same brain abnormality, as indicated in figure 3.12. Alternatively, they could have different origins in the brain. In that case, we would draw an extra component at the biological level.

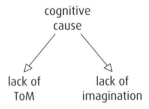

Figure 3.11

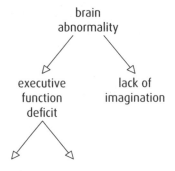

Figure 3.12

The next problem is to link the behaviour to the cognitive level. Again, we will have to deal with the executive and ToM theories separately. Taking figure 3.11 first, we can readily link the socially strange behaviour to the lack of ToM, as shown in figure 3.13. Slow language learning has also been found to be linked, fairly directly, to ToM. What should we do about low IQ? This has to be a separate element at the cognitive level, and we can call it *low general ability*. This might be caused by the same brain abnormality or by a different one. Either of these two theories can readily be diagrammed. One of them has been included in figure 3.14. If we start with executive dysfunction as in figure 3.12, the behavioural deficits will have to be added in much the same way. Deficits in ToM tasks would have to be assigned as a consequence of

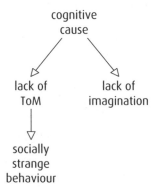

Figure 3.13

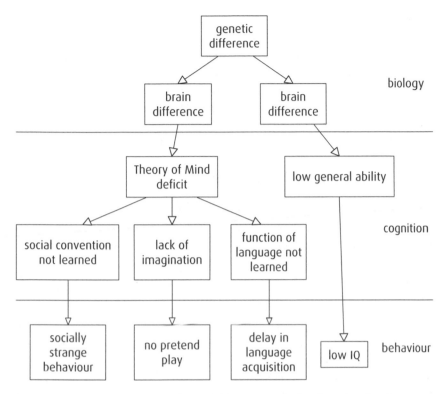

Figure 3.14 An example of a theory of autism, with the three levels of description explicitly included.

either the executive function deficit or the deficit in imagination, or a combination of these. Whichever choice was made, the decision would have to be backed up with some kind of information processing model that showed exactly how the cognitive deficit would lead to the behaviour in question.

In figure 3.14, I indicate what a complete theory of autism might look like when we explicitly indicate the three levels of description. We will go into current theories of autism in detail in chapter 6. Meanwhile, note again that you should be able to diagram in a causal model whatever theory of the cause of autism you happen to hold. In any case, the examples that I have just worked through are for illustrative purposes only.

Complications █

What I have done in the previous section is to try to give you a quick feeling for causal modelling. Inevitably, I have simplified matters, and there are a number of complications and cautions that I will briefly discuss here and then pick up at later stages in the book. These are mainly assumptions that other people have erroniously brought to causal modelling, which have got in the way of an easy understanding.

Causal pathways are never deterministic

This arises partly because of the massive interactive complexity of both biological and cognitive development. Thus, even where there is a well-specified genetic disorder, the behavioural manifestation can differ widely as a function of the interaction of the target gene with other genes. Looking further at genetics, we might note that one of two identical twins may have the full-blown disorder while the other has only a mild form. There are a number of accounts of such things in the medical literature, even where the condition is characterized by purely physical signs. The reason for this is that the precise way in which the genes express themselves during development depends not only on the genetic specification but also on the biochemical and learning environment in which the genetic programme unfolds. Small differences in the blood supply to the two foetuses at a crucial stage in development, for example, could have significant consequences. Geneticists talk about such variability in terms of the difference between the *genotype* (the genetic specification) and the *phenotype* (the range of manifestations of the genotype). But note that, no matter what is going on at the biological level, it is the cognitive deficit that leads to the behavioural shortfall.

Contingencies are not causes

Consider the proposition that, over the first three years of life, blindness causes a social impairment (Minter et al. 1998; Hobson et al. 1999; Hobson & Bishop 2003). It is certainly the case that most blind three- and four-year-olds would be behind their norms in what are called 'mentalizing' tasks (see chapter 4). Such tasks include shared attention, pretending and false belief. We can trace the reasons quite easily, by noting that a lot of the information that goes into helping a young child to learn about other people's mental states is acquired visually. An obvious example is eye-gaze. We learn a great deal about the mental states of others by observing where they are looking. But do we really want to say that blindness causes the deficit? One objection might be that since blind people catch up eventually, it does not make sense to talk about a deficit at all.[2] Another objection arises from considering how we would talk about the other factors that affect the development of these skills. One such factor is the number of siblings that you have. Single children develop mentalizing skills later than children brought up in large families (Ruffman et al. 1999). Is this delay *caused* by being an only child? To put such factors in the same class as the deficit underlying autism, by using the term 'cause' for all of them, seems to involve an excessively behavioural and time-locked viewpoint. First of all, there is no evidence, either in the case of the blind or in the case of the only child, that there is any fundamental underlying biological or cognitive deficit. The deficit that we know about is in the expression of a cognitive skill that we believe is present. What is missing is the knowledge (in terms of experience) that helps the skill to flourish. Secondly, in both cases the deficit could as well be located in the environment as in the child, since, with suitable intensification of the relevant experience, there need be no delay at all. This is simplest to see in the case of the only child of parents who share a house with another family that has children. The constant interaction with the other children will provide everything that siblings would have provided. In this case, social skills have not been affected by being an only child! Indeed, being an only child is not the *cause* of anything.[3]

These are not difficult matters, as long as we keep our heads and don't look for easy explanations! We find that it helps to consider the nature of the normal environment. A concept proposed in conjunction with my former colleague Mark Johnson is that of a Species Typical Environment (Johnson & Morton 1991). We developed this idea in order to make some sense of the interaction of innate factors with the environment. The particular context in which the idea was originally

---

[2] We might also note that the way in which blind people catch up in their mentalizing skills is not to be confused with compensation. Compensation involves using a different biological or cognitive mechanism from normal; the mentalizing skills of the blind are perfectly normal, so far as we know.

[3] This assertion is, of course, a theory waiting to be falsified.

developed was the way in which new-born infants react to faces. It seems that there is a special inborn perceptual mechanism that causes new-born infants to orient towards faces that are seen in peripheral vision. But all you need to stimulate this device is an oval shape of about the right size, together with three blobs in a triangle, corresponding to the two eyes and a mouth. It is not necessary for evolution to have specified the human face in any more detail than that, because we can guarantee, normally, that human faces will appear in the right place, and that faces of other species will not. This enables the simple perceptual device, which we called CONSPEC, to function, orienting the infant towards the nearby face. This action guarantees that the infant will learn the characteristics of the human face very quickly, probably in the first couple of months of life. Both CONSPEC and the environment are necessary to achieve this end, and the environmental contribution can be seen as being as biological in nature as the genetically programmed CONSPEC. Of course, if there were no human faces in the immediate environment, the child would not learn about the human face over the first two months. Happily, in this case, other mechanisms are available that would enable the child to do the necessary learning later on.

Suppose that CONSPEC were missing in a particular infant.[4] What would happen then? In this case, the infant would not orient towards faces that appeared in his or her peripheral vision and so would not spend as much time looking at them full on and would not learn anything like as much about them. But we could correct this problem by making sure that we put our faces at the right distance from the child and turned the infant's face so that he or she was looking straight at us. This would be an extension of the Species Typical Environment, which would compensate for the CONSPEC deficit.

The point about all this is that both CONSPEC, which is a part of the child's genetic endowment, and the normal environment of peering human faces play equivalent roles in development. Our 'normal' biology[5] includes them both. We can extend this principle to the development

---

[4] In fact, if CONSPEC were missing in practice, it would probably mean that there was quite serious subcortical damage, with gross general deficits. For the purposes of the discussion, though, I am pretending that CONSPEC can be selectively damaged.

[5] The scare quotes on 'normal', when I say 'normal' biology, are to signal that there is an enormous variability in the normal, even under the most restricted definitions possible.

of mentalizing, the problem with which I began this section. This cognitive skill depends on a special computational ability that only humans have, together with a lot of interaction with other humans, which takes a variety of forms. These interactions can be seen as a part of the Species Typical Environment. If you don't have the interactions, you don't develop the skill.[6] The more interactions you have, the faster you develop the skill. If you are an only child, you have fewer interactions of the appropriate kind; if you are blind, you get less information from the interactions. In both cases, the Species Typical Environment can be modified to compensate. In both cases, the modification works effortlessly. The contrast would be with the autistic child, where the necessary underlying mechanism is missing, and, inasmuch as there can be compensatory abilities, they have to be acquired with effort, and the environment that would be necessary in order to enable the learning to take place would have to be designed with care. Such differences between the autistic child and the blind child lead us to use *cause* for the former, but *vulnerability* for the latter.[7]

Compensation

When we discuss individual cases of autism from the milder end of the autistic spectrum, we find it difficult to reconcile them with the original simple causal model, since some of the defining behavioural signs vanish as the individual grows older. It becomes necessary, then, to introduce the notion of *compensation*. In fact, it seems likely that examples of compensation could be found with any developmental disorder.

There are three general ways of representing such phenomena, corresponding to three different underlying theories. Which of the three theories would be appropriate in any particular case would depend on the nature of the disorder and on the individual. According to the

[6]   A child who is otherwise normal but brought up in (relative) isolation will not exhibit any normal social understanding. However, after a relatively short time in human company, the child will develop the appropriate skills, indicating that the necessary mechanism was simply dormant. One such case, Kaspar Hauser, is described in detail by Uta Frith in her book *Autism* (see Frith 2003).

[7]   I wish to assure you that nothing actually hinges on the use of one term or another, as long as the differences between the conditions of autism and blindness are fully understood. If you are wedded to the use of *cause* in all cases, just make the appropriate translation where necessary, but be careful that you don't over-generalize between the two senses of 'cause' in your thinking!

first of these theories, the compensation would be purely behavioural, with the task being performed with completely different cognitive mechanisms from those used by the normal population. There is more than one way of carrying out most tasks. This is true even when we are normally biologically suited to carrying out a developmental task in a particular way. I raised this in chapter 2, when discussing the way in which Karmiloff-Smith believes that children with Williams syndrome learn language. Within such a view, we would probably want to say that the biological and cognitive deficits remained. This would be revealed by the continued existence of other problems deriving from the same deficit but not compensated for. Another way of posing the question, in a different context, might be to ask 'What do you call a dyslexic who is a fluent reader?' (see chapter 8).

The second kind of compensation would involve a change at the cognitive level, such that a weakness in or peculiarity of a cognitive process could be overcome. In this case, the same mechanism would be used as with normal development, but with outside support. Thus, suppose that a child is distractible as a result of some biological defect. An increase in the child's motivation could lead to increased attention, which could compensate for this distractibility. In this case, the original biological defect would remain as before.

The third form of compensation would take place at the biological level where, for example, the function of damaged tissue could be taken over by other areas of the cortex. This is generally known as **cortical plasticity**. I will develop a notation for compensation in chapter 4.

Protective factors and vulnerability

If we take children who experience the extremes of environmental conditions, some emerge without problems while others seem to be psychologically damaged. Those who emerge without problems are sometimes termed *resilient* (Caspi 2002). The environmental or genetic conditions associated with a good outcome are what are called **protective factors**. Kolvin et al. (1990) have used such terms in discussing the relationship between early social deprivation and later patterns of offending. Deprivation, which included marital instability, poor physical care and overcrowding, was predictive of later offending. However, the resilient, despite a background of some deprivation, benefited from protective factors such as good parental care and less adverse physical circumstances in the perinatal period and early childhood. In contrast, the *vulnerable*, despite a background without deprivation of the kind identified by Kolvin et al., were characterized by the experience of stressful social circumstances and their mother's relative youth at marriage.

What can we say about 'cause' in these situations? We can, perhaps, help to clarify our thinking by moving away from human behaviour and taking for the moment an analogous problem from medicine. Suppose that we look at the relationship between malaria and sickle cell anaemia, a genetic disorder that creates some problems of its own. It turns out that if you suffer from sickle cell anaemia, your risk of contracting malaria, even in a mosquito-infested environment, is virtually zero. Suppose that you lived in a malaria-prone area and all your family had sickle cell anaemia – except for you. You get malaria. Would you want to say that your malaria was caused by the absence of sickle cells or, indeed, by the presence of the genes that protected you from sickle cell anaemia? My investigations into this issue lead us to conclude that most people would say that the mosquito was the cause. Unfortunately, there is no equivalent to the mosquito in the example in the previous paragraph. Later in this chapter I will say more about risk, and we will see in chapter 10, when I discuss theories of conduct disorder, that the language of causality has natural limits. Meanwhile, think about the headline 'Young Mothers Cause Crime.'

Incomplete theories

What should be done where there is striking data that cannot be accounted for under the current theory? The best solution is to make the shortfall explicit at some stage just to remind you, to let the audience know that you know and to increase the chance of finding a comprehensive account. One example would be the outstanding ability of autistic children to carry out the hidden figures test (see box 4.5 on p. 92). This cannot be accounted for in a causal model such as that shown in figure 3.14 (p. 45). Until we have a complete theory, then, it might be advisable to summarize the model with the hidden figures ability explicitly excluded, as in figure 3.15.

Some easy stuff on cause and correlation ▪

In chapters 4 and 6, I will provide an extended analysis of current theories of autism, using the causal modelling framework. Before I do

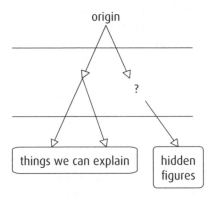

Figure 3.15

this, though, I would like to stress one kind of error that sometimes creeps into developmental theorizing. You often see claims that two things are causally related when, in fact, they are only correlated. Correlation is pervasive, partly because there are so many things to correlate, and partly because there are so many things with common cause and things with a common cause are nearly always correlated. That there are so many things to correlate means that correlations between unrelated things could be significant by chance. Remember that if the likelihood that some event could have happened at random was less than 1 in 20, we usually accept the event as meaningful; we would call it statistically significant. Now, if you took seven unconnected things and calculated correlations among all of them, you would have 21 values in total. Of these, by chance alone you would expect to obtain one that was the right size to be 'significant' by normal standards; that is, with odds of better than 1 in 20. People who do their statistics properly would allow for that, but many people do not. Let us illustrate this with a 'factlet' that never fails to astonish us. Suppose that you throw a party and 23 people turn up. You discover that two of them share the same birthday. Should you be surprised? Well, most people would be. And yet there is a better than 50:50 chance that such a thing will happen, since there are 253 different pairs of people in the room! We have to be very careful about what seems to be a meaningful coincidence. It may be chance. If it is chance, then there is nothing to explain.

Even if you have a significant correlation by the strictest standards, you cannot assume that there is a causal relationship between the two variables. If you take a random group of humans, weight and income will correlate together very well. But the correlation will be entirely due to age – remember that a random group of humans will include rather a lot of babies and children – and it isn't clear that you would want to talk about cause at all.[8]

Why is it now believed that smoking causes lung cancer? Most people will point to the fact that the incidence of lung cancer is correlated with smoking habits. But this, in itself, is not proof. It would be possible, in principle, to find that there is a gene that is responsible both for nicotine addiction and for susceptibility to cancer, as the tobacco companies have tried to argue over the years, and that smoke has no role to play at all! In fact, the proof of the causal relationship between smoking and cancer depends on a variety of data, among which are:

- the effects of passive smoking
- low cancer levels in those who have long given up smoking
- cancer of the nose for snuff addicts and cancer of the mouth for pipe users
- morphological changes in lung tissue.

Note, also, that cause does not require a deterministic relationship. The fact that Aunt Hilda smoked 40 cigarettes a day from the age of 15 and is still going strong at 93 is not an argument against the smoking–cancer relationship. I will have much cause to use the maxim

▮ There is no single cause of anything

and this means that mitigation is always possible.

To summarize this section, a causal relationship between two things, X and Y, would be diagrammed as X → Y. If the two things are merely correlated, without there being a causal relationship between them, then the appropriate description will involve a third entity, such that Z → X and Z → Y. You will find a number of examples of this in the chapters to come.

---

[8] Of course, with a selected population there could be a causal relationship between weight and income. One such population is Sumo wrestlers. That is why the 'population', the range of people for whom a generalization might be made, has to be specified.

Other notations ■

At the risk of burdening you further, I feel that the time is ripe to describe two other, related notations. The first one, psychosocial pathways, contrasts with causal modelling. This is closely related to the popular notion of cause that I discussed in chapter 1. The second notation, developmental contingency modelling, is complementary to causal modelling.

Psychosocial pathways

The concept of the psychosocial pathway was developed by Rutter and his colleagues (Rutter 1989). The main difference between this approach and causal modelling is that psychosocial pathways represent, broadly, trends over time for groups of individuals. They show the contingent relationships among events in the lives of individuals. The pathways are variously termed 'chains of adversity' or 'chains of circumstance'. Usually, these pathways are constructed from correlation or contingency tables. Causality is not explicitly claimed but it is occasionally implied. Where two events are linked by an arrow:

■ $X \rightarrow Y$

we are to understand that in those cases in which X is found, there is an increasing likelihood of Y occurring later. Note that Y could occur for other reasons, and pathway analysis seems to concentrate more on the forward implications. Thus, figure 3.16, which is based on a study by Gray et al. (1980), gives a simplified pathway from poor schooling to poor job success, controlling for other variables such as the individual's measured intelligence and social circumstance. It seems to focus more on a series of forward-pointing questions, such as

■ What are the consequences of poor schooling?

rather than backward-pointing ones, such as

■ What are the causes of poor employment records?

Thus the figure includes comparative rates of traversing each sub-path. We see that children with poor schooling are twice as likely ('2×')

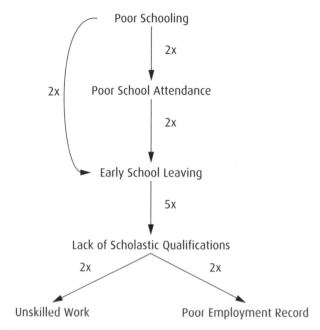

Figure 3.16 The psychosocial pathway from poor schooling to poor job success (from Rutter 1989).

to have poor school attendance (as children with good schooling). The next stage of the pathway, rather than being the continuation of the first part (that is, using only children with poor schooling), is actually recomputed from scratch, using all children with poor school attendance, whether they were assessed as having poor or good schooling. We see that, overall, the relationship of poor school attendance and early school leaving is a twofold increase over the group with good school attendance. Remember that this calculation ignores the quality of the schooling. In fact, we are also told that the poor schooling group is only twice as likely to leave school early. This means that we can infer that poor attendance with good schooling has a *worse* outcome than poor attendance with poor schooling. Poor schooling might then be seen as a mitigating circumstance on early school leaving in the poor attendance group!

In the rest of the pathway, we are not given the necessary data to see whether the same complex contingency is the case. However, it could be the case that while a child with poor schooling is more likely to lack

Figure 3.17 The psychosocial pathway described by Quinton and Rutter (1988) on the outcome of institutionally reared girls. Figure from Rutter (1989).

scholastic qualifications, a child who lacks scholastic qualifications because of poor schooling is less likely to end up in unskilled work than someone without qualifications who has had good schooling.

Rutter (1989) describes the figure from Gray et al. as 'simplified', and in this form the figure may be less than helpful as an aid to thinking about some of the problems. In the same paper, Rutter brings together a number of examples of the psychosocial pathway being used to show how outcomes can be different. One example, shown in figure 3.17, comes from a study by Quinton and Rutter (1988) on the outcome of institutionally reared girls, a third of whom manifested parenting breakdown. More detailed analysis showed that this was not due to the institutionalization *per se*, but rather to the quality of the family home. If, on leaving the institution, the child returns to a discordant family in adolescence, the likelihood of an early marriage with poor prospects is increased. This is associated with increased risk of poor social functioning, which, in turn, is associated with an increase in breakdown of parenting. Girls who return from the institution in adolescence to a harmonious home are much more likely to end up as adequate parents. It is tempting to see such intergenerational transmission as inevitable, but there is at least one other major factor, the quality of the schooling. Children's homes tend to distribute the children in their care around the local schools. This leads to a variety of school experience, which has a major impact on outcome, as indicated in the figure.[9]

I have analysed these examples in some detail as a means of contrasting them with the causal model. One clear difference that emerges from the above analysis is that while *cause* propagates down the causal model, it does not propagate down the psychosocial pathway as usually constructed. This is not accidental, I feel, but rather expresses a view of life-span development that is gaining currency. According to this view, adverse early life events are no longer seen as *determining* later outcomes (Clarke & Clarke 1999). What such events do is to place you in a disadvantaged situation, from which it is more difficult to achieve a satisfactory outcome at the next stage. They may make you more vulnerable to bad outcomes from later setbacks. The adverse early events certainly are a disadvantage, but this is not the same as life-span determination.[10] This may all look dangerously close to a social philosophy rather than a scientific analysis, but cause and responsibility are not to be equated.[11] In summary, it is possible to say that a particular behavioural sign is caused, remotely, by the genetic abnormality that is at the beginning of the causal chain. This would be the case no matter how many steps there were in between. It is clear, however, that we are not on so good a ground in saying, for example, that someone's poor employment record is caused by his or her poor schooling.

Risk

Psychosocial pathways can be seen as a special case of the more general concept of risk. As will already be apparent, the concepts in this area are tricky. The term 'risk' is used in a number of ways. One paper that

[9] Note, however, that there could well be contingencies between family background and the ability to profit from school, even when intelligence and other individual variables are taken into account.
[10] '[T]he fault . . . is not in our stars but in ourselves . . .'
[11] An extreme example of the separation is given in a guidebook to Bali, in which the traveller is warned of the consequences of being involved in a traffic accident. Irrespective of the cause of the accident, it is claimed, it is the tourist who will be deemed responsible, since if the tourist had not visited the island, the accident would not have taken place.

has attempted to bring a form of order is by Kraemer et al. (1997). I will talk a little about it just to air some of the issues, but without attempting to come to any conclusion about the specific merits of the particular approach. The approach is strictly empirical. The interest is in precursors for outcomes. The objective is to predict with the aim of informing strategies for prevention, treatment and maintenance of remission. There is no theory of cause built in to the system, although Kraemer et al. do touch on cause eventually. They propose the following definitions:

1   A *factor* is any characterization of a subject within a well defined population where the outcome of interest is found. The outcome is binary – either it occurs in an individual or it doesn't.
2   A *risk factor* correlates with the outcome and precedes it in time.
3   A risk factor that can change either spontaneously (such as age or weight) or by intervention (e.g. drug or therapy) is called a *variable risk factor.*
4   A variable risk factor that changes the risk of the outcome is called a *causal* risk factor.

According to such definitions, genes cannot be causal risk factors, although some gene products would qualify, since they are manipulable. Kraemer et al. note that they use the term 'causal risk factor' and *not* 'cause'. For them, 'cause' suggests a necessary and sufficient condition for the disorder. They point out that causal risk factors for acquired immunodeficiency syndrome (AIDS) include unprotected sex and the sharing of needles. The cause of AIDS, however, is the human immunodeficiency virus, without which unprotected sex and needle sharing would not be risk factors.

The relation between risk and cause enters into one of Kraemer et al.'s summary statements: 'Any disorder may have a myriad of risk factors, some of which play only a peripheral role in the development of the disorder or its course, and many of which will not be causal.' (p. 342). These distinctions will be useful in some of the later chapters.

Developmental contingency modelling

Another notation that has temporal sequence at its core is developmental contingency modelling (Morton 1986). This notation also is more natural when discussing the preconditions for normal development.

Let me start with the following question: 'What is the cause of the development of pretend play?' A question of this form seems distinctly odd to me. The reason that it seems odd has to do with the relative uniqueness of *A* that I expect in the claim *A caused B*. The uniqueness takes three forms:

1 There should not be many other examples of *x* for which it would be the case that *x caused B*.
2 Neither of conditions *A* or *B* should be common in the population.
3 There should not be too many exceptions – that is, people for whom *A* is true but *B* is not.

So, 'Being human is the cause of our misery' is not scientifically useful, even though the sentiment may be consoling for some. There are many other reasons for misery; most of us are human; and a surprising number of humans are not miserable.

Notice that this use of 'cause', which is the way it is used in ordinary language (including in medicine), is very much weaker than the related notion of 'implication', where, if *A implies B*, then there would be no cases of *A* without *B*. 'Cause', in the developmental domain (and, indeed, in the human domain as a whole), is not nearly so strict, for reasons I will explore below, particularly in chapter 7.

The above constraints on 'cause' mean that we normally do not talk about the cause of a normal condition. In particular, too many things would count as causes to make the notion worthwhile. Instead, we might refer to the *preconditions* for a particular aspect of normal development. It was for such reasons that I (Morton 1986) developed the Developmental Contingency Model (DCM) in the context of the emergence of mentalizing in normal development. This brings us back to the question on the *cause* of pretend play posed at the beginning of this section. But instead of asking about the *cause* of pretend play, we can think about the *preconditions* of pretend play, and related abilities. In fact, I will focus on only one of the many necessary preconditions.

Figure 3.18 is a Developmental Contingency Model, and not a flow chart or an information processing model. The horseshoe symbol on the lines in figure 3.18 is to be read as '(normally) requires the (pre-)existence of'. Thus, pairs of connected elements are related developmentally and each such pair effectively represents a hypothesis about developmental contingencies. These range in importance. The most trivial is that a certain amount of cognitive ability will be necessary

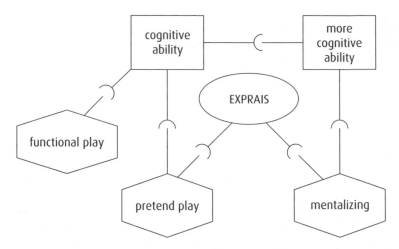

Figure 3.18 An illustrative Developmental Contingency Model (DCM) relating to autism.

for a child to be able to play. More profoundly – and this was Alan Leslie's (1987) insight – for pretend play, a special cognitive ability called the expression raiser (EXPRAIS) is also necessary. This is all described in more detail in chapter 4 (p. 87). EXPRAIS is also needed for a child to develop mentalizing skills, which normally emerge at around the age of four. The DCM is to be understood as implying that if the child either has insufficient cognitive ability (a normal three-year-old) or lacks EXPRAIS (hypothesized to be the case for children with autism), he or she will not have mentalizing skills.

The properties of the notation

In developmental contingency modelling, it is natural to trace contingencies back to the biological givens.[12] There is also the presupposition is that such biological givens will not be associated with behaviour in any simple way. Each one will be implicated in a wide range of activities and the absence of any one would have far-ranging consequences. A second presupposition is that no special environmental conditions are required for the normal fruition of the givens. That is not to say that there is no learning, but simply that the learning is effort-free. The

[12] This will be seen as the first of our maxims of causal modelling in chapter 5.

child learns about language, objects, family, causality, number and so on in an effort-free way because what is happening in the course of such learning is that the givens are being used. There is almost a teleological element about this. The processing machinery and the innate structures are constructed in the way they are in order that the goals shall always be reached. This is the achievement of evolution. The child has no choice in the matter; its 'learning' is under the control of its processes. A child can choose not to speak, but it cannot choose not to learn its native language. The biological givens that subsume language learning make sure of that.

In the DCM framework, the focus is on the prerequisites for the emergence of a particular process or structure. Such properties of the infant brain form 'elements' in a DCM. Although the direct evidence for the existence of such elements will be behavioural, the primary focus will be on the elements rather than on the behaviour. There are two main reasons for this. First, an element may be present without being visible in behaviour. Thus, a profoundly deaf infant who has no experience of sign language still has the innate component of the language learning apparatus. The presence of this component will be revealed as soon as signing starts. Before this point, the component was not able to exert any significant influence on behaviour.

The second reason for focusing on the underlying elements rather than behaviour is that a particular aspect of behaviour could be mediated by a variety of means. For example, autistic children may learn to have exchanges of utterances with adults. However, in the majority of cases, such exchanges would not, on close analysis, be confusable with the conversations that normal children have. Normally, conversations are driven by representations that depend on mentalizing (among other things) and are intrinsically 'reinforcing' for normal children. The autistic child would only slowly learn that they were appropriate modes of behaviour. These two arguments for considering elements rather than behaviour are in line with the case for cognition that was made in chapter 2.

In the preceding paragraphs, I have indicated why the focus of the DCM method is on the elements of the child's cognitive apparatus rather than on behaviour. We should now look at the elements more closely. To start with, I can make the point that elements are either primitive or not. By 'primitive', I mean irreducible. Trivially, it must be the case either that a particular element E can only emerge given that some specific element D has already emerged (to some level of specification) or that E is a primitive. The development of non-primitives depends upon the prior functioning of particular primitives plus exposure to specific kinds of stimuli. Primitives require at most a minimal environment. Note that primitives need not be present from birth, but could arise in the course of maturation. It may also be the case that the development of a primitive requires a particular contribution from the environment. Johnson and Morton (1991) explored a similar notion with their idea of a *primal* factor.

In practice, there will be a variety of patterns of contingencies. Thus, we can imagine a skill whose emergence is a function of a late maturing structure but which also depends upon the prior existence of other processes or knowledge. We would want to be able to represent all such contingencies. The general form of the contingency model is that of elements connected in a directed graph. The elements can be of a variety of kinds – processes, structures, knowledge, perceptual or other experiences, or biological elements. The symbols on the connecting lines have temporal/causal implications.

The relation between DCMs and causal models

I noted in the previous section that it doesn't make much sense to talk about the *cause* of normal development. It was for this reason that I introduced the Developmental Contingency Model. The relation between the DCM and the causal model is quite straightforward. Suppose that we are interested in the development of an ability, A; say, speech. We establish that the normal development of A (speech, for example) depends on the prior development of at least two features X and Y (ears and mouth). The DCM for this development is shown in figure 3.19.

From what I have already said, it should be clear that the normal development of A (speech) will be prevented or impeded in the case of delay of development or malfunction of either X (ears) or Y (mouth).

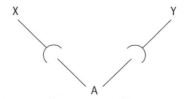

Figure 3.19 A simplified Developmental Contingency Model, claim that both of elements *X* and *Y* are necessary for the normal development of *A*.

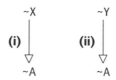

Figure 3.20 The causal implications of the DCM in figure 3.19. If either X or Y is missing, then A will not develop.

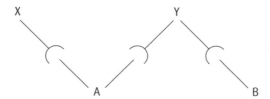

Figure 3.21 A slightly more complex DCM than that in figure 3.19. Element Y is necessary for the normal development of B as well as A.

There will thus be two different causal models of malfunction of A, depending as to whether the hearing of speech or the production of sounds is affected. The two causal models are shown in figure 3.20. If we observe the absence of A, we cannot infer the underlying cause. In a first case (i), it is possible that feature Y (producing sounds) is still intact; in case (ii), it is possible that feature X is still intact. Let us take case (i). The first step in establishing that feature Y is functioning would be to test some other ability, B, which would normally also depend on the existence of feature Y. Thus a more complete DCM would be as shown in figure 3.21.

While children who fall under case (i) would show ability B, case (ii) children would not. We would, however, expect case (ii) children to show other abilities that depend on feature X.[13] The more complete causal model for case (ii) would mention both abilities A and B, as shown in figure 3.22.

I can illustrate this principle with an example from the area of literacy development. One component of mature reading is the ability

---

[13]   The prediction of the absence of an ability depends upon the child being unable to develop the ability through a compensatory strategy. As we shall see, this is not always the case. That is, a case (ii) child might not demonstrate ability B caused by the absence of Y, but may exhibit ability A through compensation. Thus a deaf child can learn to speak via lip reading, even though the normal route for doing so was blocked.

Figure 3.22 A causal model related to the DCM in figure 3.21. The absence of Y has two consequences.

to decode letter strings into speech. There are many factors that are prerequisites for this skill. I will select two of these. One is knowledge of the visual forms of letters and the other is the ability to assemble phonological strings. The relationships among these abilities are shown in the DCM fragment in figure 3.23. If a child has failed to acquire either the letter knowledge or the phonological skills, then this child will not be able to acquire the decoding skill. These simple causal relationships are shown in figure 3.24. If we only know of a particular child that he or

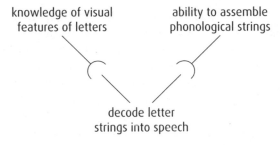

Figure 3.23 A fragment of a DCM for the acquisition of reading.

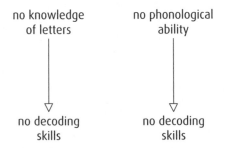

Figure 3.24 Two causal implications of the DCM in the previous figure. It is clear that the absence of decoding skills leaves us not knowing what the underlying problem is.

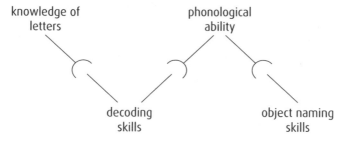

Figure 3.25 An elaboration of the DCM in figure 3.23. This theory is stronger because the extension provides us with a way of deciding whether the absence of decoding skills is attributable to problems with letters or with phonemes.

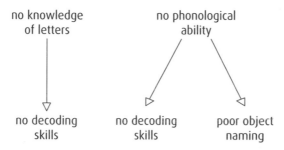

Figure 3.26 Two possible causal models derived from the preceding figure. The performance of object naming is diagnostic for the cause of the lack of decoding skills.

she has no decoding skill, we cannot tell whether this is because that child lacks one or other of the prerequisites (not to mention other possibilities). We can note, however, that the phonological abilities will reveal themselves in other simple tasks, such as an 'I spy' game.[14] This dependency is represented in figure 3.25. The causal consequences of an absence of phonological skills can now be extended as in figure 3.26. Other things being equal, we can tell the difference between the child who cannot decode simply for reason of absence of letter knowledge and the child who lacks the requisite phonological skills; we look

[14] The 'I spy' game involves one person saying 'I spy, with my little eye, something beginning with /b/' (or some other letter sound or name). The other person has to guess the object in question.

at performance on the 'I spy' game and we look at performance on a letter-naming game.

In the chapters to come, I will refer to developmental contingency modelling from time to time, and I will draw on the relationship between causal modelling and developmental contingency modelling in analysing various theories.

4 AUTISM: HOW CAUSAL MODELLING STARTED

The problem that originally forced Uta Frith and me to create and diagram the three-level causal framework was one particularly serious developmental disorder, autism. At the Cognitive Development Unit, we had spent a considerable number of working years studying this disorder and needed to take stock of where we had got to. We needed to know just where we agreed and disagreed with other people who had also spent many years' worth of work on this topic. In this chapter, I will review our approach to autism, and how it led to the causal modelling framework. In chapter 6, I will use causal modelling to describe other theories of autism. Since this book is about causal modelling and not about autism, I will outline our views on autism without giving a great deal of the history of these views or trying to provide a complete defence of them in relation to alternative theories. Anyone wishing to learn more on those topics should read Uta Frith's *Autism* (2003), which covers them at length.

For any causal account of a condition, it is vital to be able to agree on what it is that we wish to account for. 'Is there such a thing as autism?' is a question that continues to be asked when there is uncertainty about the behavioural as well as the biological level of description. 'Every autistic child is different' is a frequent cry from the bewildered carer. And yet, over the last 50 years, the consensus about autism as a clinical entity with special needs and a predictable course has grown steadily.

Where do we start? Despite continuing controversy about the precise diagnostic criteria, there is agreement that there are different variants of autism. It is a matter of debate as to whether the variants are to be described merely in terms of degree of severity – that is, 'spectrum' – or in terms of qualitative differences. From the point of view of this chapter, the outcome of this debate would only result in variation in the detail of the causal model. The basic form of the model would not change.

For simplicity, let me take the concept of the *autistic spectrum*. Disorders of this spectrum have in common three core features (Wing 1988):

1 *Impairment in socialization* – specific impairment in the quality of reciprocal interactions, ranging from aloof to passive to odd.
2 *Impairment in communication* – delay in language acquisition and poor use of verbal and non-verbal means of communication.
3 *Impairment in imagination* – lack of understanding of make-believe.

These three features were first found as a triad of impairments by epidemiological research (Wing & Gould 1979),[1] where they were discovered to form a syndrome; that is, to be closely associated in individuals and to manifest themselves in a variety of behaviours according to age and ability. Although the triad was found in children with classic autism, it was also present in children who had not been so diagnosed. Furthermore, while autism was a condition that had been thought to be invariably associated with general intellectual retardation, the triad was also occasionally found in children of average or above average intelligence.

There is in fact a lot of agreement about diagnostic criteria. Fifty years after Kanner's first description of autism (in 1943), there is a set of internationally recognized *behavioural criteria* that are considered essential for the diagnosis. These are listed currently in ICD-10 (World Health Organisation 1992) and DSM-IV (American Psychiatric Association 1994), having been gradually updated from their previous editions. As an illustration, I show the DSM-IV criteria for autistic disorder in box 4.1. To summarize these criteria, we need to focus on just three areas: impairments in social interaction, impairments in communication and the presence of stereotypical behaviours. The first impairment refers to some very *specific* problems in social two-way interaction; the second to very *specific* problems in sharing verbal or non-verbal communications, and lack of spontaneous make-believe play; and the third refers to a variety of odd and idiosyncratic interests and habits, and *specific* restricted repetitive activities.

---

[1] The phrasing of the third of the 'core features' in Wing and Gould's 1979 epidemiological study was 'repetitive activities in place of imaginative symbolic interests' (Wing & Gould 1979, p. 26).

Box 4.1 Diagnostic criteria for 299.00 Autistic Disorder – from DSM-IV

A. A total of six (or more) items from (1), (2), and (3), with at least two from (1), and one each from (2) and (3):

(1) qualitative impairment in social interaction, as manifested by at least two of the following:

    (a) marked impairment in the use of multiple nonverbal behaviors such as eye-to-eye gaze, facial expression, body postures, and gestures to regulate social interaction

    (b) failure to develop peer relationships appropriate to developmental level

    (c) a lack of spontaneous seeking to share enjoyment, interests, or achievements with other people (e.g., by a lack of showing, bringing, or pointing out objects of interest)

    (d) lack of social or emotional reciprocity

(2) qualitative impairments in communication as manifested by at least one of the following:

    (a) delay in, or total lack of, the development of spoken language (not accompanied by an attempt to compensate through alternative modes of communication such as gesture or mime)

    (b) in individuals with adequate speech, marked impairment in the ability to initiate or sustain a conversation with others

    (c) stereotyped and repetitive use of language or idiosyncratic language

    (d) lack of varied, spontaneous make-believe play or social imitative play appropriate to developmental level

(3) restricted repetitive and stereotyped patterns of behavior, interests, and activities, as manifested by at least one of the following:

    (a) encompassing preoccupation with one or more stereotyped and restricted patterns of interest that is abnormal either in intensity or focus

    (b) apparently inflexible adherence to specific, nonfunctional routines or rituals

    (c) stereotyped and repetitive motor mannerisms (e.g., hand or finger flapping or twisting, or complex whole-body movements)

    (d) persistent preoccupation with parts of objects

B. Delays or abnormal functioning in at least one of the following areas, with onset prior to age 3 years: (1) social interaction, (2) language as used in social communication, or (3) symbolic or imaginative play.

C. The disturbance is not better accounted for by Rett's Disorder or Childhood Disintegrative Disorder.

Source: Reprinted with permission from the *Diagnostic and Statistical Manual of Mental Disorders*. Copyright 2000, American Psychiatric Association.

The term *specific* is full of meaning here – it suggests: be careful, the behaviour mentioned after this word is not what you think it is. It suggests that the behaviour mentioned will be characteristic and recognizable to an expert. It suggests that not all of the area that this behaviour covers would be expected to be impaired. In other words, the criteria are deceptively full of words that you know and use in every-day life, but here they have a restricted and technical meaning.

Even if there were no arguments about the definition of the core features of autism, there are usually many more symptoms found in individual autistic children, in addition to the core features. We frequently find specific language impairments, motor coordination problems and general learning disability. Besides these, there are other features, often seen in autism, which may include anxiety and bewilderment as well as slow learning and lack of generalization. Impairments in attention, memory and perception have also been described in children within the spectrum of autistic disorders (Gillberg 1992). The range of signs and symptoms is, indeed, great, and the problem of accounting for all of them is still wide open. You can also note, from the criteria in box 4.1, that it would be possible to have two autistic children who shared not one of the diagnostic features with each other.

So, the behavioural criteria for autism are agreed – among experts, but the experts also know that there is an enormous amount of variabil-ity in the critical behaviours that might be shown. And a lot of other kinds of behaviour, not mentioned in the box, will also occur, and indeed may be, to the parents, the most pressing thing to talk about. For instance, Fred, a child with autism, was extremely destructive, and apparently enjoyed breaking glasses, lamps and windows. Clearly, this behaviour was very abnormal, distressing and dangerous, and needed attention, but, nevertheless, it was not taken into account when the diagnosis was made.

Despite the incredible differences in the stories of each individual child and family, the expert seems to be able to draw the conclusions that the child suffers from autism. Otherwise, there could never have been the agreement that went into the 'shopping list' in box 4.1. This is remarkable, because there exists no textbook that one can consult which is flexible enough to allow for all eventualities if some behaviour does not fit in with this diagnostic decision. Behaviour varies not only between different children who are all recognized as autistic, but also within one and the same child, over the years, as physical and mental growth proceeds. We must conclude that there is something more than just behaviour that the diagnostician takes into account – he or she also interprets the behaviour, and knows which instance to ignore. What makes some people so good at diagnosis was one of the questions that Uta and I had often wondered about. The answer, we felt, was that these people were able to create a model of the mental structures of the child in such a way that the autistic children all seemed the same in spite of the variation in behaviour.

At the time, Uta and I thought that life would be much easier if there were a simple physical diagnostic test for autism. Perhaps a missing enzyme might uniquely diagnose a child as suffering from autism, and this could be done at the earliest possible time. Since Kanner, many different biological abnormalities have been identified in autism. It is no longer possible to claim that the brain of the individual with autism is essentially normal – which, strangely enough, was once thought to be the case. However, we deduced from all the research papers on the biochemical abnormalities in autism that there was no way that a simple test could exist. The papers on physiological and neurological conditions left us with the strong impression that the disorder could occur (diagnosed by the same expert clinician) in individuals with quite different biological problems. So, biological methods did not seem to promise to be the solution. No simple blood test was in sight. To answer the question of what made clinicians able to intuit an underlying condition of autism, we needed to turn elsewhere.

The only solution, so far as we could see, was that there was less variability in autistics at the cognitive level than at either the biological or the behavioural level. Cognition, as we saw in chapter 2, is the level between behaviour and the brain, where in principle we can specify a single underlying cause for a variety of behaviours. Some of the hypotheses that had previously been suggested for the underlying deficit in autism suffered from the problem that it was very difficult to tell what was a cognitive cause, and what was a behavioural description. This was because the terms used were ambiguous and because no clear causal relationship was traced between the posited cause and the complex of symptoms. One instructive example was language impairment. There used to be a number of people who held most strongly the belief that the cause of autism was an underlying language impairment. One of the pieces of evidence brought forward to justify this claim was the undoubted fact that all autistic children showed some language impairment in the form of early language delay.

The thoughtful reader will have spotted the hint of circularity here, that the language deficit in autistics is deemed responsible for autism, one of the signs of which is that self-same language deficit. But I will ignore this circularity as a relatively common phenomenon.[2] Let me instead focus on the question: Is the hypothesis of an *underlying* language impairment as a cause of a variety of autism-specific behaviours (Remember what I said about the term specific?) a cognitive cause or simply a summary statement of a behavioural description? So what about testable predictions? If a language component in the mind is defective, what would one expect? Well, here goes: delay in language acquisition, poor comprehension of what people say, poor ability to tell whether a sentence is grammatically acceptable or not, poor understanding of word meaning, poor understanding of stories, poor reading, poor speaking – and so on. All of these predictions could turn out to be correct, but we would not be any further ahead. We can predict a range of behaviours in the language domain, but this is not a cognitive-level explanation for the language deficit. In addition, it does nothing to explain the other non-language aspects of autism.

Another example of circularity in explanation is provided by Kanner's (1943) original idea of an underlying **disturbance of affective contact**. This is a typical cognitive-level term. What of the testable predictions? – poor one-to-one relationships, lack of emotional attachment, inability to make friends, lack of interest in social interactions with people, and so on. Circularity is almost inevitable here, as Kanner *defined* autism just in these terms. So, if a prediction about a supposed autistic individual were not upheld, then this individual would have to be excluded from the category of autism altogether. This always follows if the definition of a condition is in the terms of a *required* pattern of behaviour. There is, by this definition, no room for variability. Prediction and diagnosis are equivalent.

How, then, should we deal with variability? If you insist on sticking to behaviour, then variability can be captured by means of the shopping list method. This is a method often used by the two major classification methods, DSM and ICD. In the description of the criteria for giving a

[2] The current manifestation of this phenomenon is the claim that the underlying deficit in autism is a 'frontal lobe deficit'. The main evidence is that autistic children all have problems with (some) tasks that (some) people with frontal lobe lesions also find difficult. I will be discussing this idea later on, but you may like to pause and think about what possible causal model may underlie the claim.

particular diagnosis, you may find something like 'any three of the following ten symptoms' as a criterion, as we saw in the DSM-IV criteria for autism given in box 4.1. However, in this case there is, again, no room for novel predictions, no way to decide whether newly observed patterns of behaviour or responses in an experimental situation belong to the basic underlying condition or are additional deficits. Nor could there be, without a cognitive account. Only with a cognitive account is it possible to move beyond what is already known. Only with a cognitive account will we be able to account for variability in behaviour as a consequence of the interaction of a basic deficit with variability in other cognitive functions or environmental factors.

Why cognitive? Why can't we deal with variability through intelligent generalization from the given criteria? That sounds good in principle, and may be the way in which good clinicians believe that they are proceeding. The problem is, however, knowing which generalizations are valid and which are invalid. Let me take criterion (3d) in box 4.1:

█ (d) persistent preoccupation with parts of objects.

What would count as a valid generalization from this? How about persistent preoccupation with parts of animals? Suppose that a child persistently pulled the wings off flies, for example. Would that count as a sign of autism? Clearly not. But why not? Because such behaviour does not fit in with the clinical picture; and because the clinical picture is more than the sum of the candidate behaviours. It has to do with the *principles* underlying the behaviour. And this is what I mean by cognition.

Another factor that we need in the account of autism is to allow for the components that lead to some of the large individual differences in the clinical picture of autistic people. These include, in particular, processes of *compensation*, and changes over time due to either internal factors such as *maturation* or external factors such as teaching. I will deal with factors such as these from time to time in the following chapters. For the moment, we can just note that these are other ways in which the primary behavioural features of autism can change. We cannot, however, infer from a change in patterns of behaviour that there has been a change in the underlying condition.[3]

---

[3] This is probably as good a place as any for me to introduce a favourite aphorism of mine: *Behaviour cannot change.* Before you start spluttering with indignation (which people do), think for a moment: *What might he mean?* The point is first that

In summary, we have to be extremely careful about using mere descriptions of patterns of symptoms as though they were causal explanations of the underlying disorder.

The biological origin of autism ■

It has now been generally accepted that there must be a biological origin to autism (see Bailey et al. 1996; Happé & Frith 1996). There are several reasons for this. First, the majority of autistic individuals show direct signs of brain dysfunction at the physiological and neurochemical levels. This shows through fMRI scans, cerebral spinal fluid investigations, brain stem auditory potentials, the presence of epilepsy and many other factors (Steffenburg 1991; Gillberg 1992). Sample findings are given in box 4.2. Given a range of possible brain impairments in autistics, we have no idea at the moment which kind of damage is actually responsible for the autism. However, it is known that people with autism have a greatly increased chance of having diverse medical conditions as background factors.[4] Secondly, there are indirect indications of brain damage, in that autism is strongly associated with mental retardation. As one takes progressively more retarded samples of children, the likelihood of autism increases (Wing & Gould 1979). A simple way of modelling this pattern is to posit that there is a specific brain system necessary for normal development, disturbance of which leads to autism. In this model we could predict that brain damage that results in general intellectual retardation could be seen as due to randomly distributed lesions. The greater the damage, the higher is the probability that the critical brain system will be affected (Frith et al. 1991).

The brain damage that causes the autism is itself the result of causal factors. In figure 4.1, we have a hypothesized single biological origin, O,

---

behaviour is ephemeral; once is has happened, it is gone. In contrast, biology and cognition remain. Secondly, if you change a *pattern* of behaviour and leave the cognitive system as it was, particularly with respect to patterns of belief, you will eventually get the old patterns back. That's why beating children doesn't work.

[4] Note that we rule out the possibility that the cognitive aspects of autism could cause the kind of brain damage found. Indeed, the only way in which cognitive activity is known to be the cause of changes in the brain that might be called 'damage' comes from traumatic experience, where the emotion resulting from the trauma is believed to result in a shrunken hippocampus (Gilbertson et al. 2002).

Box 4.2   Brain dysfunction and autism

Studies of brain dysfunction in autistic individuals have been highly competitive over the last few years. The research goal seems to have been finding the single cause. Unfortunately, it seems as though brain dysfunction is remarkably widespread in autism. A variety of claims have been made, implicating the brain stem, the cerebellum, the limbic system, the thalamus, the left hemisphere and the frontal lobes. I have not read all these references myself, but have culled them from a variety of places. So don't blame me.

The earliest findings concerning specific deficits were determined using pneumoencephalography (Aarkrog 1968; Hauser et al. 1975), CT scans (Damasio et al. 1980; Campbell et al. 1982) and MRI scans (Gaffney et al. 1989). The common finding of these studies was an enlargement of the ventricles, which suggested developmental atrophy in adjacent limbic and associated frontal structures. However, this enlargement of the ventricles has not been found in all autistic subjects (Harcherik et al. 1985; Creasey et al. 1986). A second wave of studies implicated the vermis of the cerebellum (Ritvo et al. 1986; Courchesne et al. 1988).

Again, this was not found in all studies. The above studies were the result of CT scans and they have been backed up by anatomical studies by Bauman and Kemper (1985), who found structural anomalies in both limbic and cerebellar areas of autistic patients. More recently, Piven (1990) reported evidence for cortical migrational anomalies. However, these anomalies were only found (through an MRI study) in 7 of 13 high-functioning male autistics. In addition, the malformations were not consistently found in a given lobe or even in a particular hemisphere.

Even in high-functioning autistic people, in whom we can assume that the general level of impairment is low, MRI techniques have revealed abnormalities in the cerebellar vermis (Courchesne et al. 1988). Autopsy studies have suggested neuronal disruption in a number of brain areas, particularly in the limbic system (Bauman & Kemper 1985), and some reviews of the literature conclude that there is cortical as well as subcortical involvement (Dawson & Levy 1989). However, such studies have not yet separated causal and correlative relationships between these various kinds of brain damage and autism.

PET scan studies have been particularly disappointing. Unfortunately, these have only used resting scans rather than functional imaging (Horwitz et al. 1988; Herold et al. 1997). Horwitz et al. interpreted their results as indicating dysfunction in a distributed system that subserves directive attention.

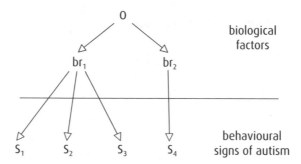

Figure 4.1 A causal model of a theory that claims that O is the origin of autism leading to two forms of brain damage, one of which leads to the behavioural signs of autism (S_{1-3}) and the other, correlated damage, has other consequences (S_4). The arrow represents the causal relationship. A horizontal line is used to separate the biological and behavioural levels.

which could be a particular genetic condition, for example. This could also give rise to other damage that is unrelated to the autism. The arrow represents the causal relationship. A horizontal line is used to separate the biological and behavioural levels. The genetic condition gives rise to two kinds of abnormal development in the brain, which I have labelled br_1 and br_2. In the example, br_1 is solely responsible for the cluster of behavioural signs S_{1-3}, which are the main diagnostic criteria for autism. However, in this not implausible scenario, the kind of damage that I have termed br_2 will always be found, but will, by the terms of the scenario, have no causal role in the autism. This, then, illustrates the difference between correlation (br_2) and cause (br_1). To give a concrete illustration of the principle, it is possible that the cerebellar damage found in many autistic people has no causal effect on the defining symptoms of autism. In figure 4.1, S_{1-3} would then represent the autistic signs and S_4 the effects of cerebellar damage.

The symbol S is used for signs and symptoms at the behavioural level. I have indicated subcategories S_{1-3} without specifying them. The subcategories would be easily formed; for instance, by using the distinction between positive and negative signs, or between signs and symptoms. Signs are the objectively observable behaviours. They are positive if they are abnormal by their presence and negative if they are abnormal by their absence. On the other hand, we only know about symptoms through the patient's self-report or through indirect inference. For instance, if we saw a person talking and listening intently when no-one was there, we might infer that they were hearing 'voices'. Whether we use signs or symptoms will depend upon the particular causal theory being proposed. The general form of the causal model will remain the same.

I have mentioned a variety of kinds of brain impairment that have been associated with autism. These are abnormalities found at the end of an early developmental process and are thought to persist throughout life. The adult autistic brain is just as good a source to provide data about these abnormalities as that of the child. However, the damage itself must have a cause in the developmental history of the autistic individual. With respect to the biological origins of autism, genetic factors have received particularly strong confirmation (Bolton & Rutter 1990; Rutter et al. 1990; Rutter 2000). The results from both twin and family studies suggest that the genetic causes are themselves likely to be heterogeneous (Szatmari & Jones 1991). While genetic factors may well be the major cause of the majority of autistic disorders, other causal factors, such as viral disease, are still being considered as additional, independent causes (Nunn et al. 1986; Tsai 1989). There have been recent claims that the MMR (measles, mumps, rubella) inoculation has led to severe autistic symptoms in previously normally developing children. The causal pathway for such effects, according to the supporters of this position, would clearly have to differ from other paths, but would affect the specific system br_1 in figure 4.1.

At the biological level, then, there are a variety of possible prime causes that can lead to autism. Since we assume that all cases of autism have something in common, we suppose that all the prime causes will eventually be shown to affect the same brain system in some way or other.[5] By brain system I mean that part (or parts) of the brain that performs a particular identifiable function.[6] The possible causal effects include destruction of the system, disconnection from other parts of

[5]   There is an underlying assumption that I make here, which is that diagnostic categories such as autism will reflect a common disorder that will be definable in terms of cognitive and brain factors. The argument in this section would not apply to a diagnostic category that was essentially behavioural, such as conduct disorder, since any behaviourally defined disorder will be liable to alternative cognitive (and brain) causation. This issue is taken up in chapter 5.

[6]   The framework is neutral with respect to whether any cognitive function is localized or distributed in the brain, and as to whether any particular region of the brain is dedicated to a single function or can subserve a variety of functions.

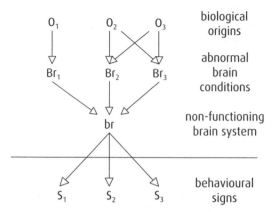

Figure 4.2 A causal model for autism, showing a convergence on a particular non-functioning brain system as the defining feature. The biological origins would include genetic and viral factors, and the abnormal brain conditions would include non-specific classes such as abnormal cell migration or problems with a specific neurotransmitter system.

the brain, or damage or changes in structure leading to malfunction. In any individual case, even if we lack precise information, we can still discuss the available biological evidence in terms of a causal analysis, while marking the gaps in the reasoning for filling in when the appropriate information is available.

In figure 4.2, I represent the material that I have just summarized. The items at the top level, called O_{1-3}, represent the postulated biological origins – genetic and other factors. This diagram represents a summary statement, ideally across the full range of the disorder. For any one child, it is possible that only one of the biological origins will apply. Each of the biological origins causes a variety of abnormal brain conditions over the course of development in a way as yet to be established. I have symbolized such non-specific brain conditions as Br_n.[7] Having identified the place in the model for the autism-critical brain condition, we can go a step further in our causal theorizing. The kinds of general brain abnormality (Br_n) required for a causal account will be

---

[7]   I use Br, with an upper-case 'B', to refer to general conditions such as abnormal migration of cortical cells or an imbalance of neurotransmitters: br, with a lower-case 'b', is used to refer to specific conditions such as a network that fails to perform an expected computation.

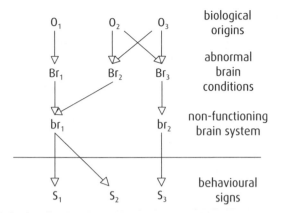

Figure 4.3 A sample causal model in which two different brain systems contribute to the behavioural phenotype of the disorder.

all those that affect a common system, here called br. In the model, it is damage to the specific system br or interruption of the functioning of system br that causes autism. In this figure, then, I have added another link to the causal chain on the biological level. Note that we could do this even though very little is as yet known about the anatomical and physiological, let alone molecular biological, facts. Having added the link, we immediately see an interesting consequence: it may turn out that there are two or even more identifiable cortical systems the abnormal development of which is jointly responsible for the autistic behavioural complex.

I have illustrated the possibility of two responsible cortical systems in figure 4.3, where, in addition, I model a theory that includes two specific biological systems, br_1 and br_2, which are responsible for different aspects of the behavioural manifestations of autism. This exercise illustrates what it means to say that different symptoms, even though they co-occur, are not necessarily traceable to the same underlying biological fault. How would we know when this was the case? We would see dissociations between otherwise related behaviours. Thus S_2 and S_1 would be seen together far more often than S_3 and S_1. An example will be considered later on.

We have claimed elsewhere that the causal chain between candidate biological factors and the resulting behavioural impairment requires an intervening *cognitive* level (Frith et al. 1991). Some of these arguments

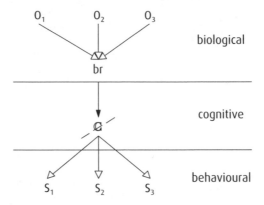

Figure 4.4 A sample causal model that includes an abnormal cognitive system as part of the common pathway for a disorder.

were reviewed in chapter 2. The final form of our diagram, then, must include the cognitive level. Within this level there will be a number of further links in the causal chain. The general form of this causal model is shown in figure 4.4, with just a single link in the cognitive level and with the biological level simplified slightly for the purposes of exposition. The struck-out 'C' symbolizes a cognitive system, found in normal development, that is missing in the abnormal developmental path being described.

Causal models are not determinate

All the primary elements of the causal model are now in place. Note that I might have given the impression in the preceding paragraphs that outcome in the causal model is determined. As a matter of empirical fact, as discussed in chapter 3, all outcomes of developmental abnormalities appear to be probabilistic, and causal diagrams should be interpreted in this way. The reason for uncertainty in outcome is that abnormal development is nearly always caused by multiple factors. Thus, it is rare that variation in a single gene alone can give rise to the full-blown manifestation of any particular condition. Huntington's disease and phenylketonuria appear to be two exceptions (Plomin et al. 2000). The condition will more usually depend upon a combination of genes. The target abnormal gene may be necessary – if the gene is normal then the condition will not appear –

but it will rarely be sufficient.[8] In an equivalent way, we would expect some aspects of the causal chain to depend partially upon external factors, such as the intra-uterine environment. Similar interactions will be found at the cognitive level, where the manifestation of a disorder may vary with intellectual or emotional aspects of the individual from moment to moment. In summary, we expect that variability can occur at any stage in a causal chain.

After these preliminaries, we are now ready to proceed with the task of representing specific theories of autism in the causal modelling framework.

The role of cognition in defining autism ■

In causal modelling, as with other frameworks, there have to be objectives and a set of ground rules. I will expand on these in chapter 5. However, from what I have already said, it should be clear that one of the ground rules of causal analysis is that all of the *core* features of autism will eventually have to be accounted for. In addition, the model will have to account for all of what have been called the *associated* features. It should also be clear that specific accounts are only developed if general accounts do not suffice. Thus, we do not have to account for the consequences of mental retardation in individuals with autism in the same way as we account for the triad of impairments and their consequences. That is to say that while any account of the biological origins of autism must also explain the accompanying mental retardation, it is not required to attempt a single cognitive account of the two. I explore this concept in figure 4.5(a). Here we have two specific consequences, br_1 and br_2, of one and the same general damage, Br. They have different consequences at the cognitive level C_1, which leads to impaired intellectual function, and C_2, which leads to the criterial signs of autism. In any child who suffers from this general type of brain damage, we will always find autism in conjunction with severe mental retardation. It would, of course, be possible to create a different theory, whereby a particular cognitive deficit led both to the intellectual deficit and the autism. This is shown in figure 4.5(b).

---

[8] We can note, for example, that autism and dyslexia are much more common in boys than girls, without anyone suggesting that it is the girl's extra X-chromosome that contains a protective gene.

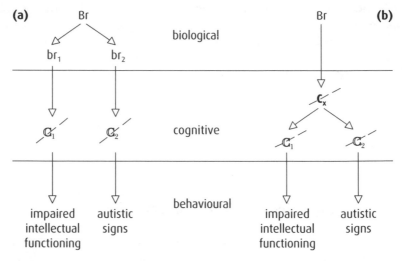

Figure 4.5 Two simplified causal models for autism. An account of the biological origins would need to encompass the entire tree. In (a), there are different biological and cognitive origins for the impaired intellectual functioning and the autism. According to this theory, a cognitive account of autism need only deal with the right-hand portion of the tree. The intellectual functioning would seen as secondary. General theories of mental retardation would be used to deal with the left-hand side. In (b), I have shown a theory that derives both kinds of deficit from the same cognitive source.

Primary and secondary features

Causal analysis must allow for the principled explanation of all the features, including secondary ones. However, the nature of the account of the two will differ. It is often a matter of controversy as to what constitute primary and what secondary features. Let me take as an example anxiety, a frequent symptom in autism. People who regard the anxiety as primary see it as springing directly from a malfunction of the arousal mechanism, which, in turn, is seen as being directly caused by the biological conditions underlying the disorder. In contrast, anxiety can be seen as a secondary and not a primary feature. In this case, I would derive it as a result of the autistic child's incomprehension of features of the environment, particularly the behaviour of other humans. In other words, I believe that autistic anxiety is a normal (and possibly functional) response to the consequences of the condition. I do not want to argue the case here. Our point is that there are two ways of thinking about anxiety, and they can both be expressed as causal models. When you do this, it is easier to understand the comparative claims of the models and decide how the differences might be tested. I suggest that you try to draw these two models as an exercise. My solutions are given in box 4.3.

One particular claim that I make is that pathological features involving a component of the environment in their causal chain will nearly always be secondary and not core features (this is explored later in the context of figure 6.5 – see p. 111). The reason why I propose this is that such sub-chains could be broken by appropriate manipulation of the environment. In the case of anxiety in autism, the manipulations that seem to be successful include the maintenance of a fairly rigid routine. The routine seems to have the desired effect of reducing anxiety through increasing the predictability of events. Hence I would classify the anxiety as secondary rather than primary. What I seem to be doing is interpreting the terms *primary* and *secondary* first in terms of the scope of the causal link from the biological origin to behaviour and, secondly, by the role of the features in diagnosis. The terms should not be seen as indicating relative importance in management or treatment. Note also that the terms primary and secondary do not refer to the probability of a feature occurring. If a secondary feature arises through interaction of the core disorder with an aspect of the environment, and that aspect of the environment is universal, then the secondary feature would always be present. A primary feature, on the other hand, modulated by some other cognitive variable (such as intelligence), may or may not be present. Note that such a definition of secondary features is independent of causal modelling.

Is autism a unitary disorder?

From the brief review above of current work on the biology of autism, I have concluded so far that autism has no single biological origin. Nevertheless, autism, or rather the developmental disorder underlying the spectrum of autistic features, continues to be seen as a single diagnostic category. If there is no single origin, nor any single kind of damage that can be used as criterial, what, then, justifies the application of a single label?

There are two factors that, at first glance, seem to provide sufficient justification. These are the frequent co-occurrence of the triad of impairments (social, imagination and communication) together with

Box 4.3 Anxiety in autism

These are my solutions to the alternatives posed on pages 82–3:

(a) Anxiety as primary:

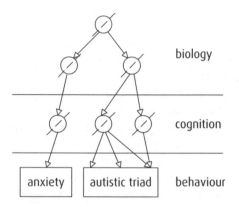

(b) Anxiety as secondary:

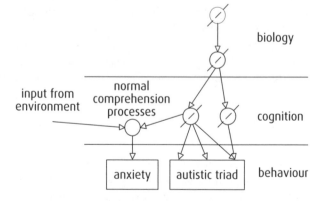

In this case, anxiety is seen as a normal outcome of the failure to understand the environment. The comprehension functions themselves are seen as normal (allowing for MA); however, they lack the appropriate support from other cognitive functions and, in particular, they lack the ability to attribute a causal role to the mental states of others.

the principle of variability, which would give rise to a spectrum of behavioural manifestations, encompassing different degrees of autism. However, the triad, or any similarly defined behavioural phenotype, is simply a collection of symptoms whose co-occurrence is meaningful. In other words, although the term *behavioural phenotype* has descriptive value, it has no explanatory value.

But what if we take another look from a cognitive point of view. As I have already remarked, the common constellation of signs and symptoms could, at a cognitive level, point to a single, underlying cognitive deficit. Clinical experience and the history of autism itself suggest that there could be such a diagnostic entity, which is much more than a chance constellation. Despite proven heterogeneity at the biological and behavioural levels, Uta Frith and other colleagues and I (Frith et al. 1991) decided to explore the possibility of justifying a single label within a causal account. We therefore proposed that what all autistic people have in common is a single *cognitive* deficit. Furthermore, we proposed that this deficit gives rise to the core symptoms in the course of development.

In order to define the specific deficit that might underlie the triad of impairments, we focused our attention on a particular aspect of normal development (Astington et al. 1988; Butterworth et al. 1991; Whiten 1991). This is the development of Theory of Mind[9] (Premack & Woodruff 1978), or 'mentalizing' (Morton 1989), our ability to predict and explain the behaviour of other humans in terms of their mental states. Our ability to **mentalize** is revealed in our use and understanding of such words as *believe, know, wish, desire, intend* and *pretend,* which are acquired remarkably early (Wellman 1991). A central feature of our proposal is that autistic children lack this ability (Baron-Cohen et al. 1985; Leslie 1987). I will explain below how this may account for the core behavioural deficits of autism.

---

[9] The term *theory* in the phrase 'Theory of Mind' has led to certain misunderstandings of our position. In particular, it has led to the belief that we are talking about conscious constructions concerning not only other individuals, but also other minds in general. This is most certainly not what we – or, indeed, Premack and Woodruff (1978), who coined the term – intend to imply, although some theorists in this area do seem to use the term in this sense (Meltzoff & Gopnik 1993; Russell 1997). Human beings certainly do develop explicit theories concerning other minds, and autistic people are notably deficient in such development. However, this is not the difference that we consider fundamental to autism. (Here I also speak for both Uta Frith and Alan Leslie.)

What is mentalizing? ▓

The ability that I am talking about, mentalizing, is primarily uncon-
scious or implicit. It is a property of our cognitive apparatus that comes
into action when triggered by particular stimuli, and it 'makes sense'
of other people's and our own behaviour fully automatically. The
hypothesis is that the ability to mentalize is dependent on a primal[10]
mechanism and cannot be explained entirely by learning. The ability
manifests itself gradually in behaviour over the first five years. By age
one, infants already attend to behaviour and internally represent
many physical states of the world. That is, they can remember and
manipulate in their heads what they perceive in the world. These
are what we call first-order representations.[11] From some time in their
second year (or arguably even earlier), children have at their disposal
second-order representations and can represent mental states as well as
physical states (Leslie 1987).

What is the difference between first- and second-order[12] representations? We know that ⟨ducks are fowl⟩ and we can represent that idea
in memory as a first-order representation. At the same time, we can
represent the idea ⟨ducks are fish⟩ as long as we ascribe it to someone
else, in a form such as ⟨Some monks believed that {ducks are fish}⟩.
Second-order representations, in this case the representation of someone's belief, can be used to predict people's behaviour. For instance,
monks could eat ducks on Fridays if they believed them to be fish.
In this way we can establish relationships between external states of
affairs and internal states of mind. To create sentences that express

[10] 'Primal' is defined by Johnson and Morton (1991) as the interaction of the
genotype with the internal environment and the non-specific component of the
Species Typical Environment (see p. 47). In this way, we avoid ascribing responsibility for a feature of development solely to the genes. See the discussion on *variability* earlier in this chapter (pp. 72–3).

[11] Note that when I talk about representations, I mean *mental* representations, not
pictures.

[12] I use the terms 'first- and second-order representation' as these two terms make
a clear and unambiguous contrast. In other places, Alan Leslie has used the term
'meta-representations' when referring to what I have called 'second-order'. Unfortunately, there are other meanings of 'meta-representation', and the 'Theory of Mind'
literature has become very confused due to lack of distinction between the various
senses of this term.

second-order propositions, we require particular lexical items (such as 'believe', 'desire', 'pretend' and 'intend') as well as special punctuation (the curly brackets) which we don't need for first-order propositions. Equally, in the brain we will need a special cognitive process to enable us to create second-order propositions. We have called this process EXPRAIS.[13] I say something more about the nature of EXPRAIS and about its history in an appendix to this chapter.

We postulated that the cognitive cause of autism is damage to EXPRAIS. We argued that this could explain the difficulties that autistic children have with pretend play. More importantly, this hypothesis enabled us to predict special problems with other mental state computations. In particular, we predicted that autistic children would have problems in a situation in which another person had a false belief about the world. At the time, no-one had supposed that autistic children had any such problem, so the prediction was very powerful. We set out to test our hypothesis as follows: Would autistic children, taking into account chronological age and mental age, have special problems with understanding someone's false belief about something, as opposed to understanding a real state of affairs? The hypothesis was confirmed by the Sally-Anne experiment (Baron-Cohen et al. 1985) described in box 4.4.

According to the strong form of this theory (Frith et al. 1991), the deficit in EXPRAIS and the consequent deficiency in mentalizing ability would form part of an expansion of the element C_2 in figure 4.5. In line with this, Frith et al. show how the mentalizing deficit goes some way to explaining the three core features in the autistic spectrum.

However, it may well be that in the final analysis the autism spectrum demands explanation in terms of more than one cognitive deficit. Some symptoms whose precise status as part of the behavioural phenotype is as yet unclear, notably those associated with repetitive actions, special skills and so-called frontal signs, may need additional explanation. These would also be mediated through the cognitive level, but could require a second component at the biological level as in figure 4.5 in the same way that the intellectual deficit is separated

[13] EXPRAIS is short for 'Expression Raiser'. This, in Leslie's 1987 paper, is the single most crucial computational process in forming representations of other people's beliefs, desires and intentions.

Box 4.4   The Sally-Anne task

The Sally-Anne task is a scene acted out in front of the child. It can involve dolls or real people. The essence is that one individual, Sally, puts something away, out of sight, and then leaves the scene. Another character, Anne, moves the object to another location and also leaves the scene. Sally returns to the scene and wants the object. The child is asked 'Where will Sally look for the object?' This question determines whether the child would know that Sally will look for her toy in the place where she hid it, in spite of the fact that it has been moved elsewhere. If so, then the child can represent Sally's false belief about the location of the object as well as representing the true state of things.

   Normal children have no problems with this sort of task from about four years of age. Down's syndrome children with a mental age of five or six can also answer correctly. However, we found that of a group of 20 autistic children, with a mean mental age of nine years, 16 failed the task in spite of being able to answer correctly a variety of questions of fact about what happened. They knew where Sally had put a marble; they knew that it was Anne who had moved it and that Sally had not seen the move. Their problem did not lie in perception, in memory or in language. The autistic children just could not conceptualize the possibility that Sally believed something that was not true. A number of experimenters have now carried out similar studies worldwide, confirming that autistic children have a specific impairment with beliefs (for a recent review, see Happé & Frith 1995).

---

from the central autistic deficit. I will explore this idea later on in this chapter and in chapter 6.

Changes over time

In all of the studies reported so far, there is a minority of autistic children who perform mentalizing tasks correctly. Uta Frith and her collaborators have now tested over fifty able autistic children on the false belief and related tasks. So far, they have found that for autistic children to succeed on a mentalizing task they have to have a much higher chronological and mental age than is the case in normal development. On the whole, those autistic subjects who pass Theory of Mind tasks are teenagers with a mental age in excess of eight years

(Frith et al. 1991; Happé 1995). Could the successful autistic children have acquired some mentalizing ability after all? If so, how? I consider two possibilities.

I represent compensation in the causal model by use of a special symbol, an ellipse, which I have illustrated in figure 4.6 in the form of compensation at the cognitive level. The idea behind this concept of compensation is that early in life the child will show the usual range of behavioural signs arising from the cognitive deficit. The supposition is that the individual develops particular knowledge or skill in response to social interactions in order to cope with the problem. This knowledge or skill could be specific to the problem or could be an unusual application of a general skill. In the case of false belief tasks, the nature of the compensation could be an exhaustive compilation of information concerning the class of puzzling events. This will end with a generalization, which could be summarized as something like the following:

> Suppose that an action, A_p, by person P, at time t_A, changes the value of a variable V from its initial state V_i to its final state V_f. Suppose, also, that a second person, Q, does not observe P perform A_p. Subsequently, Q will act as if the value of V is V_i.

In other words:

> When something in the world changes, people who just happen not to have seen the change occur behave (for some reason) as if they do not know about these changes.

In figure 4.6, we have a non-functioning cognitive component, C_1, which gives rise to the three classes of symptom, S_{1-3}. I will indicate the proposed compensation, brought about by the operation of component C_2, with the ellipse over the arrow from C_1 to S_3, together with the rectangle around S_3, which indicates that the relevant pattern of behaviour, normally seen in autism, is no longer present.

The non-social features of autism: how to diagram ideas on weak central coherence in autism ▮

In their extensive review of the subject, Bailey et al. (1996) contrast narrow and broad accounts of autism. Narrow theories include the

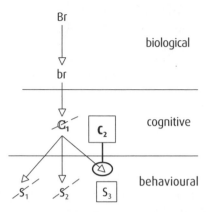

Figure 4.6 A causal model including compensation. The model is to be understood as saying that breakdown in behaviour S_3 is a normal consequence of the disorder, which follows a non-functioning process C_1. In some cases, the (normal) process C_2 can be used to restore behaviour S_3, this being indicated by the solid box, which is thus not connected to the causal tree.

EXPRAIS hypothesis and other specific social or social-cognitive theories. The broad theories include central coherence and executive dysfunction. I will discuss executive dysfunction in chapter 6.

The need for developing the notion of central coherence arose from the problem that the mentalizing hypothesis did not cover a number of features of the extended phenotype (Frith 2003). To give one clear example, Shah and Frith (1983) showed that an autistic group had overwhelming superiority in the hidden figures test (see box 4.5). There seems no way in which such a perceptual/attentional advantage could be plausibly derived from a deficit in mentalizing. Central coherence addressed some of those problems. In brief, the theory proposes that people with autism place very much less stress on the context in which a stimulus is found, compared to normal processing. Weak central coherence could not be a consequence of mentalizing problems, although it remains unclear as to whether the mentalizing deficit could be shown to derive from the central coherence deficit or whether we would have to postulate two cognitive deficits. This will be a matter for empirical research. Here, I diagram both possibilities. In figure 4.7, I represent the theory that mentalizing derives from the central coherence deficit. In figure 4.8, I show the causal model that represents the claim that there are two basic cognitive deficits. Note that in the latter case I

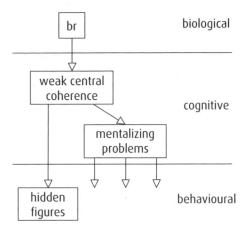

Figure 4.7 A causal model of the hypothesis that mentalizing problems are caused by weak central coherence.

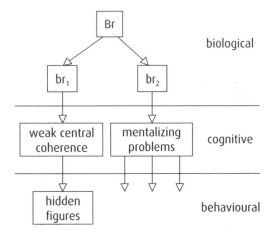

Figure 4.8 A causal model of the hypothesis that mentalizing problems and weak central coherence are correlated rather than having a causal relationship.

postulate two separate deficits at the brain level. This is forced on us. If we showed just one brain deficit with the two cognitive deficits, there would be no way of mapping the brain deficit on to a cognitive primitive without the model collapsing to that shown in figure 4.7 (for further discussion, see Happé 2000).

Box 4.5   Hidden figures

In the hidden figures test, a small target shape has to be located in a drawing of a larger shape. The larger shape is designed so that the small shape is not immediately obvious, as the viewer is more aware of the larger form and its components. In effect, the target shape is swallowed up by the bigger figure. For more details of this work and its implications, see Frith (2003).

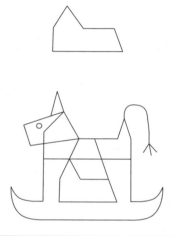

Summary ▨

I have taken you from autism as a diagnostic category, through the Theory of Mind account to some ideas for the future. In the course of doing this, I hope it has become clear how causal modelling helps to clarify the ideas. Adding clarity to the ideas does not, of course, make them any more correct. However, it increases the chance of our finding accurate ways of verifying or falsifying the ideas. At the moment, I would rather that you understood what I was trying to do with causal modelling than have you believe the theories that I have just been illustrating. Apart from anything else, I may change my beliefs about the cause of autism, if the evidence arrives, but I will express any new theory – my own or yours – using causal modelling.

In this chapter, we have examined a concrete example of the way in which causal modelling can be used. It seems to be time to take another look at what we are doing. So, in chapter 5, I draw together some of the general principles that have arisen here, and that have guided work on causal modelling. The story of autism continues in chapter 6, where I consider ways of representing other theories of the disorder. If you wish to postpone chapter 5 until you have finished autism, however, there will be no great harm done.

APPENDIX

The Expression Raiser – EXPRAIS

The theory of the cognitive basis of autism that was developed at the Medical Research Council's Cognitive Development Unit (CDU) was based on an idea of Alan Leslie's in 1983. The essence of the theory is quite beautiful and simple in structure. In my own (no doubt purified) memory of the history of the ideas, it emerged during one of the theoretical seminars that we had twice a week during the first year or two of the CDU. The structure of the seminars was that we all told each other about everything we had done and explained the major ideas we had elaborated, in the belief that there would be interesting cross-fertilization. Uta Frith had talked to us for two or three sessions about her work on autism and had discussed at length the then available theories of autism. All of them were unusable. Shortly afterwards, Alan told us about some ideas that he was developing on the relation between pretend play and mental state terms.

What are mental state terms? They are words that describe mental states, such as *believe, intend* and *desire.* Now, the thing about such words is that they don't have to refer to truth. So, we can say

▌ Kate believes that George is home.

when, in fact, he isn't. We can say

▌ George intended to be home that evening.

when, in fact, he wasn't. We will return to mental state terms in a moment.

Equally, we can say

■ I pretend that this banana is a telephone.

or we can play with the banana by speaking into it, and so on. At the
same time, we know that the banana is not a telephone.

What might be going on in the brain while one is pretending? There
has to be a special kind of representation that contrasts with ordinary
representations. An example of an ordinary representation is

■ ⟨a banana is a fruit⟩

where the angle brackets ⟨⟩ indicate that this is a mental representation, not a spoken sentence. A child who learns this proposition will be
able to generalize about bananas – where they will be kept, when they
will be eaten and so on. All this generalization would take place
automatically as a part of the properties of the semantic system. But the
child would be in trouble (as would we all) if, while pretending, we had
representations such as

■ ⟨this banana is a telephone⟩

and our semantic system arrived at all the supposedly valid generalizations concerning both bananas and telephones.

So, when we pretend we have to avoid setting up normal representations. Instead, we have to *raise* the propositions referred to into *second-
order propositions*. We can indicate this by putting the propositions in
quotation marks, thus:

■ ⟨I pretend 'this banana is a telephone'⟩

This does not mean that generalizations cannot be made or inferences
drawn, but the generalizations or inferences also remain part of the
pretend universe, effectively staying in quotation marks themselves.

The same principle applies in the other cases. So, if I know that Kate
believes that George is home, the proposition

■ ⟨George is home⟩

cannot be allowed to have the status of knowledge in my mind. My
representation has to be

⟨Kate believes 'George is home'⟩.

I can draw conclusions about what else Kate believes, but I cannot draw conclusions about what George is doing.

To deal with words such as *believe* and *pretend*, then, we have to be able to do the mental equivalent of putting on the quotation marks. Alan Leslie called the device that would do this the Expression Raiser (which I have shortened to EXPRAIS). So an EXPRAIS would be needed before a child could either pretend or use mental state terms – or have representations about other people's mental states. We wondered whether this was why a three-year-old could not solve the false belief task (see box 4.4), but we rejected that idea because pretend play is often found shortly after a child's first birthday. Other people (e.g. Wimmer & Perner 1983) had suggested that a three-year-old lacked a Theory of Mind, and the obvious next move was that the Expression Raiser was necessary but not sufficient for a Theory of Mind (ToM), the other factors being developmental.

In my memory play, when Alan had finished his exposition of his theory and we had made sure we had understood, Uta dropped into the silence:

'You know, it is a funny thing, but autistic children never pretend play.'

There was a silence – dramatic, of course – and we all drew the same conclusion. Suppose that autistic children cannot pretend play because they do not have an Expression Raiser. If they do not have an Expression Raiser, then they will not be able to form the appropriate representations for other people's mental states. If they cannot form these representations, then they will not be able to solve the false belief task. This was a totally new idea, which was successfully tested in Baron-Cohen et al. (1985). Alan took another couple of years before he published a paper on pretend play (Leslie 1987) and the autism theory came at about the same time (Leslie & Frith 1987; also see Frith 2003).

Note that this theory has been interpreted as though autism is caused by a lack of ToM. Indeed, one of the reviewers of the first draft of this book ascribed such a belief to me, in spite of my care with the text. The lack of ToM cannot be responsible for autism, for a number of reasons. The most obvious one is that ToM does not emerge in normal children in its fully fledged form until the fourth birthday or so (if we take it to be indexed by passing the false belief task), and the signs of autism precede this by a couple of years or more. We need to talk about a mechanism that develops, and the phrase Theory of Mind Mechanism,

ToMM, is used. The point of the original theory was that EXPRAIS was necessary, but not sufficient, for the development of ToMM. A related error is made by Russell (2002), who attacks Leslie on the grounds that children do not have the *concept* of pretending until age four or five, yet solo pretend arrives at 18 months. This would only be an argument if meta-representation (what you need to have concepts about one's own mental processes) was the same as second-order representations (which is what EXPRAIS enables you to do). Meta-representations require second-order representations, but also require extra cognitive ability and perhaps more besides. In figure 4.9, I show an extended

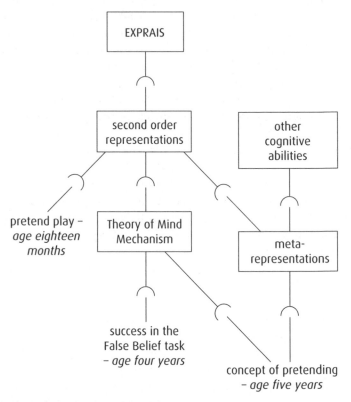

Figure 4.9 A Developmental Contingency Model for the various skills involved in mentalizing tasks. Some developmental features, relating to both maturation and the acquisition of knowledge, have been omitted. Note that a Theory of Mind, as something that a child can talk about, would require meta-representational skills.

Developmental Contingency Model to represent the position that I have just elaborated.

In chapter 6, I note that blind children are delayed in their development of a ToMM, but this is presumably since they lack some of the environmental input that is necessary, rather than any problem with EXPRAIS. There are other disorders in which the passing of the false belief task is delayed, such as Down's syndrome and, in accordance with the principles developed in this book, we must be cautious in interpreting task failure in non-normal populations. We cannot infer that children with Down's syndrome lack EXPRAIS.

I elaborate in chapter 11 the idea that EXPRAIS is a cognitive primitive. It could be localized or it could be a computational option that is available widely in the brain (for example, in the form of a special kind of synapse). Its role in a causal model would not differ in the two cases.

5 ▪ THE WHAT AND THE HOW

In the previous chapter, I showed how the causal modelling framework evolved to allow Uta and me to express our views about the developmental causes of autism. In particular, we wanted to indicate that autism had a biological origin but a cognitive core. We also wanted to make sure that we separated clearly the cognitive core of autism from its behavioural consequences. Finally, we wanted to produce a framework through which we could clearly mark the continuity of ideas as they evolved. Our own views are continually in the process of modification. We do not know, for example, what the relationship between central coherence and Theory of Mind is going to be, or, indeed, whether central coherence will survive as a concept or will be broken down into more precise computational elements. However, what will remain constant is the form of expression of our ideas and certain principles of scientific practice that have evolved over the years. In box 5.1, I mention three of the broader principles. Others, which bear most directly on the practice of causal modelling, Uta and I have gathered together as a set of ground rules or maxims (Morton & Frith 1995). Most of these have been illustrated already in our analysis of autism, and most are adaptations of standard practice into the framework of causal modelling. Over the years, the rules of causal modelling of a developmental disorder have been informally well established – the good practice that we hope to maintain. Uta and I first expounded them in print in 1995. They have changed a little, but not much. Here, I first list them and then proceed to expand and illustrate them.

Box 5.1   How my colleagues and I have tried to progress

In looking at what we have done over the years, it has become apparent that our progress has not been random. While attempting to look down upon ourselves is encouraging divine retribution, there do seem to be some constants – shared, of course, by many other scientists:

1   The principle of accumulation – single experiments are rarely critical.
2   The principle of theory driving – it is one of the canons of classical science that predictions have a power in inverse proportion to their *a priori* probability. The failure of autistic children on the Sally Anne (false belief) task was *predicted* from the expression raiser theory (finally published by Leslie 1987). There was no other reason to expect the predicted result, either in theories of autism or in folk wisdom about their abilities.
3   The principle of inheritance – if a theory is to be replaced, then the new theory should explain as much or more of the existing data set as the old theory.

Ground rules of causal modelling ▌

Maxim 1: 'Start with biology!' Let the causal chain start with the biological origins.

Maxim 2: 'Build causal chains!' The causal chain should be specified, or at least sketched, from the hypothesized developmental origin to current behaviour.

Maxim 3: 'Give a full account!' All major signs and symptoms of the disorder must be accounted for (or at least mentioned).

Maxim 4: 'Specific over general!' A distinction between specific and general conditions must be made. Features that can be accounted for as part of a general condition need not be mentioned within the causal theory for the specific condition.

Maxim 5: 'Distinguish cognition from behaviour.' Maintain the distinction between cognition and behaviour. Remember that all psychological tests measure behaviour.

Maxim 6: 'Be cognitively economical.' Cognitive elements should not be generated to map one-to-one on to the behaviour that they are meant to account for. (This is a general rule of cognitive theorizing, not restricted to causal modelling).

Maxim 7: 'Correlation is not causation!' Do not confuse correlation with cause. Statistical association may be indicative but is not sufficient.

Maxim 8: 'Avoid circularity.' The thing to be explained cannot be the explanation. In other words, don't redescribe the behaviour as if it were a cognitive mechanism.

Maxim 9: 'There is no single cause of anything.' There is no single cause of anything.

Maxim 10: 'Nothing is determined.' There are many sources of variation, internal and external.

Maxim 1: 'Start with biology!'

The precise biological origins of developmental disorders are very rarely known. This does not mean, however, that they should be ignored. As much information as is known should be included in the causal model. This applies even in the case in which we wish to rule out any biological component explicitly. For example, the biological origin of autism has often been ignored. Some time ago, in the absence of evidence, this was understandable. Autism manifested itself most obviously in terms of social isolation and it was easy for people to believe that social problems must have a social cause. However, purely non-biological psychosocial causes of autism can no longer be invoked, since the evidence for a genetic origin is clear.

While many developmental disorders are currently believed to have a biological origin, there are some conditions where the environmental contribution is thought to dominate, and there are theories of particular disorders in which biological factors are assumed to play no role. Some theories of conduct disorder fit this bill (see chapter 10). The approach I am taking in this book is neutral with respect to such issues (although the particular theories that my colleagues put forward elsewhere tend to include a biological component). The notation will allow us to represent theories proposing an environmental origin of a disorder just as well as those proposing a biological origin. This common notation makes it easier to make comparisons between these theories, without ideological baggage. Cases in which an interaction between biological and environmental origins is proposed present no special problem for the notation.

Maxim 2: 'Build causal chains!'

A claim such as *limbic system abnormality causes social impairment* is unhelpful in the context of a causal model. Even if the statement were true in that it pinpointed correctly a critical brain structure, we would still have an insufficient account of social impairment. A single causal statement is not the same as a causal model. We need plausible links in the causal chain from origin to signs and symptoms. Distinctions have to be made between long-range (distal) and proximal causes. Without such a philosophy, there will be the eternal danger of mistaking other kinds of relationships for causal ones. Such relationships include vulnerability, risk and correlation.

Maxim 3: 'Give full account!'

The problem of unified theories in psychology is created by the tendency to theorize about a small segment of data while ignoring the constraints from related areas. Thus, for example, it continues to strike me as strange that most theories of short-term memory phenomena, while focusing on the phonological basis of such phenomena, have historically failed to take serious account of the cognitive structures required for speech production, as Monsell (1987) has highlighted. The equivalent practice with developmental disorders is to succumb to the temptation to give an account of only a selected sub-sample of the signs and symptoms. A number of early cognitive explanations of autism suffered from this problem. When the job is to explain all of the symptoms, it is hazardous to choose one symptom as the most important and suggest an underlying process fault for this single symptom, ignoring the other symptoms or assuming that they derive from the same underlying psychological dysfunction. The remaining symptoms are in as much need of causal explanation as the supposed primary ones. It is tempting to relegate all problems not accounted for in the primary explanation to the position of indirect, secondary consequences.

For example, in a social deficit account of autism, the social deficit would be assumed to result in poor learning of language, while, conversely, in a language-based account of the disorder, the language deficit would be assumed to result in poor social relations. In either case, the particulars become important: Would the particular language deficit be expected to lead to the particular social deficit and vice versa?

What are we to conclude from the continued social deficit after language has been learned? These are not easy matters. If you ask too few questions it is bad science; too many and there is no progressing.

For any causal model, the quality of the information is of vital importance. While we try to use the most up-to-date epidemiologically based evidence, as well as clinical practice as laid down in DSM-IV (American Psychiatric Association 1994) and ICD-10 (World Health Organisation 1992), we must leave open the possibility that received wisdom as to the symptomatology will be overturned by new research. On the other hand, as I have already pointed out, the inability to account for some major fact should not hold up the modelling. Just make sure that the gap is visible.

When the modelling is more detailed and computational, the same kinds of dangers occur. Computational modelling of disorders – and in the developmental arena this is mostly of the connectionist variety – usually cover a very reduced set of the behavioural phenotype. Because of this, there is very little of relevance to the enterprise of providing a full causal model. Hopefully, in the future, this state of affairs will no longer apply.

Maxim 4: 'Specific over general!'

The developmental disorders that I am concerned with here are all specific disorders. In other words, there is a particular deficit (identifiable at some level – biological, cognitive or behavioural) that has particular consequences for development, which may occur in a pure form; that is, with all other psychological functions intact. The pure form may be rare, and more often there are other associated problems of a variable kind. If the original brain damage were large, for example, then many cognitive functions might be affected and this might lead to general deficits. Specific deficits have to be demonstrated over and above general deficits.

Mental retardation is an example of a general deficit that is present, to varying degrees, in about a third of autistic individuals. Mental retardation affects almost all cognitive functions and is manifest in a very wide range of behaviour. It implies brain abnormalities of the type that would affect the basic efficiency of biological processes. This would manifest itself in general deficits in cognitive information processing. The effect of such damage on development is grave. Widespread cognitive delays are common in autism. These have to be taken into account separately from specific deficits. After controlling for developmental level (mental age) and chronological age, many supposedly typical symptoms have been found to be neither unique to nor universal in autism (Hermelin & O'Connor 1970). They can therefore be attributed to the general condition of mental retardation, and they should not be accounted for in the causal theory of the specific condition of autism.

Of course, there will be theories of genetics in which the mental retardation and the autism will be related, but at the biological level. There will also be theories of the biological basis of mental retardation in which the mental retardation of people with autistic symptoms might be contrasted with that of other well defined groups. However, most specific causal theories of autism do not have to derive the retardation. The causal model in figure 4.5(a) (p. 82) implies that we need not ask the question 'How could the lack of a Theory of Mind lead to a drop in IQ?' The theory represented by figure 4.5(b), on the other hand, does presuppose a cognitive theory that covers both the mentalizing problems and the retardation.

Maxim 5: 'Distinguish cognition from behaviour'

Remember that all psychological tests measure behaviour. This is a very difficult principle to put into practice. I have already talked about the difference between intelligence and intelligence tests in chapter 2, where I pointed out that the two could only be taken as equivalent to each other under special circumstances. Remember that all tests, all surveys, and all reports on self or other are behaviour, irrespective of the label. In fact, it is not the test that we see, but the performance on the test. Thus, an anxiety scale that is a self-report cannot be taken to measure anxiety by most uses of the term. What it does is yield a number that is an index of anxiety. Equally, ratings by their teachers of the disruptiveness of children cannot be taken as corresponding directly to any cognitive characteristics of those children (although they may directly reflect traits of the teachers concerned). In the case of autism, the underlying cognitive deficits, in EXPRAIS and in the Theory of Mind Mechanism, are different from, and are not obviously related to, the false belief task that indexes the disorder in behaviour.

Maxim 6: 'Be cognitively economical'

Cognitive elements cannot be mapped one-to-one on to the behaviour that they are meant to account for. This is a general rule of cognitive theorizing, which is not restricted to causal modelling. While it is true that differences in behaviour require corresponding differences at the cognitive level, it is also the case that common cognitive elements are pervasive. The high correlations between almost any pair of abilities indicate that some notion of general intelligence, ability or facility partakes in almost any task (see Anderson 1992). We have to avoid the route blazed by phrenology/trait theory in referring to such supposed primitive (irreducible) entities as 'ability to withstand peer pressure'. These are descriptions of behaviour. There has to be a theory of the cognitive processes underlying the behaviour, and that cognitive theory should contain elements that are already established in some other theory put forward to account for other data. If this is not possible, then any cognitive element that is postulated should be specified in such a way that predictions can be made about the consequences of its absence in contexts other than the data currently in question. An example of this occurred in our analysis of the reading abilities of Italian Down's syndrome children (Morton & Frith 1993a). In this account, we supposed that phoneme awareness tasks required both a meta-cognitive ability, M, and a phonological ability, P. Down's syndrome children lack M and therefore would also be unable to perform other meta-cognitive tasks; dyslexic children lack P and would be unable to perform tasks requiring that ability. Down's syndrome children would, however, be able to perform other phonological tasks that did not require meta-cognitive ability; and dyslexic children would be able to perform other meta-cognitive tasks (see chapter 8).

Maxim 7: 'Correlation is not causation!'

The temptation to interpret correlation as causation is ever-present. Examples of using correlational evidence as causal proof abound in all areas of psychology. It would be a violation of maxim 4 to single out autism researchers for specific blame.

Maxim 8: 'Avoid circularity'

There is an almost irresistible urge to select one aspect of a behavioural phenotype and regard it as the cause of the phenotype as a whole, and then adduce the deficit in question as evidence of the truth of the hypothesis. Examples abound and are referred to throughout this book; for example, poor language as a cause of autism, poor balance as a cause of dyslexia, and executive dysfunction as a cause of autism. A clear separation of cognitive and behavioural factors together with a cognitive theory of the behaviour in question are what is necessary to avoid the problem. Then it becomes possible to predict, from the theory, some other deficit in the target population that has not hitherto been observed. This sort of requirement is normal science.

Maxim 9: 'There is no single cause of anything'

It will often be convenient to act as though there might be a single cause of something, but if you do, don't be surprised if someone takes you seriously.

Maxim 10: 'Nothing is determined'

Increasingly, causal accounts of developmental disorders are being produced that implicate multiple causes. This is the means that the scientific community has adopted to account for lack of determinism and variability of outcome. The variability may be due to genetic factors or environmental ones. Notions such as *potentiation*, where some biological factor makes a person more susceptible to a particular environmental influence, and *compensation*, where cognitive factors overcome a biological disadvantage, are essential parts of any system for representing theories of cause. Note that such factors create problems for the business of diagnosis. Consider the following question: Is a diagnostic category to be determined by its origin, such as a genetic specification; by the resulting state, specified in terms of brain anatomy or cognitive function; or by the behavioural outcome? Variability of various kinds creates the gaps among these criteria. I do not have answers to such questions, but the framework that I use makes it easier to think about the alternatives.

6 ▦ COMPETING CAUSAL ACCOUNTS OF AUTISM

In chapter 4, I illustrated the use of the causal modelling framework by representing versions of the model of the origins of autism that treats *mentalizing* as the core deficit. This was one of the original motivations for developing causal modelling (Morton & Frith 1995). However, our intentions were much broader than that. What we wanted to do was provide a notation that enabled us to compare alternative accounts of the causes of autism. This is the idea that I am expanding on in this book. Such a notation, as we have seen, requires us to have all of the biological, cognitive and behavioural levels represented. Most of the current competing accounts have the same general structure as the ones already discussed. However, as we shall see, the formalism of the present framework helps us to focus on the crucial differences between these accounts.[1]

Almost everyone now agrees that there is a biological disorder at the root of autism. Using our framework to describe the situation gives us a three-tiered causal model, which is essentially as shown in figure 6.1. This figure says that there is some biological origin, O, of the condition with one of a set of possible biological consequences, Br. This has a specific effect on a particular brain system, br_{aut}, which underlies the cognitive function C_{aut}. As discussed in chapter 4, I identify C_{aut} with the Expression Raiser – the function required to create second-order representations. Other theories will identify C_{aut} differently. The model in figure 6.1 goes on to state that damage to C_{aut} affects the development of the set of cognitive functions, c, which, in turn, leads to a variety of signs and symptoms, S.

---

[1] I will, in any case, only mention a few of them.

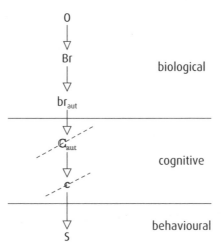

Figure 6.1 A generic causal model for autism, starting with a general biological origin and with brain and cognitive states specific to autism.

Representing the effects of environmental factors ▪

The standard causal model of autism, as represented in figure 6.1, can be varied by postulating the involvement of external factors in the development of the disorder. There are two general ways in which this can be done. First, there could be an influence of environmental factors on the biological aspects of development. In particular, there could be some external event that creates a changed brain state. The causal model for this kind of theory is shown in figure 6.2. The first part of the biological chain that we saw in previous diagrams is missing from this figure, since the claim in question would relate to a child without genetic or other developmental abnormality. An illustration would be the occasional report that a child has developed normally until the age of three or so but then had a viral condition leading to brain damage, with a rapid regression of language gains and subsequent autistic symptoms. A similar account would be given for the theories concerning the possible link between MMR (measles, mumps, rubella) vaccination and late-onset autism. In both examples, it would make sense to enquire whether the brain damage was equivalent to the br_{aut} occurring in the more typical case with a purely genetic origin. Note that there could

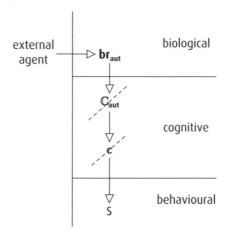

Figure 6.2 Representing possible effects of an environmental agent in a causal chain leading to autism.

also be a genetic component to the causal chain in the MMR theory, such that some children are genetically more susceptible. Diagramming these options is left as an exercise.[2]

For other examples of environmental influence on developmental disorders, I will leave autism aside for the moment. Such environmental factors would include the intra-uterine environment – for example, the children of mothers who take drugs while pregnant are known to be at risk for a variety of developmental disorders. A second class of influence would be materials present in the atmosphere. For example, it is believed that children brought up in neighbourhoods where the traffic pollution is particularly high suffer from some intellectual deficits brought about by the lead in the air. Any theory of developmental disorder that specified dietary factors would also fall within this class.

The second way in which the environment can influence development is through cognition.[3] Thus, our account of autism in chapter 4 included the possible role of parenting style in the development of

---

[2] Remember that whether or not you believe the MMR story shouldn't affect your ability to accurately represent the underlying theory.

[3] I have had difficulty conceptualizing cases in which the environment acted directly at the behavioural level. The only exception is tying someone up or otherwise restricting them. In all the other cases that I have thought of, it has turned out that

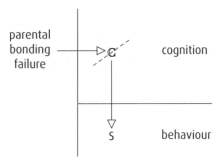

Figure 6.3 The causal model underlying the claim that autism is caused by a failure of bonding between parent and child.

secondary symptoms. There are two other hypotheses concerning autism that involve the environment in the primary symptoms. These are the psychoanalytical accounts (e.g. Bettelheim 1967; Tustin 1981) and the ethological account (Tinbergen & Tinbergen 1983). In fact, the published forms of these hypotheses put the responsibility firmly on to the parents. The term 'refrigerator mother' gained a brief currency a few decades ago, and implied that there were no variables internal to the child that contributed to the condition. Such a theory, in its simplest form, ignores all the evidence already cited concerning the biological contribution to autism and would be represented in outline as in figure 6.3. Of course, the causal model shown in figure 6.3 leaves a large explanatory gap. We would need to know exactly how the parenting weakness could give rise to the specific cognitive deficit.[4]

the important aspect causally has been the influence of the intervention on cognitive development. For example, physical punishment for particular actions may lead to changes in the patterns of behaviour of the child, but long-term changes in development will be a function of changes in the cognitive structures. Such causal chains are part of some accounts of conduct disorder, for example (see chapter 10). You might like to think through the appropriate analysis of the effects of jailing thieves.

[4] In fact, the consequences of weaknesses in parenting are being extensively charted in the literature on attachment (Bowlby 1969; Belsky et al. 1996; and for a recent overview, see Thompson 1999). Rather than leading to a specific cognitive deficit, failures of attachment security lead to differences in cognitive style – in the way in which the child interprets the world, not only at the time, but into adulthood. This might be seen as setting different parameters within the same cognitive architecture.

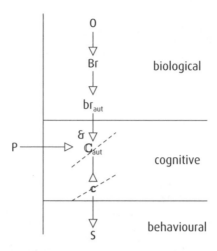

Figure 6.4 A causal model to represent the theory that autism is caused through an interaction of parental factors with a biological predisposition. The use of '&' indicates that both of the factors have to be present to trigger the causal chain.

A modification to such an extreme view would allow that only some children were susceptible to bad parenting of this sort. These children, having a particular 'temperament', perhaps, could then be described in terms of the causal chain shown in figure 6.1, with a specific cognitive function, C_{aut}, being damaged or absent. On such a hypothesis, however, this would not be sufficient to cause autism, What would be needed is a particular input from the environment. I have shown this in figure 6.4. The external circumstances – let us suppose for the moment that these are parental factors, P – are seen as affecting the cognitive function, C_{aut}. One possibility that the logic of the formalism allows would be that the two factors, damage to br_{aut} and external factor P, are both required for autism to occur. To indicate this conjunction, I have used the symbol '&'. Whenever this symbol is used, it is to be understood as saying that both causal factors have to be present for the effect to occur. If only one of the two factors is present, then the condition will not arise.

The theory expressed in figure 6.4 would next be obliged to specify, or at least indicate, the nature of C_{aut} such that there is (or, at least, that it is plausible that there might be) a brain state that maps uniquely on to it. Such a constraint would, for example, rule out knowledge states

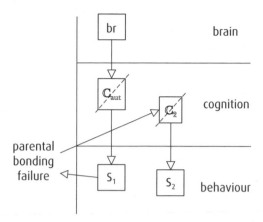

Figure 6.5 A causal model for the view that problems with parental bonding are secondary rather than primary in autism. The primary causal chain leads to behaviour S_1. This impacts on the parents, whose behaviour leads to other cognitive changes in the child, C_2, and, thence, to unwanted behaviour S_2. Compare this with figure 6.4, where the parental involvement is seen as primary.

(such as a belief or a feeling about mother) as candidates for C_{aut} unless these beliefs were seen to be innate.[5]

Psychodynamic accounts emphasize the role of interpersonal factors as both cause and effect of conditions such as autism. Interpersonal factors clearly exist, but their causal role is not clear. In our own account of autism, we would want to allow a place for secondary problems that were the reaction of the child to its parents' response to the manifestation of the child's basic disorder. This is sketched in figure 6.5. The basic biological/cognitive autism problem gives rise to behaviour S_1. This behaviour has an effect on the parents who react to it. The parents' reaction (lack of normal care, incomprehension and inconsistency, perhaps) would have its effect on the child, causing a dysfunctional cognitive change, symbolized by C_2. This, and the resulting behaviour,

---

[5] Knowledge states are variable such that one might believe P one day, then be given information that made you believe not-P only to be told that the information was false, leaving you believing P again. However, there will have been brain activity between the two identical belief states, which means that the brain state will have changed. This, in turn, means that a belief, P, cannot be equated uniquely with a brain state. See chapter 11 for further discussion.

S_2, might be reversible in a way that the damage to C_{aut} would not be, since C_2 is not anchored in a brain state. The effects of psychotherapy would be limited to such a reversal.

Cognitive theories of autism ■

Lack of imitation as a cause of autism: the need for a core cause

Rogers and Pennington (1991) have proposed that the root cognitive cause of autism is an inability to imitate. They point to 'the potential power of an early deficit in imitation to disrupt other early developing interpersonal processes' (p. 137). While they accept that there is no evidence pointing to any deficit in this respect in autistic children during the first year of life, Rogers and Pennington point to deficits in imitation skills in older autistic children.[6] In addition to deficits in imitation, Rogers and Pennington suppose that autistic infants also lack the ability of emotion sharing. These defects 'would greatly affect the baby's ability to organize *social* information concerning other people by depriving the baby of primary sources of social data' (p. 147, original italics). These two deficient skills, together with the Theory of Mind deficit that emerges later, are viewed by Rogers and Pennington as 'increasingly complex expressions of the ability to form and coordinate certain representations of self and of another and to use these representations to guide the planning and execution of one's own behaviour' (p. 150). Such functions are, apparently, supposed to be mediated by biological circuits involving the prefrontal cortex and the limbic system.

Rogers and Pennington (1991) depict their own model in the form shown in figure 6.6. The underlying cognitive deficit in the theory is 'Impaired formation/coordination of specific self–other representations'. In this formulation, it is not easy to envisage a deficit in any single function in a cognitive model.[7] Rather, it seems to be a description of

---

[6] Note, however, that it is unlikely that early imitation skills are mediated by the same mechanisms as later skills. For example, they differ in the intentional component. It is worth thinking about why a two-year-old would imitate – that is, what set of beliefs and expectations they might have – and how this might differ from the six-month-old who is imitating.

[7] Of course, the function of EXPRAIS is to enable the creation of separate representations of self and other with respect to mental states. This would be a prerequisite for the creation of self–other representations.

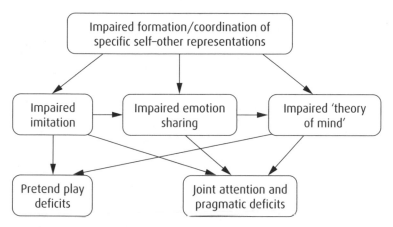

Figure 6.6 Rogers and Pennington's (1991) own depiction of their theory of autism (copyright © 1991 Cambridge University Press; reproduced with permission).

the outcome of a variety of information processing operations spread out over developmental time. In the Rogers and Pennington theory, this underlying problem in representation leads initially to the deficit in imitation. This, in combination with the continuing representational problem, leads to impaired emotion sharing, which, in turn, again in combination with the representational problem, leads to a deficit in Theory of Mind. The theory could not, then, be represented formally in the same way as our own theory, with a number of possible biological origins converging on to a single cognitive core (as in figure 4.4). Rather, the core impairment seems to be at the biological level, iden- tified as a limbic/prefrontal disorder. I am inclined, then, to represent the Rogers and Pennington model inside our framework in the form shown in figure 6.7. Looked at from within the framework, a number of interesting questions arise concerning the links among the cognitive elements.

In the Rogers and Pennington model, impaired imitation is seen as deriving from impaired self–other representations. This is an advance on the more simple view that a deficit in imitation is the primary cog- nitive cause. Such a formulation has the disadvantage that imitation is a complex cognitive skill and cannot be readily mapped on to a simple biological substrate. Thus it would be necessary to specify the elements

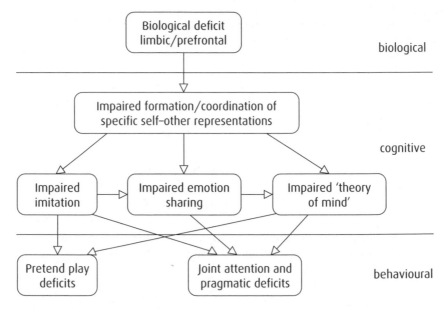

Figure 6.7 Our version of the Rogers and Pennington (1991) model in figure 6.6, attempting to separate the three levels.

of this skill in such a way as to make the possibility of a biological mapping plausible. This is much the same kind of problem as would arise with our own model if the underlying deficit were seen simply as an inability to create a Theory of Mind. This complex, cognitive, conscious activity is clearly the result of a good deal of cognitive development and interaction with the environment, and not at all the kind of factor that I would want to introduce into a developmental theory (though others do). The mentalizing theory, however, reduces to a core computational ability – that necessary to create second-order representations.[8] This is the order of thing that could well correspond to a simple biological deficit that might have no clearly visible signs over the first year of life (Johnson et al. 1992). If we wanted to fit 'ability to imitate' into a causal, developmental, multi-level representation, then it would need to be broken down in a similar way.

[8]   In chapter 11, the notion of a core computational ability is captured with the term 'primitive'. Thus the computational primitive necessary for mentalizing is EXPRAIS.

The role of joint attention

Theoretical explanations close to our own that postulate a cognitive deficit are also provided by a number of workers, including Sigman and Mundy (1989). Similar to Rogers and Pennington's approach, which I discussed in the preceding section, these authors postulate a seemingly simple and early appearing cognitive function as the basic underlying fault in autism. Sigman and Mundy focus on joint attention and the component of shared affect in this particular cognitive function. Now it seems plausible to attribute deficits in joint attention to an early manifestation of deficits of second-order representational skills (Mundy et al. 1986). However, Mundy et al. (1990) reject this 'in the light of developmental data indicating that gestural joint attention skills emerge prior to meta-representational skills in normal development' (p. 126, fn 3). The Sigman and Mundy view of the CDU theory (Frith 1989; Frith et al. 1991) is given in figure 6.8. This represents a confusion between an underlying ability and the manifestation of that ability. Baron-Cohen et al. (1985) initially demonstrated the specific mentalizing deficit with a task that normal children could not do until they were around four years old. But that task also requires a number of other abilities, and it is those other abilities that are not developed until the child is four years old, on average. However, the underlying computational process, EXPRAIS, is supposed to be innate and will operate in other situations earlier. The model that we actually support is shown in figure 6.9. Within the theory we espouse, there is no early limit for the manifestation of mentalizing. We would, for example, be happy to include joint attention skills such as pointing (Leslie & Happé 1989; Baron-Cohen 1991), eye-gaze engagement and teasing (Reddy 1991),

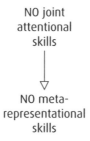

Figure 6.8 The Sigman and Mundy view of the Frith, Leslie and Morton theory of autism.

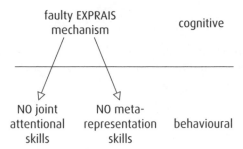

Figure 6.9 How we actually think about the relationship between attentional and meta-representational skills. Compare with figure 6.8.

all of which occur with the first year.[9] All of these abilities seem to require the ability to form second-order representations. The special feature of the false belief task is that it requires more complex skills, which allow reasoning to take place about mental states. These do not develop until the fourth or fifth year.

The affective theory of autism

We can turn now to the model of autism proposed by Hobson (1989, 1990; see also Leslie & Frith 1990). Hobson postulates that the primary deficit in autism is a disturbance of affective contact. He would accept that there is a biological origin to this disturbance of affective contact – this much he has in common with us. He would also agree that it would be necessary to provide a causal chain from the affective disorder to the full range of autistic symptoms. How can we represent Hobson's core affective disorder within the framework that we have created?

At first glance, it might seem as though there is a clear contrast between Hobson's *affective* theory and our own *cognitive* theory. But if we diagram Hobson's theory as a causal model, then we can see that the 'affective' level has the same relationship to biological and behavioural levels as does what we have called the cognitive level. That is, Hobson would not want to say that the affective problem that he alludes to was either biological or behavioural. The affective and the cognitive are different domains but belong at the same level of description. In terms of the contrasts that I have been using (biological, cognitive and

---

[9] For links between mentalizing and early eye-gaze detectors, see Baron-Cohen (1997).

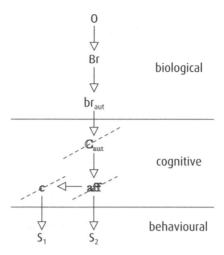

Figure 6.10 A causal model representation of Hobson's (1990) theory of autism, stressing the primacy of an affective disorder.

behavioural), Hobson's theory is at the same level as other cognitive models.

The most convenient way to represent Hobson's theory, then, is as in figure 6.10. The affective disorder gives rise to a set of symptoms, here called S_2. In addition, it will lead developmentally to a further cognitive deficit, which is equivalent to the problems with mentalizing that I have already discussed. The set of symptoms arising from this is summarized with the label S_1.

In the expansion of our own theory, we would interpret the affective disorders as secondary consequences of the child's interaction with the environment – usually in the form of the parents of the child. One way of doing this is shown in figure 6.11, where the affective disorder, *aff*, is seen as a consequence rather than the cause of the cognitive disorder, *c*. The nature of the environmental contribution is spelled out more fully in figure 6.5. Given that all the models are represented in the same format, comparisons between them should be facilitated.

The non-social causes of autism: frontal lobe dysfunction

A number of researchers have proposed that autism, rather than arising from specific abnormalities, is caused by more general difficulties in the

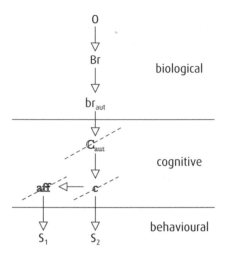

Figure 6.11 A causal model for autism, including an affective disorder as secondary, in contrast to figure 6.10. There is a similar model in figure 6.5, with an explicit involvement of parenting in creating the affective disorder.

high-level planning and control of behaviour (Pennington et al. 1997; Russell 1997). A particular claim in this theory is that it implicates directly a brain area, the frontal lobes and its functions, which are often described as 'executive'. The frontal lobe hypothesis states that the problem with autistics is that they have frontal lobe damage – or else damage in a system that involves the frontal lobes. At present, the reason for supposing this is that autistics tend to fail on so-called frontal tasks.

Frontal tasks are operationally defined as tasks that a group of adult patients with frontal lesions do worse on than a control group of patients with posterior lesions. However, the following facts should also be considered about patients with known frontal lobe lesions:

- few, if any, frontal patients fail all 'frontal' tasks while passing tasks that are failed by patients with posterior lesions
- few, if any, frontal tasks are failed by all frontal patients
- frontal tasks tend to be complex and thus can be failed for a variety of reasons.

These facts mean that there is no simple characterization of 'frontal'. While certain parts of the frontal lobes seem to be involved in all tasks

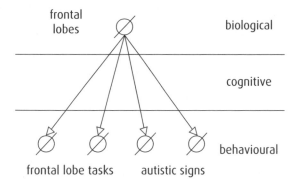

Figure 6.12 A causal model based on the frontal lobe hypothesis.

that require decision-making, attention-switching and other complex cognitive functions, there has been no characterization of the components of the tasks, nor any indication of the localization of any particular functions. Grouping all of these tasks together under the 'frontal' heading does not allow us much inferential power. For example, there is no means of distinguishing autism from non-autistic frontal lobe disorder. The need for differential diagnosis requires that we make such a distinction. In addition, as it stands, the claim of autism as a frontal disorder does not address what is going on at the cognitive level of the disorder. We are left guessing about the chain of causality from the neuroanatomy to the specifically autistic signs. The simplified causal model is shown in figure 6.12. The separation of autistic signs from poor performance in frontal lobe tasks is necessary because of the different cognitive abilities that mediate the two sets of tasks and that have to be included in any reasonable model.

That autism might be caused by a lesion or abnormal development somewhere in the frontal lobe (quite a lot of territory, it should be remembered) is a perfectly reasonable hypothesis concerning the possible site of damage, but it is only a very small step in creating a causal model of autism, and it is far from being an explanation.

Executive function disorder

The idea that autism is a problem with executive function looks more hopeful as a causal hypothesis compared with the frontal hypothesis, if for no other reason than that it moves the core of the hypothesis into the cognitive level. One argument in favour of the executive hypothesis is that whereas only 80 per cent (or 70 per cent or 60 per cent) of high-functioning adult autistics fail the simplest of the Theory of Mind tests, *all* autistic adults, including Asperger's, are impaired at executive function tasks. However, the conclusion is that 'executive function disorder' is the *cause* of autism, without further justification, would violate one of the underlying principles of causal modelling – our maxim 8, 'Avoid circularity', referred to in chapter 5.

In addition, there are problems in defining what counts as an executive function disorder. Duncan (1986) says bluntly that executive function is a cognitive construct used to describe behaviours thought to be mediated by the frontal lobes. If this were the case, then the executive function hypothesis would have all the disadvantages of the frontal lobe hypothesis. Various kinds of definition have been tried. Bailey et al. (1996), rather than treating executive function as a single ability, talk about a set of abilities involved in maintaining an appropriate problem-solving framework. They provide the following non-exhaustive list:

> Included in this set are the ability to disengage from the external context and inhibit inappropriate responses; to plan sequences of willed actions; to sustain an appropriate cognitive set for staying on-task; to monitor own performance and make use of feedback; to flexibly shift attentional set. (Bailey et al. 1996, p. 101)

Recent findings in the area are that children and adults with autism have problems in planning and organization (Ozonoff et al. 1991; Hughes et al. 1994), in using feedback (Prior & Hoffman 1990), in switching to a new cognitive set (Rumsey & Hamburger 1988; Ozonoff et al. 1991; Hughes et al. 1994) and in disengaging from perceptually salient stimuli (Hughes & Russell 1993; Bíro & Russell 2001). It should be noted that these descriptions (actually taken from Bailey et al.'s summary of the findings) do not constitute a cognitive model, but are, rather, a pre-theoretical redescription of the experiments that have been carried out. Thus, if one takes the list:

• problems in planning and organization
• problems in using feedback
• problems in switching to a new cognitive set
• problems in disengaging from perceptually salient stimuli

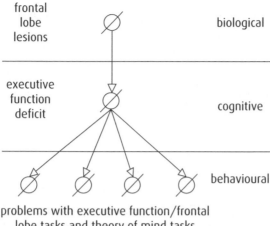

Figure 6.13 A bald model of the simple claim that autism is caused by executive function deficits.

there is no theoretical means of predicting whether, given that one of the list items holds for a particular individual, which of the other items is most likely to hold. In other words, this formulation, for all its cognitive language, has all the problems of a behavioural shopping list. We still lack a testable cognitive theory of the tasks that could be tested on an autistic population.

The resulting causal model is shown in figure 6.13. The problems are much the same as those found with the frontal lobe hypothesis. First, there is no means of distinguishing between the signs to be expected from individuals with autism and those shown by individuals diagnosed as suffering from executive function disorder. The second problem is that there is no distinguishing between the 'executive function' signs and those signs that classically characterize the autistic phenotype. That is to say, in such a formulation there is little acknowledgement of the classical nature of autism, as might be represented by figure 6.14, and still less is there any idea proposed that the mentalizing or central coherence deficits (together with plausible causal models worked out for these – discussed in chapter 4) could be a separate cognitive consequence of 'executive function disorder'.

Instead, proponents of an executive account of autism propose that the primary causal factor is executive dysfunction, rather than something

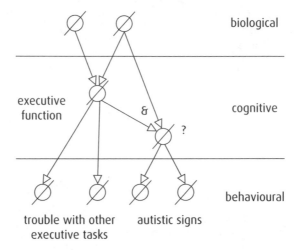

Figure 6.14 A model of the executive function deficit model of autism, which separates out autistic and executive dysfunction signs. The identity of the cognitive function marked with a question mark would have to be established. The two biological origins are required because of the difference between the executive and autistic phenotypes. The model remains incomplete.

to do with Theory of Mind or central coherence. That may be so, but the proponents of such a theory still have to account for the phenomena associated with Theory of Mind and central coherence. That is, to achieve explanatory sufficiency, their theory should have the form of that shown in figure 6.15. This makes it clear that the precise causal relationship between (some kind of) executive dysfunction and weakness in central coherence remains to be spelled out. In this model, the relation between the Theory of Mind deficit and the autistic signs could be exactly the same as the one traced out in chapter 4. There is a further change that will be necessary to make the model consistent. At the moment, there is no way of distinguishing between the two kinds of biological cause, one of which would give rise to the autistic spectrum, the other just giving rise to executive dysfunction. It seems to me to be impossible to do this without changing one of two things. The first option is to split the executive dysfunctions into two kinds, one of which gives rise to the autistic spectrum. One way of doing this is given in figure 6.16. This model implies that there are two ways of failing executive tasks. This is indicated by the cognitive function marked *C*, which has two inputs,

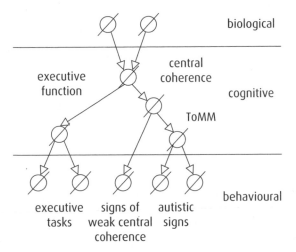

Figure 6.15 An expansion of the model in figure 6.14, specifying that the central coherence (CC) deficit derives from an executive function disorder. The Theory of Mind Mechanism (ToMM) deficit follows as in the standard theory, although there is still a problem with the relation between the biological and cognitive levels.

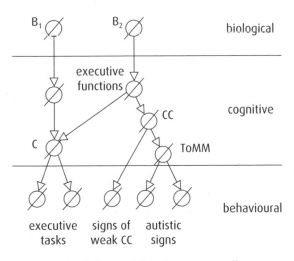

Figure 6.16 An extension of the model in figure 6.15, allowing an independence of the biological origins of executive and autistic dysfunctions with two separate phenotypes.

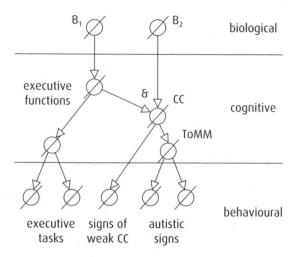

Figure 6.17 An alternative model to figure 6.16, which also allows the executive dysfunction to be primary in the creation of autism. Malfunction in CC requires problems with both B_1 and B_2.

both of which are required for this process to function. So, if the biological element B_1 is affected, the cognitive function below it will be affected which, in turn, will affect function C. This leads to executive dysfunction in behaviour. If the biological element B_2 is affected, the cognitive function below it will be affected, which will not only affect function C, leading to executive dysfunction in behaviour, but will also affect central coherence (CC), creating the autistic and central coherence characteristics. What we have managed to do here is to allow executive dysfunction either with or without the autistic signs.

The other option, given in figure 6.17, is to have one kind of biological problem, B_1, which leads to both the executive dysfunction and to a central coherence (CC) weakness. Since we still have to distinguish between two groups with executive dysfunction, one with and one without the autistic signs, the CC weakness would need to be potentiated in some way separate from B_1. In figure 6.17, I have accomplished this through B_2. If B_2 is intact, there will be no problem with CC and no autistic signs.

In the preceding paragraphs, I have been focusing on the theoretical insufficiency of the frontal lobe/executive dysfunction accounts of autism as currently expressed. It is, perhaps, in order to say a little more about

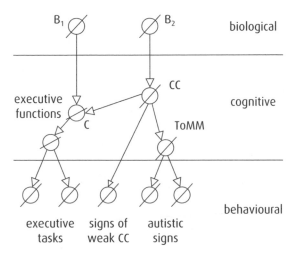

Figure 6.18 A model within which the executive dysfunction in autistic people is derived from a central coherence weakness, itself caused by brain damage B_2. Cognitive function C would also be affected by B_1 breakdown, giving rise to executive dysfunction without autistic signs.

how this position arose in the first place. Ozonoff et al. (1991) pointed out that there are high-functioning autistics who succeed on ToM but fail on executive control, but not any who succeed on executive control but fail on ToM. This would have to be interpreted as saying that the development of ToM required the presence of certain executive functions. The absence of these executive functions would then lead to the loss of function that leads to the autistic signs, as in figures 6.15–6.17. However, no-one has yet proposed a causal relationship. What seems to me a much more promising view is that some executive function breakdown is derivable from a central coherence weakness. This would give a model something like that shown in figure 6.18. This account resembles that put forward by Russell (2002). Executive dysfunction on this theory could occur either for direct biological reasons, through B_1, or, for cognitive-developmental reasons, with an origin in B_2.

Suppose that we want to allow for the existence of autistic signs without weak central coherence. This requires a different configuration, and I propose one answer in figure 6.19. You might like to take a close look at this figure and work out what the possibilities are. In this theory, brain damage B_3 gives rise to autistic signs without weak central coherence. B_2 would give weak central coherence without the autistic

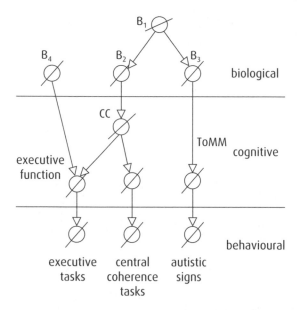

Figure 6.19 A model within which the executive dysfunction in autistic people is derived from a central coherence weakness, itself caused by brain damage B_2. Damage B_4 would give rise to executive dysfunction without autism.

signs, while B_1 would give both sets of problems. In addition, the model specifies a different kind of damage, B_4, which produces executive problems (in fact, the same executive problems as are produced by B_2) without any other problems. There are a number of alternative options to this particular formulation that we might choose, depending on how we saw the relationships among the various components.

This analysis of the possible relationships between executive dysfunction, autistic signs and central coherence shows that causal modelling can be used in a computational way. It is a simple simulation device that can be used either in a binary way or thinking in terms of variables. The binary mode of operation involves treating each causal connection as an inference engine. So, if A is connected to B you can compute:

▨ If not A, then not B.
▨ If not B, then . . .

and so on, down the causal tree, deriving the possible patterns of behavioural dysfunctions from the patterns of breakdown at the biological level.

More subtly, you could think in terms of the efficiency of the elements and have malfunction propagate down the graph. Causal modelling makes this easy. With a little practice, you can look at a figure such as figure 6.19 and see the relationships among the possible kinds of breakdown.

Getting specific about executive dysfunction

There are a number of complicating factors that have to be considered carefully in evaluating these options with respect to executive dysfunctions. Of these, the most important is that many other diagnostic types fail on one or more executive task. Examples include schizophrenia and Parkinson's disease in adults (e.g. Morris et al. 1988; Pantelis et al. 1994), Korsakoff's amnesia, obsessive–compulsive disorders, Fragile-X syndrome, ADHD (Chelune et al. 1986), conduct disorder (Lueger & Gill 1990), treated phenylketonuria (Welsh et al. 1990) and Tourette's syndrome (Bornstein 1990). This creates clear problems when it comes to differential diagnosis. I spell this out in box 6.1. At its simplest, this means that you cannot diagnose autism on the basis of executive dysfunction.

This issue has been addressed by Ozonoff and Jensen (1999), who talk about the 'discriminant validity question'. Their hypothesis is that 'specific types of executive impairment may be associated with specific neurodevelopmental disorders' (p. 171). They start with the observation that every study that has examined the performance of an autistic population on the Wisconsin Card Sorting Test (WCST) has found that autistic subjects are highly perseverative compared to controls. The same result has been found with studies using the Tower of Hanoi (ToH) or Tower of London tests. In contrast, the only two studies that administered the Stroop test (also supposed to index executive disorder) to autistic groups both failed to find any differences from controls (Bryson 1983; Eskes et al. 1990). On the other hand, studies with children diagnosed as having ADHD have shown no general dif-ference from controls on the WCST. Both the ToH and the Stroop test, on the other hand, have shown consistent differences with ADHD children. Ozonoff and Jensen (1999) compared a high-functioning group of autistic children with groups of ADHD and Tourette's syndrome children together with controls. The interest of the Tourette's children is that they show involuntary movements and vocalizations, which have been thought to be due to a lack of frontal inhibition. However, most previous studies have found no impairment on the Stroop or the Wisconsin for this group. Ozonoff and Jensen replicated the majority findings on the three tests,

Box 6.1   Shared cause and differential diagnosis

If a number of disorders share an underlying condition, then we cannot say simply that the latter is the *cause* of any of the former. For example, if we wish to say that there is a condition *executive function disorder* (henceforth, EFD), and we claim that autistics manifest EFD and children with conduct disorder (CD) manifest EFD and children with ADHD manifest EFD, then it cannot be the case that EFD causes autism, that EFD causes CD and that EFD causes ADHD as in figure 1. Otherwise, simple rules of inference would require that all CD children were autistic and so on. Since there are differential diagnoses among autism, CD, and ADHD we have to find an alternative way of proceeding.

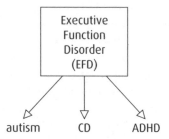

Figure 1 Not a differential diagnosis.

Anyone who wishes to persist with the idea of an entity such as EFD might say, instead, that autism is caused by the conjunction of EFD together with another disorder A. Conduct disorder would be caused by EFD together with another disorder C and so on. The resulting causal

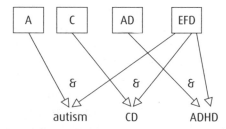

Figure 2 A differential diagnosis with a common cause.

model would look more like figure 2, where it is clear that the main scientific task is to identify the additional disorders as well as specifying the nature of the EFD. This resembles the theory represented by figure 6.20.

The alternative approach is to abandon the notion of EFD as an indissoluble whole and, instead, specify sub-types. So the appropriate way of phrasing the causal hypotheses would be:

(EFD)$_1$ causes autism
(EFD)$_2$ causes CD
(EFD)$_3$ causes ADHD

where (EFD)$_1$, (EFD)$_2$ and (EFD)$_3$ are different from each other. This causal theory is shown in figure 3. Such an adjustment may clarify the intentions of the hypothesis but does not help with diagnosis, since knowledge that some child has shown executive dysfunction cannot be used to diagnose autism or CD or to confirm a diagnosis of autism or CD made by other means. This could only be done when (EFD)$_1$, (EFD)$_2$ and (EFD)$_3$ are specified in such a way that they can be identified. This was the objective of the Ozonoff and Jensen (1999) paper, which is discussed in the main text. Use of the phrase *executive function disorder* can then be restricted to a general, pre-scientific context. So as to make this point absolutely clear, I am not saying that there are no such things as executive function disorders. They do exist, there are lots of them, and in various combinations with each other and other cognitive problems they are responsible for a number of developmental disorders. What I do claim is that saying 'X is caused by EFD' is scarcely more helpful than saying that 'X is caused by a brain problem'. We have to do better than that. I will say this again in chapter 10.

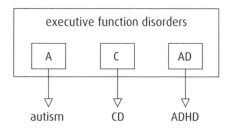

Figure 3 A differential diagnosis with no common cause.

showing differences on Wisconsin and ToH with the autistic group and on the Stroop with the ADHD group. The TS group was indistinguishable from the controls.

Ozonoff and Jensen conclude that the 'discriminant validity problem' is only a problem at a superficial level of analysis, since the disorders can be discriminated on the basis of their executive profiles. They conclude 'Such executive "fingerprints" may be useful aids in identification of the conditions, as well as in designing best practices for their remediation' (p. 175). That may be the case, but I draw the conclusion from this study that the term 'executive function' is not a very useful one, since it does not clearly refer to anything. Certainly, the term cannot be used in any causal model without the most severe restrictions. The best that I could come up with was to hypothesize a common biological problem that interacts with three different other factors to give the three profiles. The resulting combined causal model is sketched in figure 6.20. Following Ozonoff and Jensen, I label the resulting cognitive deficit for

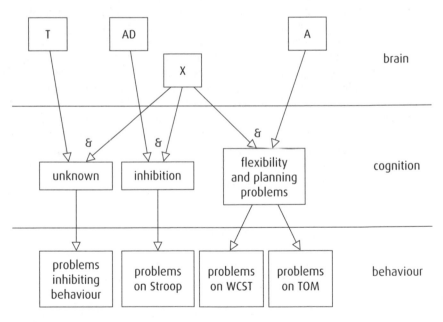

Figure 6.20 A causal model to represent the ideas of Ozonoff and Jensen (1999). Four deficits are specified at the brain level: T for Tourette's syndrome, AD for ADHD and A for autism. The fourth deficit, X, is damage that we suppose the three groups to have in common by virtue of their common label as executive disorders.

autistics 'flexibility and planning problems' and that for ADHD 'inhibition', although it should be clear that the terms lack theoretical precision. Further, their scope is uncertain, so that it would be hazardous to take any other task and predict how well the groups would perform. In addition, the relation of the autistic executive problem to the rest of the autistic behavioural phenotype is unspecified.

Given that we solve the problems raised by Ozonoff and Jensen in relation to the need for differential diagnosis, we would still have to derive the classical signs of autism in the causal model. The question is from where, exactly, in the causal model, would the divergence come? There are a variety of possibilities. At one extreme, the problems with the false belief task would be diagrammed as arising directly from a cognitive deficit of the executive class – although, it should be said, no such deficit has yet been proposed. At an intermediate level, one might hypothesize that the mentalizing deficit arises, developmentally, from an executive deficit. As I understand it, this is the option being pursued by Russell and by Ozonoff and colleagues over the years, and this is the option shown in figure 6.17. Another possibility is that executive functions and mentalizing functions are carried out in developmentally related parts of the brain.[10] The co-occurrence of executive dysfunction with autistic symptoms would then be seen as correlational rather than causal. This is shown in figure 6.21.

The emphasis on executive tasks has arisen from the observation that a large proportion of high-functioning autistics manage to pass the Theory of Mind tasks and, in particular, the Sally-Anne (or false belief) task. The conclusion that seems to have been drawn here is that these individuals are no longer suffering from a 'Theory of Mind deficit'. (I will not elaborate here, yet again, on the distinction that I feel is procedurally necessary between a Theory of Mind deficit – as revealed by meta-cognitive tasks – and the mentalizing deficit, which is the cognitive precursor.) However, autism is a developmental disorder, and it is not contested that *all* autistics have a developmental history of delay in the ability to pass the Theory of Mind tasks. That they can now pass some of these tasks does not change their developmental history. In addition, as Bailey et al. (1996) comment, most, if not all, of the individuals who pass the laboratory tests still seem to suffer profound

---

[10] By 'developmentally related parts of the brain' I mean parts of the brain that are adjacent, that have common neurodevelopmental origins or that are affected by the same neurochemicals.

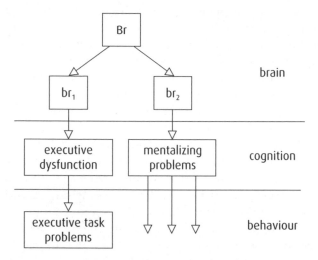

Figure 6.21 A causal model for the theory that executive problems and mentalizing problems have a common brain origin but are not causally related.

impairment in everyday life in situations requiring the on-line use of Theory of Mind.[11] Whatever one's bias is, it is important to keep the distinction clear between on-line influences and developmental cause (Happé 2001).

Having completed the review of theories of autism, we have seen a variety of models expressed and compared within the framework and have extended the notation a little. In the next chapter, I become more general again and see what the technique of causal modelling can contribute to the problem of diagnosis.

---

[11] This is one example of a laboratory test revealing more of the person's abilities than is revealed in naturalistic surroundings. Often, it is claimed, laboratory tests fail by virtue of not being naturalistic. The reason for success in this case is that the structure of the laboratory test focuses the individual's attention on the critical factors of the situation, enabling that individual to use other resources to overcome an underlying deficit.

7 ■ THE PROBLEM OF DIAGNOSIS

In the discussion of theories of autism in chapters 4 and 6, I alluded to the problem of defining what autism really is. Put at its most stark, the problem is whether autism is to be defined in terms of a particular genetic make-up, the presence (or absence) of certain brain structures, the presence or absence of particular cognitive structures, or a particular pattern of behaviour. Or is some combination of the above to be preferred?

This issue – How is a disorder to be defined? – is relevant over the full range of developmental disorders. It is of special interest to people who are concerned with the question of whether a particular child falls within the responsibility of a state educational provision or other quasi-legalistic situations. It is also of importance for questions of management or treatment. Hence, there are very large manuals in which the definitions of words such as autism can be found, in the form of a list of the behavioural criteria appropriate for that label (as in box 4.1 on p. 69). However, we must be careful not to fall into the trap of thinking that because there is a word, 'autism', there has to be a single, universal, incontrovertible category that any individual is either included into or excluded from. There are two issues here. The first is that there are grey areas. Thus, in the case of autism, you will find reference to 'the autistic spectrum' and see descriptions of individual children, or adults, as having 'autistic features'. The second issue is more radical. The nature of categories depend on how you are looking at them.[1] Diagnosis

---

[1]   This is not the same as Humpty Dumpty claiming that words mean exactly what he want them to. So the meaning of 'autism' does not vary in the way in which the meaning of the word 'pet' can vary, for example, which can change as a result of the

involves categorization, and in this chapter I will look at some of the issues of diagnosis in the context of causal modelling.

Diagnosis and cause: relying on behaviour ▪

Diagnosis is a serious business looking for respectability. The serious part is that management, treatment and prognosis depend upon it. The respectability is the scientific background. Examples of diagnostic errors abound. How could it have been in the olden days that deaf and dumb people were considered to be subnormal and placed in mental asylums? Even accepting that they might have been slightly developmentally retarded with respect to the hearing population because they had not received normal language input, today I am saddened and surprised by this history. The answer is that people were focused on the behaviour alone, not on the cause of behaviour. At that time, there was a belief that diagnosis and management was based on more than behaviour, that the underlying condition was being addressed. Specifically, the results of intelligence tests would be interpreted as reflecting underlying deficiencies. But nowadays we understand (well, some of us do) that tests of intelligence, on which the notion of retardation depends, are essentially tests of behaviour. In addition, we can now see that the behavioural end point can be the outward manifestation of a variety of inner states. Thus, a low score on an intelligence test does not necessarily reflect a low intelligence; it could mean, for example, that the child was preoccupied with love or pain. This clear separation of the behaviour from the underlying cognitive state is central to causal modelling and to our approach to diagnosis.

Problems for clinicians

How do you diagnose children with developmental disorders when the only basis you have is the child's behaviour or, even worse, what is

---

interaction between a thing, or object, and an individual. A notice appeared on trees around Hampstead Heath this summer, saying 'Unusual pet found. Is it yours?' You can have fun imagining what the notice might refer to, realizing that lots of strange things could qualify. Whether or not an individual could qualify as 'autistic', however, would have to be as the result of the application of some generalizable set of rules. The question is 'Which rules?'

reported about the child's behaviour? Only a fraction of the possible relevant behaviour can be observed directly by the busy clinician, and he or she has to rely on the report by parents and teachers. The parents are the main source of information about the child's first years of life. In all developmental disorders, it is crucial to establish when problems first manifested themselves. Was there always something wrong? Was there normal development, with problems gradually revealing themselves as the child grew up? Was there regression in development? Mistakes in classifying a child as having a specific disorder when in reality there is nothing wrong could have serious consequences for the child. Sensational stories about diagnostic errors are often found in the health pages of the daily newspapers – for instance, a highly anxious child being mistakenly diagnosed as suffering from attention deficit disorder and prescribed drug treatment. On the other hand, mistakes in classifying a child as 'perfectly normal', or as showing only temporary problems that he or she 'will grow out of', are just as serious. Equally sensational stories can readily be found along the lines of 'I dragged my child from one clinic to another for ten years. Nobody believed me that there was a serious problem.'

The Spanish Inquisition example: the dangers of labelling ▮

Our own view of autism at the CDU, discussed in chapter 4, placed *mentalizing* at its core. From what I have said earlier, it should be clear that this is partly a definitional choice. We felt that the social oddness of the autistic population in all its manifestations was more coherent and closer to the intuitive definition of autism than any other, and that the three core factors, identified by Lorna Wing, *impairment in socialization, impairment in communication* and *impairment in imagination,* can be shown to arise computationally from a problem with mentalizing. This was the power of Alan Leslie's original insight, discussed in chapter 4 (p. 93) – it created that computational link and put the underlying theory on a firm footing. Remember also that this insight led to the *prediction* of a problem with the false belief task for the autistic children. This finding, which is commonplace and, apparently, self-evident nowadays, was revolutionary at the time.

What, then, do we do with those children, previously diagnosed as autistic, who now pass the standard false belief task? If our position is that there is an underlying brain problem that manifests itself in a cognitive dysfunction and that neither of these are reversible, then we would have to insist that the diagnosis must remain in spite of differences in behaviour. Our position would have to be that the child was compensating for the dysfunction, and was succeeding on the task by some other means than those available through normal development (Frith et al. 1991). In the limit, this could be a dangerous position to find oneself trapped in and, as a self-corrective, I should point out that there are possible dangers in excessive or exclusive reliance in such a belief in the unchangeability of cognitive factors. These can be illustrated historically.

Suppose that you firmly believe in the existence of a particular cognitive entity (but, of course, have never seen it; only inferred it) and you are convinced that the component in question is faulty in a particular developmental disorder. You may have good reasons for your belief – a good theory, in other words, which has withstood some tests and some criticism. So, what would happen if a child independently diagnosed with this disorder – say, autism – were to perform very well on a test that your theory says he or she should fail on? Most people would do another test to check on the first. The more different the test the better, because they would hope that the theory was right and that a very different prediction from the theory would be borne out after all.

Suppose that the child were to perform well on a number of such tests. Would this case then disprove the theory? Most people, including ourselves (being human) would rather believe that the diagnosis was incorrect. But suppose that, for historical reasons, we were committed to the diagnosis. We would then conclude that the child was performing brilliantly in some completely unusual way, compensating for his or her disability. Hence the relevance of the Spanish Inquisition. What must the poor child do to convince us that he or she is 'innocent' ('normal'), and that the theory is wrong or not applicable in this case?

We have here a process of diagnosis that takes as its basic assumption that behaviour or the verbal report of a person diagnosed as 'heretic' (likely to suffer a fate much worse than death itself, namely eternal hell), is untrustworthy. Lack of transparency of the relationship between the inner (cognitive) state and the outward appearance is the rule. Hence no revision of diagnosis is necessary. However, guided by the diagnosis, there is a sure method (almost sure) of achieving transparency: by confession after torture. Presumably, the inquisitors believed that their extreme methods were justified by the possibility of a genuine cure for the (in their eyes) horrific disorder and by the role of confession in the cure. Here, I hope, the analogy breaks down, but I hope to have pressed it sufficiently to demonstrate that diagnosis has more than one function, and that fixation of belief on the part of the clinician, or the experimental psychologist, should not be one of them.

Labelling versus denying special need

The practice of psychiatric diagnosis has often been attacked on the grounds that it is not just a bad thing to wrongly diagnose a person who is perfectly normal, but that it is bad to diagnose at all. The idea is that if you attach the label of a diagnosis to an individual, that label will make other people expect a particular pattern of behaviour and will in fact increase such behaviour. One small step from here is the superstitious belief that if you don't name the devil, he will not come and get you.

To illustrate: the argument is made that we will condemn a child to conform to a particular pattern of behaviour merely by expecting this pattern. For example, some people believe that a child will do more poorly in school for being labelled dyslexic. The reasoning is that the child who knows that he or she is dyslexic will have the 'excuse' for not learning, while the teacher will not be motivated to teach the child because he or she thinks that improvement is unlikely to occur. Is this a realistic worry? Not according to our experience, which suggests that both the child and the teacher have the motivation to improve performance and often feel a strong challenge to overcome problems once they have been identified. The opposite argument holds that failing to label a child who is in fact dyslexic denies this child the right to have his or her special needs recognized and to be given appropriate help. Of course, labelling a child dyslexic who is, in fact, depressed, or lazy or being bullied would not help. The concern with errors of diagnosis is appropriate, but the concern with the effects of correct diagnosis is a different kind of matter and the two should not be confused.

Concern for one type of error, overdiagnosis, should be balanced by a concern for underdiagnosis. Both need to be avoided. How? Diagnosis is clearly a difficult and dangerous tool. How can we protect ourselves from the dangers? We may start by distinguishing two separate issues, which are unnecessarily confounded: the purposes of diagnosis and the role of cause in diagnosis. The first issue concerns the different purposes of diagnosis. Each purpose has a different underlying rationale

and therefore a different scientific basis. One purpose is to guide decisions in medical treatments or educational interventions. Another purpose is to help weigh up the costs and benefits of long-term invasive
treatment. Yet another is to determine the prognosis. In this case, the
origin is particularly likely to be important. A fourth purpose is that of
research. To investigate a disorder, we need a group of individuals with
the disorder. We can only get the group through diagnosis. But one
objective of the research is to establish the diagnostic category. Care is
needed to avoid the danger of circularity. This can be done by being
prepared to move from the original notion concerning the disorder and
come to a set of differential diagnoses based on cognitive or biological
principles. Notice that you can't get out of the problems by deciding to
research a symptom. You just end up with a bunch of heterogenous
people who may not have anything cognitive in common.

Our interest is focused on the second issue – that of cause. Cause
and treatment/management are related, but unsystematically. With a
broken leg it doesn't matter much what you were doing at the time.
The surgical procedures will depend on the state of the bones, even
though, according to surgical folklore, the rate of healing is related to
the mental condition of the patient.

What are the disorder categories through development?

Categories as defined above are collections of behaviours. What forms
the collections? In practice, sets of symptoms have been found to
go together in such a way as to create criteria for disorder categories.
A certain constellation of symptoms (rather than a single symptom)
suggests a certain disorder. After the disorder is recognized, the clinician
can consider the appropriate treatment – not before. The situation in
the case of mental disorder is more complicated than in the case of most
physical disorders in one important respect: the variability of the disorder
over the life-span of the individual. How does this come about? Consider
what happens after birth when the brain of the infant has the kind of
abnormality that we theorize about. Its further development in interaction
with the social and physical environment will be affected by this abnormality. Not only will the brain have a deviant pattern – a different cell
structure, for instance, or different connections – but so will the mind,
since, as I have already observed, the mind is entirely contained within the
brain. This will have consequences in behaviour and will be observed in
different forms throughout development – and, indeed, throughout life.

Plasticity

The effect of abnormality early in development will be mitigated by the phenomenon of plasticity. Plasticity in development means that damaged or abnormal tissue can be repaired, or that other brain areas can be redeployed to take over the function of a damaged part. Nevertheless, there are limits to plasticity and the concept of brain damage makes clear that impairment of function is to be expected as a consequence.

What is normality?

Let us take for granted the assumption that there *are* mental disorders, and that these disorders result in behaviour that is symptomatic; that is, not developmentally normal and causing disability. We have to appeal to common sense and medical practice here, since it is notoriously difficult to agree on what is meant by 'normal' that one can deviate from.

The simplest, but not likely, causal diagram is shown in figure 7.1. Here the view is represented of a single cause in the brain, leading to a single specifiable cognitive consequence, which in turn leads to a circumscribed impairment in just one type of behaviour. This might, for example, be an idealized description of nerve deafness. The problem even here is that for a full account it would be necessary to represent the consequences of deafness according to whether sign language was available early on or whether the child grew up essentially without

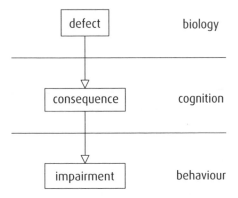

Figure 7.1 An idealized form of the simplest possible causal model.

language. In the latter case, a number of secondary cognitive effects might be expected, including an inability to think verbally. Even with the deaf child who grew up with language through a signing environment, other cognitive and behavioural consequences are likely.

Problems of diagnostic practice ■

In the study of developmental psychopathology, there appears to be a gap between clinician and academic. As I noted in chapter 2, the ICD-10 classification of mental and behavioural disorders, in its clinical descriptions and diagnostic guidelines, is quite explicit in saying 'These descriptions and guidelines carry no theoretical implications. They are simply a set of symptoms and comments that have been agreed . . . to be a reasonable basis for defining the limits of categories in the classification of mental disorders' (World Health Organisation 1992, p. 2).

The multiaxial classification scheme for psychiatric disorders in childhood and adolescence (Rutter et al. 1975), which underlies the ICD classification, has at its base the belief that a number of categories must be used systematically in diagnosis. The axes employed are as follows:

1 Clinical psychiatric syndrome.
2 Specific delays in development regardless of their origin, other than delays *solely* due to poor schooling.
3 Intellectual level 'regardless of whether the retardation is part of a psychosis, a consequence of sociocultural retardation or a result of a medical condition such as Down Syndrome' (p. 4).
4 Current non-psychiatric medical conditions.
5 Current abnormal psychosocial situations – not past psychosocial stresses: 'When an abnormal psychosocial situation is present it should be coded regardless of whether it is thought to have caused the patient's psychiatric disorder' (p. 5). The intention is '*not* to attempt any overall categorization of the theoretically inferred "basic" or "underlying" family pathology, but rather to categorize the several different dimensions that may have differing types of impact on the child' (draft axis 5, 1988, p. 4, original italics).

The axes were chosen to provide 'unambiguous information of maximum clinical usefulness in the greatest number of cases' (p. 1).

Note also that 'The scheme is essentially descriptive and *non-theoretical* . . . the aim is to record the presence or absence of different conditions or situations *irrespective* of whether the clinician considers them to be causal in relation to the psychiatric problem.' The care of this wording is deemed necessary 'in view of the continuing theoretical disputes about the importance or otherwise of biological, psychosocial and cognitive factors in aetiology' (p. 2). For similar reasons, the classification is seen as applying 'only to a person's current situation and problems and *not* to the person himself' (p. 2, original italics throughout).

One can see that the pragmatics of needing to agree international standards of assessing signs and symptoms, and the need for some set of classification labels, took priority when the international group faced the difficulty of agreeing aetiology. The causal modelling framework can be seen as facilitating the scientific resolution of the theoretical disputes by permitting simultaneous representation of alternatives. Of course, the ideological issues are likely to be more resistant to resolution.

While the multiaxial classification works by side-stepping theoretical arguments, I offer the causal modelling notation as a way to advance theory. One crucial first step is to disentangle facts and hypotheses into biological, cognitive and behavioural levels. In many cases, descriptions of disorders show that the levels are mixed haphazardly and, in the case of the cognitive level, intuitive psychology often takes over from scientific concepts. Intuition is not necessarily wrong. However, in the history of medicine and the understanding of physical disease, science has proved stronger. This is also to be expected in the understanding of mental disorders.

Diagnostic entities

In our thinking, we have found it useful to start from the assumption that the disorders that we are concerned with are natural entities. We trust clinical intuition to the extent that we believe that the disorders in question are not mere collections of randomly occurring symptoms. The simplest analogy is the disease model, where the disease – diabetes, for instance – can be traced through all its forms.

Strong forms and weak forms

Basically, the definition of an entity can have a *strong* form or a *weak* form. The strong form of a disease definition involves a single identifiable cause. For the weak form, the definition will include additional causes. In diabetes, the strong form specifies a metabolic disorder involving one particular enzyme. Whatever variability can be found in the origin of this disorder and in the course of the disease, the absence of the enzyme is the defining criterion. Generalizing this example, we can say that the strong form corresponds to a singularity in the causal nexus. Of course, in real life the weak form may be more frequently found, but for the purpose of clarity I will use strong forms for the following illustrations that can be produced by the fairly mechanical application of the causal modelling notation. When we initially began to diagram different disorders, we noticed very early on that there were three possibilities of strong forms, each with a singularity somewhere in the causal nexus.

A, X and V shapes

The three letters A, X and V have shapes that each have a 'singularity'; that is, they come to a single point either at the top, the middle or the bottom of the shape. Our causal diagrams revealed the existence of three types of causal model, the first resembling the shape of the letter A, the second the letter X and the third the letter V. These are shown in figure 7.2. Each of these letter shapes shows a convergence of paths at a single point: the top, the middle and the bottom, respectively. These three locations of 'pinch-points' correspond to biological, cognitive and behavioural levels. The convergence or pinching means that

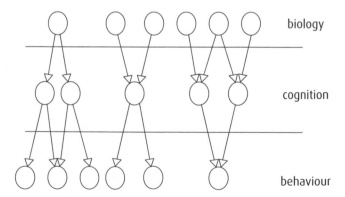

Figure 7.2 The strong forms of the A-, X- and V-shaped causal models, with a single causal nexus at one of the three levels.

there is just one single feature at some point in that level or sub-level. In the weak forms of the three types (in the sense of the previous section), there would be two or more nodes at the pinch-point. In the superstrong form (if it actually exists – I don't know any), we have the shape of a letter I, as already shown in figure 7.1.

There seems to be a trend towards defining a disorder genetically if that is possible. With Williams syndrome, for example, we know a great deal about the cause, in that the location of the genetic defect has been isolated. Indeed, the genetic defect seems to be the definition of the syndrome, although there is a wide range of expression of the condition among individuals with the diagnosis (Donnai & Karmiloff-Smith 2000). We still know relatively little about the cognitive consequences, although description of the behavioural phenotype is receiving a lot of attention at the moment. In contrast, in the case of autism we know nothing of the cause and a great deal about the underlying cognitive condition. In these and other cases, what we aim for ultimately is a full account of how a brain condition leads to the pattern of symptoms.

A-shape syndromes

A typical example of a strong biologically defined syndrome would be a specific genetic defect, such as phenylketonuria (PKU). This would be an A-shape definition, a form of which is represented in figure 7.3, with a single genetic defect leading to a biochemical imbalance, and where C_1 and C_2 represent the cognitive and emotional consequences of this imbalance. These can be overcome if the child follows a diet that counteracts the biochemical imbalance. There are a number of intermediary biological stages missing from this representation. In PKU, there appear to be global cognitive impairments as well as emotional disorder (Taylor 1991). The S's represent signs and symptoms, the behavioural manifestations.

There are two aspects of figure 7.3 that need to be strongly marked. The first is that, as I have already stressed, the notation should not be taken to imply that there is a deterministic relationship between origin at one end and signs and symptoms at the other. The notation is descriptive, not prescriptive, and causal theories of any degree of complexity can be represented to any required level of detail. Thus, one might want to represent the fact that the presence of the particular genetic defect characteristic of PKU is not sufficient for the full cognitive and behavioural expression of the disorder, but that certain other biological, environmental or cognitive preconditions would be

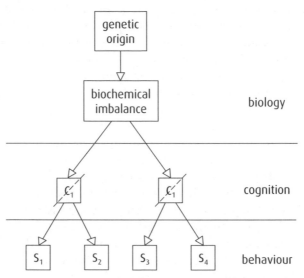

Figure 7.3 An example of the A-shaped causal model for phenylketonuria (PKU). See the text for further qualifications. The S's represent various signs and symptoms.

necessary as well. This would be done by indicating the requirement of the conjunction of causes (as illustrated in figure 6.4) in order to capture the fact that the difficulties of PKU children depend strongly on how well the prescribed diet is kept to. To give another dramatic example of the amazing diversity that follows from a single major gene disorder, we could take neurofibromatosis. Manifestations in a single family may vary from a few skin blemishes, that require an expert to note them, to multiple nerve tumours, that cause gross deformity.

The second aspect of figure 7.3 is related to the first. The diagram could be seen either as the description of an individual or as the description of a type. If we are describing an individual, then we enter only those elements germane for that individual. In such a case, we represent the specific determinants of the signs and symptoms for that individual. The causal links would then be seen as clinically real. On the other hand, we could use the diagram for the description of a type in order to answer the question: 'What is the range of clinical picture possible for PKU?' In this case, the causal connections should be seen as probabilistic, rather than deterministic: this is the more usual form of the causal model. Mostly, I will address the modelling of disorders as

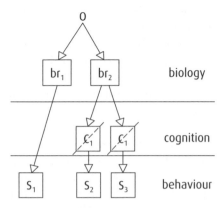

Figure 7.4 An example of the A-shaped causal model, where S_1 is a behavioural symptom that has a biological cause without mediation by cognitive factors.

types. Thus they should fit all possible cases, but will lack the specific information that would make the diagrams useful in individual cases.

Note that a number of variations are possible in this general form of the diagram. One example is that the primary biological defect has a number of biologically defined consequences. This would be represented by a causal nexus entirely within the biological level. A second variant is that a biological defect may directly lead to behavioural consequences without cognitive mediation. Thus, dopamine deficiency in Parkinson's disease (in interaction with other factors) can lead to tremor. The way in which these two examples would be incorporated into our diagram is shown in figure 7.4. In this case, br_1 and br_2 are biological consequences of the primary deficit. Damage of the form br_1 is shown as directly causing the behavioural consequences S_1. In contrast, br_2 has cognitive consequences C_1 and C_2, which together have a variety of signs and symptoms S_{2-3}. All of these variations would still roughly conform to the A-shape.

Another example of a strong biologically defined syndrome would be a specific metabolic defect, such as is present in **Lesch–Nyhan syndrome**. This is a developmental disorder that affects brain development in a very disastrous way: a single enzyme, hypo-xanthine-guanine-phospho-ribosyl-transferase, is missing. This can be tested for unequivocally to establish the diagnosis. It is fortunately a very rare disease, and no-one would think of carrying out the appropriate biochemical test unless alerted by the behavioural features. The referral would most likely come from a child psychiatrist. The dreadful symptoms that will have brought family and child to his clinic will be self-injury and mental retardation. The affected child will also suffer from gout, an invariable result of the metabolic disorder. Treatment is possible in these cases, at least for the gout. The mental retardation is sadly irreversible and the self-injury has to be managed by physical mechanical methods; for instance, putting the arms of the child in splints so that the hand cannot automatically reach to the mouth, where sharp teeth inexorably chew it. It is not at all clear how the self-injury and general learning disability are to be explained, and particularly why it should be hand-to-mouth injury and not any other type of self-injury that afflicts these individuals. Reports indicate that the patients are relieved when mechanical prevention is applied. They seem to be unable to help themselves and behaviour modification has not proved very successful. This example is useful as it shows that the diagnosis of the disorder can be unequivocal, and yet the explanation of the disorder is crucially wanting. This is because the different levels of description have not yet been linked.

X-shape syndromes

An example of a cognitively defined syndrome is that of autistic spectrum disorder. This can be represented as an X-shape, as shown in figure 7.5, with a variety of possible biological causes O_{1-3} all leading to the same cognitive deficit. The single cognitive deficit then results in (some subset of) a large number of signs and symptoms. Again, variations at all three levels are possible, as I have already shown in our

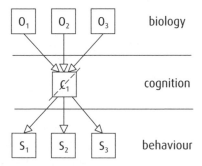

Figure 7.5 The X-shaped causal model such as we saw in chapter 4 for the core disorder in autism.

discussion of competing theories. All would maintain a relative convergence at the cognitive level. Even if it were necessary to postulate two or three separate cognitive deficits for a full explanation of the condition, the causal analysis could still roughly conform to the X-shape. This would remain the case as long as the cognitive description of the syndrome was an order of magnitude more compact than the behavioural, and as long as there was no adequate single biological definition either at the genetic, neuroanatomical or neurochemical sub-levels.

Note that the links from biology to cognition in figure 7.5 are meant to represent disjunctive rather than conjunctive causation. That is to say, the diagram is to be interpreted as saying that C can be caused by O_1 or by O_2 or by O_3. It may be necessary in a full causal account of a particular disorder to allow for restrictions such as that C is caused by the *conjunction* of O_2 and O_3. This should be explicitly noted in the model by the inclusion of an '&' between the relevant links. This principle has already been illustrated in figure 6.4.

V-shape theories

Finally, we can represent the behaviourally defined syndrome. This would have the general form of a V-shape, as shown in figure 7.6. In this figure, S represents the defining behaviour or behaviour pattern which,

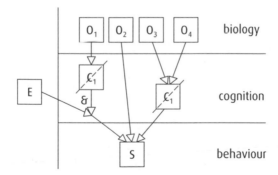

Figure 7.6 An example of the V-shaped causal model wherein a disorder is defined by the symptoms, S, irrespective of their origin. Elements labelled O_n correspond to biological origins postulated in a particular theory, and the C_n correspond to cognitive functions. The line through these indicates that they are damaged or abnormal. In chapter 9, we analyse theories of hyperactivity as having such a form.

in the example, can be caused directly, as from biological origin O_2, through cognitive mediation through C_2, a deficit that could be caused by O_3 or O_4 or, indeed, by the interaction of a cognitive deficit, C_1 with environmental factors. In chapter 9 I use the example of hyperactivity, which is defined as a diagnostic entity at the behavioural level.

Variability ■

One of the irritating as well as fascinating problems in developmental psychopathology is that of the variability among individuals. If a group of people are selected because of their identity by some definition, then it will inevitably be discovered that they are different – sometimes wildly different – by some other definition, particularly at a different level. Thus, a group of Fragile-X children will display a range of severity of symptoms from mild hyperactivity to full-blown autism. All biological systems, such as the system that is damaged in autism, develop under multiple influences. Variability in any one of these could lead to mal-formation in the system and the resulting cognitive deficit.

Variability can be handled in a number of ways. Sometimes we have the discomfort (in a scientific context) of the DSM style of definition of hyperactivity within ADHD where any six out of nine symptoms counts as a manifestation of a behaviour category. This is discussed in chapter 10. Such pragmatics – categories at all costs – have little scientific con-tent and could even be thought of as anti-scientific. In some accounts of hyperactivity, there are signs of uneasiness with this approach and indications that some more consistency might be found through redefining the concept at a cognitive or biological level. In this case, what looks initially like variability within a single diagnostic category becomes multiple diagnostic categories.

Another way of handling variability is to order symptoms in terms of severity. In the ideal case, one would be able to assign a degree of severity to each patient. Any patient, then, would manifest all the symp-toms, from the mildest up to the most severe found in that patient. In such a disorder, what you will not find in an individual patient is a scattering of symptoms of different severity, with some medium-severity symptoms missing. The underlying model for the concept of variability would then be that of a quantitative disorder, either at the biological or the cognitive level. At the biological level, you could imagine gauging the severity of the affliction in terms of the amount of tissue damaged or the level of a particular neurotransmitter. Another way of referring to this would be in terms of the particular combination of quantitative trait loci (genes of small effect size contributing probabilistically to the manifestation of a trait – Plomin et al. 2001). At the cognitive level, the diagnostic tasks could be ordered in terms of their information processing demands. Patients would then be located on this continuum as a function of some cognitive measure; for instance, the available working memory.

Let us look at one simpler example of variability, a genetic condition where in some cases we find signs S_1 and S_2 but in others we only find S_1. How can we conceptualize this? Of the possibilities available to us, let me illustrate a couple where I examine explanations in terms of a second biological factor that can either be protective (in which case only S_1 results) or precipitating. In figure 7.7, I model the assumption that the pathogenic condition would normally give rise to two brain abnormalities, br_1 and br_2. These cause the abnormal development of the two cognitive systems, C_1 and C_2, which gives rise to the symptom complex in its full-blown form. In figure 7.8, I introduce a protective factor, and see how this factor serves to counteract the effect of the pathogenic factor on br_2, which will then develop normally. The cognitive structure C_2, then, will be intact. This is symbolized by the box around it. In this case, the extra factor can be seen as protective.

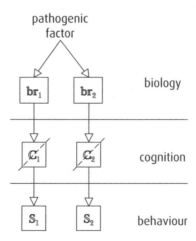

Figure 7.7 A causal model for a condition in which some pathogenic factor leads to a pair of brain conditions, each of which leads to a cognitive deficit and consequent symptoms.

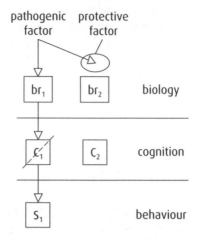

Figure 7.8 Variability in the condition illustrated in figure 7.7 can be brought about by the presence of a protective factor – symbolized by the ellipse around the arrow, which is being inhibited. The protective factor prevents one of the usual biological consequences, br_2, from being created. Observe that since the causal model is for the disorder, you don't bother to put links between elements that are functioning properly.

A second possibility occurs where the assumption is that the extra factor works in a negative way. For this, we take a completely different hypothetical example. In this case, by itself, the pathogenic factor only gives rise to br_1. This is illustrated in figure 7.9. In such cases br_2 is

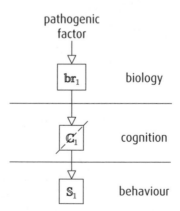

Figure 7.9 An illustrative causal model for a condition that normally gives rise to only a single causal chain.

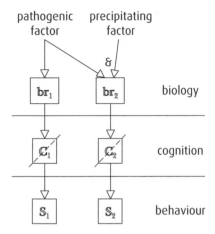

Figure 7.10 A variation on the condition diagrammed in figure 7.9, whereby an extra factor interacts with the original pathogenic factor to produce a second biological problem.

not found unless the extra, precipitating factor is present, as shown in figure 7.10. The two factors are seen as acting in concert – symbolized by the '&' sign – in producing the br_2 condition. The extra factor in figure 7.10 can be seen as making the individual vulnerable to the effects of the genetic condition.

In principle, precipitating factors of this kind could be environmental or genetic. Johnson and Morton (1991) have discussed the sense in which genetic and environmental effects could be equivalent. Thus, differences between individuals can be brought about by 'normal' variations within the genotype. Such differences give rise to the range of colour, body type and some characteristics of the central nervous system that lead to differences in speed of processing. This is the kind of variation that is usually referred to when the phrase *individual differences* is used. 'Normal' variations in lower-level environments (especially the *in utero* environment) would be functionally equivalent here. Thus, maternal variations in diet shift the average height of their children without affecting the genotypic variation.

Finally, we can consider cases in which the condition has a known biological origin. For this, we move outside the developmental area. Take the case of a left middle cerebral artery infarct. The variability in symptom following a haemorrhage will surprise no-one and calls for no special principles of explanation. Lesions will differ in their extent both as a function of the exact location of the problem and the individual variation in distribution of the artery. In addition, the effects of two roughly equivalent lesions can be widely different (Poeck et al. 1984) because of the differences between individuals in the way in which particular psychological functions have become implemented in a particular region of the cortex. Of course, all patients who have suffered from a left middle cerebral artery infarct will have symptoms that are related. All will have some form of aphasia and most, if not all, will have some form of dyslexia. At one time, such a description might have been thought sufficient to justify the single diagnostic category, but work in cognitive neuropsychology has established a number of clear categories of dyslexia with different patterns of symptoms and different possibilities of compensatory strategies. The variation, then, is most economically described in terms of malfunction in particular components of cognitive models of the reading process (Patterson 1981; Shallice 1981).

Changes over time: improvement and deterioration ▮

Developmental disorders can be grouped according to their most likely time course. Some disorders show gradually improved adaptation over time. This is the case for Asperger's syndrome, a high-functioning variant on autism (see Frith 2003). It is not clear whether the improvement is due to biological versus cognitive changes. It is clearer with dyslexia, which is discussed in chapter 8. One of the characteristics of intelligent people with dyslexia is that they eventually learn to read quite fluently. This must be due to their adopting different strategies, with the biological deficit remaining unchanged. In contrast, there are disorders that are characterized by inexorable deterioration of cognitive function. I presume that this is due to degenerative brain processes. One example is Rett's syndrome. Down's syndrome has also been mentioned in this category because of its association with the degenerative Alzheimer's disease, which afflicts many Down's syndrome individuals, and starts from a far earlier age than with ordinary people. There is no convenient way to represent in a single causal model the different stages of such disorders. The best idea seems to be to have a number of different models for each stage.

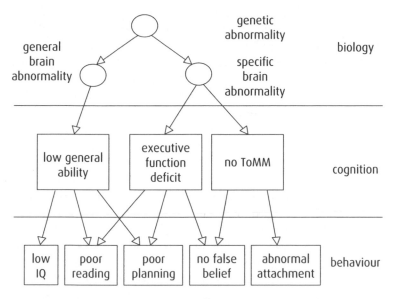

Figure 7.11 A candidate causal model for a complex genetic disorder, including two independent brain abnormalities, one giving rise to intellectual impairment and the other producing executive function impairments together with the kind of autistic impairment discussed in chapter 4. The contributions of the three cognitive impairments to various tasks should be regarded as illustrative rather than being specific claims. Nothing hinges on their accuracy.

The variability of the phenotype ▊

We can illustrate the relationship between theory and diagnosis most dramatically with an example. Let us take a relatively complex theory of autism, a disorder with a strong genetic component. The causal model is given in figure 7.11. It assumes some genetic abnormality that is unspecified. This gives rise to a couple of abnormalities in the brain. The first of these gives rise to a general impairment in mental abilities, as indexed particularly by low IQ. The second brain abnormality, presumably in the frontal lobes, is the cause of some executive function deficit as well as the classic mentalizing problems discussed in chapter 4. Various hypotheses have been put forward in this model as to the reason for poor performance on various tests. You may prefer other analyses of the various tasks, but that would not affect the general moral that I wish to illustrate from the example. The general point that

I want to make is that performance in most tasks – no, let me be firm and say *all* tasks – could arrive from breakdown in more than one cognitive function. Thus, in the figure, we have a lack of Theory of Mind Mechanism (ToMM) leading to abnormal attachment patterns with parents, as well as leading to a failure in false belief tasks. The latter failure is in conjunction with an executive function deficit, which also leads to poor planning and poor reading.

Suppose, for the purposes of argument, that we know this causal model to be the case and that we wish to define, for the purposes of diagnosis, a category that we will call *autism*. How could we go about it? If we were to assume for the moment that the most important clinical defining characteristic of autism was failure in the false belief task (and the corresponding social deficits), there would seem to be at least four ways in which we could arrive at a definition. These would be in terms of the genes, the brain, the ToMM deficit or the executive function deficit. If we chose the genetic specification as the basis for the definition of autism, then the behavioural phenotype would include all five of the tasks that we have included: low IQ, poor reading, poor planning, no false belief and abnormal attachment. Suppose, instead, that we took the brain deficit as the defining feature. We can take another look at the model, with the brain deficit and all the downstream elements in the causal chain highlighted, in figure 7.12. The behavioural phenotype of autism in this definition does not include low IQ, but does include the other four indicators.

The two definitions of autism that we have tried up to now have been at the biological level. But we could well define autism in terms of a cognitive deficit. Suppose that we chose the particular executive function deficit as the defining feature of autism. This is illustrated in figure 7.13. The result is that the behavioural phenotype includes poor reading, poor planning and no false belief, but ignores attachment and IQ.

Finally, suppose that we regard the absence of a Theory of Mind Mechanism as being the basis for our definition. The consequences are shown in figure 7.14. Now, the behavioural phenotype only includes no false belief and abnormal attachment. The other tasks in the original model – low IQ, poor reading and poor planning – are now all irrelevant.

I summarize our findings in table 7.1. The ticks indicate which symptoms enter into the behavioural phenotype of 'autism' under the different definitions of the disorder.

What we should notice here is that there is an apparent conflict between the four definitions as to what exactly constitutes 'autism'. We

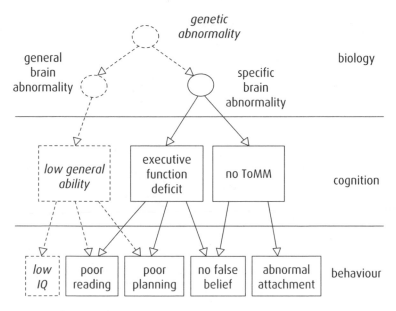

Figure 7.12 The causal model from figure 7.11, taking the brain deficit as definitional of autism.

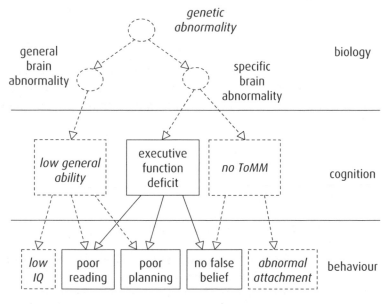

Figure 7.13 The causal model from figure 7.11, taking the executive function deficit as definitional of autism.

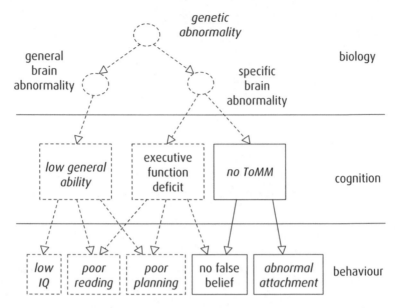

Figure 7.14 The relevant causal model when the absence of ToMM is taken as definitional.

Table 7.1 The symptoms for a disorder depend on the underlying defining factor

	Symptoms				
Underlying defining factor	**Low IQ**	**Poor reading**	**Poor planning**	**No false belief**	**Abnormal attachment**
Gene abnormality	✔	✔	✔	✔	✔
Brain abnormality	✘	✔	✔	✔	✔
Executive function deficit	✘	✔	✔	✔	✘
ToMM deficit	✘	✘	✘	✔	✔

should also notice that all four definitions come from the same causal model and, therefore, must be compatible with each other. In other words, we have a choice of diagnostic definitions without changing the underlying model of the spectrum of disorders. This being the case, it would be pointless to dispute whether, for example, 'autism' includes abnormal attachment in its definition. That would solely be a question of definition of the term 'autism' rather than a matter of fact. Of course, with this example – which, you should remember, is to some extent hypothetical and simplified – there is a disorder which includes all five symptoms that has a particular genetic origin, and is fully specified in figure 7.11. In principle, these five symptoms will always occur, irrespective of the definition of 'autism'. However, the figures make it easy to see that there could be another disorder, unrelated to that described in figure 7.11, which gives rise to a subset of the symptoms. This disorder would start with a different genetic abnormality and would involve a different specific brain abnormality. For example, this disorder could give rise to an absence of false belief and abnormal attachment. People with that particular genetic phenotype would then fit into the behavioural phenotype of autism by the ToMM definition in figure 7.14 and table 7.1. The question would then be whether it would be acceptable to someone who used the ToMM definition to include both genetic groups under the same heading. I leave further consideration of this as a exercise. I have provided figure 7.15 as an aide. When

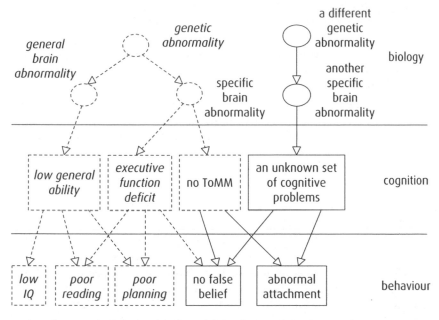

Figure 7.15 A compound causal model for two disorders, the autism of figure 7.14 and a second, different hypothetical disorder, the effect of which is simply absence of false belief and abnormal attachment. The puzzle is whether you want to say that people with the second disorder have autism.

a real example occurs, as it does in the next chapter, we will be able to see some of the implications.

Of course, the search for a 'real' definition becomes more complicated when we take *variability* into account (see p. 148). Thus, we may find an individual who qualifies as autistic by virtue of having the appropriate genetic abnormality but, because of other genes, does not have the general brain abnormality and so is normal with respect to IQ, reading and planning.

On co-morbidity and the question of residual normality ■

One of the changes that has taken place over the past few years is a shift from categorical diagnosis to descriptive labelling. Thus, a child may be described as *having* ADHD rather than *being* ADHD. One of the reasons for this is that a child may present with a number of disorders. This complicates both the diagnostic and the explanatory tasks since, in principle, the signs and symptoms have to be partitioned into those with one cause and those with the other causes before we can progress. In practice, both problems are approached gradually. Diagnosis progresses by a process either of expansion or contraction as the diagnostic criteria are refined. Thus, the diagnosis of autism – or, more broadly, autistic spectrum – has expanded over the years as, for example, the requirement for mental retardation has been removed. The diagnosis of dyslexia, by contrast, has contracted, as the social and emotional causes of some reading backwardness have been factored out (see chapter 8).

From the point of view of explanation, what has been necessary has been a creative division of the apparent signs and symptoms into theoretically coherent sets. In chapter 4, I discussed the process of conjecture that led to the Theory of Mind account of autism. What was required in order to make this great leap forward was to ignore a lot of the evidence. We had to ignore all the evidence of mental retardation, the behaviour such as head banging and flapping, and the good performance in tasks such as hidden figures. What we did was to ask 'What would a child who only had a problem with EXPRAIS look like ?' The answer was that such a child would fail the false belief task, whereas other children of the same mental age would succeed. At no stage in this process was it imagined that *only* autistic children had this

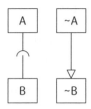

Figure 7.16 The DCM that says that A is required for the normal development of B, and the parallel causal model saying that the absence of A is the cause of the absence of B.

deficit. The choice of Down's syndrome children as controls made that clear. With such controls, the retardation of the autistic group was excluded from the theory but allowed for in the experimental design. From a practical point of view, developmental disorders are difficult enough to account for without ignoring normal development. With our limited capacity of comprehension, we need to make the equation between what is needed for normal development and what is missing in abnormal development. This is summarized in the relation between DCMs and causal models already discussed in chapter 3 and re-exemplified in principle in figure 7.16. The specific theories of normal development, using a DCM, and of the developmental disorder, using a causal model, are given in figure 7.17. The causal model in this figure is not for autism, but merely for an aspect of autism. Once the theory is established, we can go back to the signs that have been ignored and begin to account for them. The intellectual problems are then seen

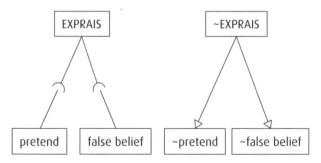

Figure 7.17 The DCM representation of the theory that the normal development of skills with pretend and false belief requires the expression raiser (EXPRAIS) (left) and the causal model of the derived theory that the absence of an EXPRAIS will lead to an absence of both skills (right).

as co-morbid, the emotional problems are seen as secondary, and a third set of behaviours are seen as arising from problems in central coherence. All of this has been explored in chapters 4 and 6. But it is unlikely that these steps would have been possible without the original simplification.

It is easy to confuse the steps taken in the history of autism with a general principle called 'residual normality' by Thomas and Karmiloff-Smith (2002). This is the assumption that 'in the face of a selective developmental deficit, the rest of the system can nevertheless develop normally and independently of the deficit' (p. 729). As a working hypothesis, this assumption seems sensible. It gives us a chance to conceptualize an idealized disorder and plan experiments accordingly. The problem would be if it were seriously taken as a universal law.

To summarize ■

In this chapter, I have covered a number of topics around the theme of diagnosis. Diagnosis is not simple. Even if the aim of diagnosis is clear – to help the clinician cure or ameliorate a condition, for example – there are still a number of principles on which the diagnosis could be based. As a sample conclusion, you could try the following: if you want to be a brilliant diagnostician, get a multi-level theory.

8 ▪ A Causal Analysis of Dyslexia

The dyslexia debate: Is there such a thing as dyslexia? ▪

Dyslexia is an ideal topic for causal modelling. To start with, it is defined and diagnosed in different ways by different people, the major division being between those who give it a behavioural definition and those who focus on the cognitive or biological underpinnings. Secondly, there is a major issue as to the contribution of environmental factors – notably, the role of teaching. Thirdly, even where the general approach is agreed, there are a variety of detailed accounts, particularly with respect to the underlying cognitive deficits. We will see that causal modelling has already played a significant role in helping to clarify the issues.

There seems to be increasing agreement among scientists and educationalists that dyslexia can be given a reasonable operational definition, which is separate from any causal accounts. Thus, the recent report of the Working Party of the British Psychological Society on 'Dyslexia, Literacy and Psychological Assessment' (henceforth, BPS 1999) adopts a working definition:

> Dyslexia is evident when accurate and fluent word reading and/or spelling develops very incompletely or with great difficulty. This focuses on literacy learning at the 'word level' and implies that the problem is severe and persistent despite appropriate learning opportunities. It provides the basis for a staged process of assessment through teaching. (BPS 1999, p. 8)

Such a definition does not imply that reading is simply a matter of decoding and writing words, and that the teaching of reading can stop once the word level has been mastered. Nor does it imply that the word level (as opposed to the sentence level) should be taught completely before other aspects of reading are tackled. However, it does imply that the word level is associated with particular problems that can be treated independently of problems at other levels – those of comprehension, for example. It also implies that reading problems at the word level that persist despite 'appropriate learning opportunities' are different in some important ways from similar reading problems that arise *because of* lack of suitable learning opportunities. Needless to say – no, I need to say it – this is not a value judgement. Both kinds of problem require handling at the educational level, but could well need handling differently. Certainly, they can be seen to be handled differently at the level of psychological theory, and such differences are reflected in the causal models that follow.

We certainly do not need to become involved in discussions as to what 'dyslexia' *really* is. Indeed, like 'reading', it may best be regarded as a pre-scientific term, one that is descriptive of a symptom rather than of a developmental disorder. This will become clear by the end of the chapter.

The first distinction that we need to make is between *true dyslexia* and reading difficulty of the type that is sometimes called the 'garden variety' (Gough & Tunmer 1986). This is not as easy a task as might initially appear (Stanovich 1988). The relevant difference is between those children who are delayed for reasons to do with the relationship between the child and the educational process, and those children who have some clear and specific cognitive deficit that gives rise to a reading problem. There appear to be major, not trivial, differences in the literature with respect to the delineation of these groups. On the one hand, we have the biological school, exemplified by Galaburda and his team. The advance publicity information for a conference co-sponsored by the New York Academy of Sciences in September 1992 and organized by Galaburda contains the following (from Tallal 1988):

> Despite normal intelligence some 10% of our school children have great difficulties in learning to read and write. This severe handicap, which is often combined with developmental language impairment (dysphasia), seems to have a neurological etiology.

The implication is that all 10 per cent are to be seen as neurologically impaired. The basis of the claim is work comparing the brains of dyslexics and normals with respect to certain parameters (Galaburda 1989; Galaburda et al. 1989; for a review, see also Hynd & Semrud-Clikeman 1989).

This position contrasts with that of educationalists such as Marie Clay, who see reading difficulties as a largely educational problem (Clay 1979). Clay's work in New Zealand involves retesting children after a year's reading instruction (on their seventh birthday). Those children in the bottom 10–20 per cent in reading attainment, irrespective of the apparent cause, are given half an hour a day remedial teaching by highly trained specialists for 12–20 weeks. Clay reports that between 70 and 90 per cent of these children respond to this special teaching by attaining age-appropriate performance (Clay 1987). The children who do not respond include some who arrive at satisfactory performance levels the following year without further intervention and other children who turn out to be significantly handicapped. The implication is that there remains less than 1 per cent of the original population with a permanent, specific handicap.

How are we to reconcile these two sets of ideas and facts? There are a number of possibilities:

1 Educationalists such as Clay use a purely behavioural definition of reading difficulties and are concerned only with children at primary school age. Neurologists such as Galaburda tend only to consider cases in which there was a lifelong handicap in reading and reading-related skills, regardless of systematic improvement over time.
2 Educationalists might argue that the Galaburda team has sampled a set of extreme dyslexics with brains not typical of the reading-impaired population (they were a sample who were self-referred by willing their brains for scientific research). The vast majority of dyslexics, by this argument, would not be expected to show any brain abnormalities.
3 Neurologists such as Galaburda might argue that all people with developmental reading difficulties have some kind of cortical abnormality, but only in a minority of cases is the difficulty not remediable. This account also requires some assumption, such that most cases of reading difficulty are remediable if caught in time, or are only remediable if they are treated by a method that includes some particular feature that the Clay method contains.

I will attempt to take these possibilities into account in the discussion that follows.

The discrepancy definition of specific reading disability ▪

It is well known that there are great difficulties in defining reading failure as opposed to generally low academic achievement. The pioneering work in studying the total population of a particular age group in the Isle of Wight (Rutter et al. 1970, 1976) showed that it was hard to establish clear-cut differences at the behavioural level between children who were specifically reading disabled and those who were merely backward. Their reading patterns were equivalent. To identify the target sub-population of dyslexics, then, intelligence had to be taken into account. Using a discrepancy definition based on the regression between reading test scores and intelligence test scores, a group of under-achievers could be identified who had 'specific' difficulties; that is, who were unexpectedly failing to become literate at the pace of their peers (Rutter & Yule 1975). This definition, you might note, excludes children who have a low IQ from also having dyslexia. You could not be backward and dyslexic!

Ultimately, this method, which seemed very promising as a basis for identifying dyslexia, was defeated by its own strength: its behavioural descriptive basis. In the measures available, no consistent and meaningful neurological correlates could be found that would allow the delineation of a biologically based syndrome. On the contrary, it was the *backward* group, not the 'dyslexic' group, who exhibited neurological symptoms such as clumsiness, deafness, visual problems and epilepsy.

The next step, which proved irresistible to critics, was to deny that there is such a thing as dyslexia (Treiman & Hirsh-Pasek 1985; Bryant & Impey 1986; Prior 1989).[1] However, this is a step too far (Miles & Haslum 1986). There is good evidence that reading and spelling problems can be influenced by genetic factors (Stevenson et al. 1987; Schulte-Korne 2001). On the other hand, the discrepancy definition of dyslexia does not map on to such a concept, as is already apparent in the Isle of Wight studies. How could this state of affairs come about?

---

[1] The simplest argument is that a $1\frac{1}{2}$ year, a 2 year and a $2\frac{1}{2}$ year discrepancy between mental age and reading age only differ quantitatively, not qualitatively. From a teaching point of view that does not matter; you pick out certain children for special treatment. From a scientific/diagnostic point of view, such an argument cannot be easily countered behaviourally.

The behavioural definition of reading difficulties is not the same as a cognitive definition. A discrepancy definition is a definition at the behavioural level and can only distinguish between two broad categories. First, there are children who show no discrepancies. If such children, with low scores on intelligence tests, also have poor scores on reading tests, this could be a consequence of general developmental delay, general learning disability or adverse external circumstances, which could lead to poor performance on intelligence tests and be accompanied by a lack of reading experience. Secondly, there are children with poor reading test scores relative to IQ. This could be a sign of a *specific* cognitive deficit, but not necessarily. Thus, some children may be found to be reading disabled relative to their IQ for rather tangential reasons: they may not speak the language, they may have missed out on schooling because of illness, they may have emotional problems due to bullying or abuse, or they may suffer from poor teaching. Some children may appear to be specifically reading disabled simply because they are growing up in a subculture in which schooling and literacy are not valued. All of these children would be picked up in big sweeps of educational tests and would look worse off even than true dyslexics in terms of their reading test scores. They may be shown to be dyslexic in terms of a discrepancy definition; however, they are only pseudo-dyslexic. The Clay sweep at the end of the first school year gathers up the bottom 15 or so per cent of readers to place in a remedial programme and includes these types of children. One would expect particularly high success rates when teaching these children individually in a situation in which they might be given their first real chance at learning to read.

Current reading test scores do not identify particular types of specific disability. Therefore, the category of specific underachievement necessarily lumps together children whose deficit could also be due to, say, visual impairment. Clearly, not all children with an unexpected reading failure suffer from a specific underlying cognitive deficit. Let us stress the causal asymmetry here. I agree that if there is an underlying cognitive problem, then there will be behavioural signs at some stage of development.[2]

---

[2] I put the qualification of 'at some time in development' here because it will alway be possible that the individual would be able to compensate behaviourally by utilizing other cognitive abilities than those normally employed for a particular task. However, I suspect that even when the primary sign of a disorder has been compensated for, there will always be residual minor behavioural deficits resulting from the original cognitive deficit.

However, the presence of such behavioural signs does not necessarily imply an underlying cognitive problem. A further reason for not trusting the behavioural discrepancy definition is that it excludes dyslexics who are well compensated sufficiently to be accurate readers while still reading very slowly and with effort.

Within the framework that Uta Frith and I have set up, we can readily make the required distinctions within the area of specific reading difficulties. We can represent true dyslexia as well as pseudo-dyslexia, the reading failure that is due to external and often reversible causes. And we can easily represent different causes for dyslexia, or subtypes of dyslexia. In the end, as you will see, the problem can be addressed from the point of view both of psychology and of behaviour genetics.

Towards a cognitive definition ■

Beginning with the Isle of Wight studies, there has been a large body of work on specific reading difficulty, which has succeeded in sharpening the distinction between specific and general effects and in laying the foundations of genetic studies of a particular type of dyslexia that seems to run in families and that seems to be more frequent in boys than in girls (Critchley 1970; Pennington 1989). The main outcome from the genetic studies (twin studies and family pedigree studies) is that the phenotype for the disorder – that is, its characteristic feature – is a phonological processing problem (Olson et al. 1989, 1990; Stevenson et al. 1987). This outcome was independently arrived at in a wide variety of psychological studies comparing dyslexic readers and reading age matched normal readers. I shall focus on this particular condition as a prototype of dyslexia and will model it in an X-type causal diagram (see chapter 7).

Why is there continuing disagreement as to the existence of such a prototype? It has been suggested that a simple yet sensitive behavioural measure that will distinguish dyslexics with phonological problems is performance on non-word reading and spelling (Snowling 1987; Siegel 1989; Rack et al. 1992). Ordinary reading tests that consist of real word recognition and text comprehension are likely to camouflage the problem, since by sheer rote learning a child may acquire a large sight vocabulary and by sheer intelligence may be able to use sentence context

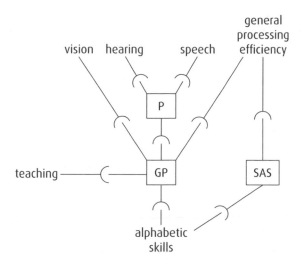

Figure 8.1 A Developmental Contingency Model (Morton 1986) for literacy. The horseshoe symbol indicates that one element is necessary for the normal development of the other. P indicates the phonological system, GP the grapheme–phoneme system and SAS the supervisory attentional system (Shallice 1988).

to guess the gist of the message.[3] The question that fires the debate is this: What is special about dyslexic readers that is not also shown by garden variety poor readers or, indeed, by young normal children before they have learned to read? In other words, are there differences among these groups at the cognitive level? Before I can address these questions we need to look at the prerequisites for the normal development of literacy. I do this because what applies to deficits also applies to normal development.

Contingencies in literacy acquisition

In figure 8.1, we see some of the main contingencies for learning to become literate in an alphabetic script. One important internal

---

[3]   That the vocabulary score correlates very highly with all other reading measures, including those that stress comprehension at the most abstract level, is another problem. The correlation is valid only for the normal population. Where there is a cognitive deficit and the child has adopted a compensatory strategy, large group statistics are no longer applicable.

prerequisite is a minimum of general processing efficiency.[4] Further-more, we need to assume that there is adequate vision and hearing, since these are the normal input channels for the skill to be learned. (Children with impairments in these channels would have to be catered for separately.) In addition to these very basic prerequisites, which figure as prerequisites in a great many developmental contingencies, we also require two additional cognitive capacities that are specifically relevant: one is a normally developing phonological system, P, which many researchers have proposed is damaged in true dyslexics; and the other is a normally developing **supervisory attentional system (SAS)** as proposed by Shallice (1988). This general attentional system needs to function efficiently for any formal learning to take place, and I assume that when this system is immature or damaged, the acquisition of any taught skills, including reading, would be difficult or impossible, even if all other prerequisites were available. This might be the case with certain types of attention disorder that can occur co-morbidly with dyslexia (Stevenson et al. 1993; see also chapter 9). External input – specifically, teaching – will be required for any progress in learning to read. If all of these internal and external conditions are fulfilled, then an automatized system for handling grapheme–phoneme (GP) corres-pondence will be established, as a result of which alphabetic skills will be evident.[5] Only after achieving a certain degree of proficiency with alphabetic skills will the child go on to become an orthographically skilled reader (Frith 1985; Morton 1989).

An X-type causal model of dyslexia ▌

As in the case of autism, there are enough facts available at both the biological and the behavioural level of description to suggest that there is a diagnostic entity. This is despite two things: first, the specific biological origins of dyslexia are unknown and are likely to be multiple; and, secondly, the signs and symptoms are extremely variable and have

---

[4] The concept of general processing efficiency is discussed extensively by Anderson (1992).
[5] The alphabetic skills will, of course, depend on other things than GP. Thus, the ability to segment at the level of onset/rime enables children to use spelling patterns in familiar words (*beak*) when decoding unfamiliar words (*peak*) (Goswami 1986, 1990).

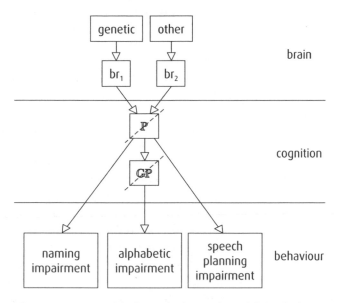

Figure 8.2 A simplified standard causal model for dyslexia.

not yet been sorted out into core symptoms, additional associated problems and secondary consequences.

The causal model for dyslexia that seems to be well supported by the weight of the evidence is given in figure 8.2. It includes alternative biological origins, a single, defining cognitive deficit, and a variety of core and other signs and symptoms. It would not be surprising, however, if, in the future, different or additional deficits were considered necessary for a full explanation of the many varieties of reading problem.

Biological factors

As yet, the precise biological basis of dyslexia is a matter of speculation. The genetic findings (Smith et al. 1983; Stevenson et al. 1987; Olson et al. 1989) all agree on there being an identifiable, single component underlying dyslexia; namely, a deficit in phonological processing. Scarborough (1990) studied children whose parents were dyslexic. Of these children, 65 per cent, a remarkably high level, were later themselves diagnosed dyslexic. These children had tended to show deficits in certain speech processes by age three. In a theory concerning brain lateralization, Annett (1992) proposed that there is a risk for poor phonological processing due to normal genetic variation associated with a single right-shift gene – that is, a gene that affects handedness. In a large sample of dyslexic children, an excess of children were found at both extremes of the right-shift continuum; that is, those who showed a marked discrepancy between left-hand and right-hand skills (Annett & Kilshaw 1984).

Galaburda (1989) reviewed the anatomical evidence from 8 brains analysed up to that time. The details need not concern us, but abnormalities were found in particular parts of the brain that are thought to subserve speech and language. Livingstone et al. (1991) reported further anatomical findings, this time concerning the visual cortex. Here too, abnormalities were found in dyslexic brains, specifically in the magnocellular system, which is responsible for low-contrast, high-speed visual processing. Experimental evidence for a deficit in this process has been provided by Lovegrove et al. (1990). Although a connection between a visual cognitive deficit underlying reading failure is a perfectly reasonable option (see the models below, in figures 8.6 and 8.12), we cannot jump to the conclusion that there is a deficit that is different from our previously assumed P-structure. We will have to await further evidence before we can talk about contrasting biological causes, which may or may not be connected with contrasting cognitive deficits.

It is notable that virtually all current theories of the origins of dyslexia have implicated genetic factors. A possible exception is the somewhat speculative Geschwind–Galaburda hypothesis, which explains abnormalities in brain asymmetry that might be relevant to dyslexia in terms of complex interactions of the intra-uterine environment and the sex of the foetus (Geschwind & Galaburda 1985). On the other hand, Bishop (1990) provides a critical evaluation of both Annett's and Geschwind's theories of cerebral lateralization and dyslexia, and concludes that there is little support for theories that individual differences in the direction and degree of laterality of language representation are the basis for developmental dyslexia.

For such reasons, the biological level in the causal models that follow will have only one starting node at the biological level, corresponding to genetic disorders, although it is anticipated that in the future a number of different types of genetic disorder will be identified. Indeed, at least five different chromosomal regions have already been implicated (Fisher & DeFries 2002).

Cognitive factors

The consensus of the best available research is that a proportion of poor readers, garden variety as well as true dyslexics, are deficient in the formation of a particular cognitive structure; namely, that responsible for grapheme–phoneme correspondence (Johnston 1982; Frith 1985; Snowling et al. 1986; Snowling 1991; Jackson & Coltheart 2001). This can have a number of different causes. In *true dyslexia*, as I have described it in the X-type model, the cause is a deficient P-structure. This deficit not only results in a faulty GP structure and poor alphabetic skills, but in additional impairments as well. Some agreement has been reached as to the crucial impairments (Catts 1989; Pennington 1989). These all concern problems in the phonological processing of spoken language and are termed by Pennington 'name retrieval', 'verbal short-term memory' and 'speech production'. It will be apparent from this description that the proposed deficit will reveal itself well before the normal onset of literacy.[6]

There is widespread agreement that the developmental deficit in system P that we assume characterizes dyslexia (Shankweiler et al. 1979; Snowling 1987; Stanovich 1988; Olson et al. 1989; Jackson & Coltheart 2001) can be indexed by a variety of phonological tests. Such tests include alliteration and rhyming (Bradley & Bryant 1983; Bryant et al. 1990), non-word reading (Rack et al. 1992), and rhyme matching (Lenel & Cantor 1981), all of which involve the use of certain components of phonological skills.[7] Many studies have shown that the critical component P is also absent in normal children below school age, as indicated in figure 8.3, due, presumably, to a relatively late process of maturation (Liberman et al. 1980; Lundberg et al. 1988; Byrne & Fielding-Barnsley 1989).[8]

---

[6] It also follows that the deficit underlying dyslexia in English-speaking children should be found in all cultures, including non-literate cultures and non-alphabetic cultures.

[7] At the moment, it is unclear how this developing process might be characterized. Its identification at the cognitive level is the major goal for serious researchers in the field. Ramus (2001) has summarized the current state of play.

[8] There is reason to believe that another component of phonology is derivative on alphabetic skills, and only develops in individuals who have a minimum of experience with alphabetic scripts. Thus, Morais et al. (1979) showed that adult illiterates found it difficult to understand for instance, what was meant by the request to say 'Ted' without the 'tuh'. Because letters are visible manifestations of the artificial concept *phoneme*, it is not surprising that so-called 'phoneme awareness' is dependent on knowing letters.

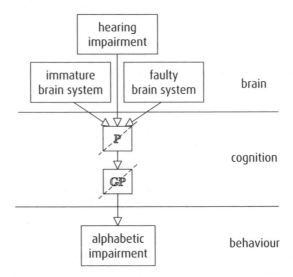

Figure 8.3 A causal model for the phonological impairment P, which could arise for reasons unconnected with dyslexia.

A third reason for the lack of development of the critical component, P, could be hearing impairment, including intermittent impairments such as Otitis Media with Effusion (OME).

Difficulties of the beginning reader

The reciprocal relationship between literacy acquisition and phonological skills (Ehri 1984; Stuart & Coltheart 1988; Cataldo & Ellis 1990; Perfetti 1991) means that clear causal pathways for reading failure are difficult to establish. For instance, subsyllabic segmentation and blending skills appear simultaneously with alphabetic reading skills. However, it seems likely that different components of phonological processes are evoked when typical phoneme awareness tasks are given to a person who is literate and when given to a pre-literate child (Morais 1991).

While there is a clear correlation between the emergence of P-indexed skills in pre-school children and their subsequent smooth and early entry into an alphabetic system, there is also evidence from training studies (Lundberg et al. 1988) to strengthen the notion of a causal relationship. Wimmer et al. (1991) have shown that pre-readers with poor P-indexed skills (e.g. not being able to substitute one particular vowel for another vowel in single-word 'mis-repetition') could be divided into two groups after the first school year: those whose P-component was simply delayed compared to that of their peers but subsequently became competent readers; and those who remained persistently poor readers, with the possible explanation that their P component was faulty.

In its simplest form, this hypothesis supposes that, at pre-school age on standard tasks, an immature P-system is not distinguishable from a faulty P-system. The implication of this theory is that the brain systems involved in figure 8.3 above should be the same in the case of fault and delay. The study by Scarborough (1990) of pre-school children at risk for dyslexia suggests, however, that a careful analysis of speech processes may pick out a dysfunctional from a merely immature P-system even at this early stage. On this view, we would expect the biological components in the causal chains of the two to be different from each other. I would also expect remediation in the case of delay to be much more straightforward than in the case of deficit.

Associated and secondary problems

There are, however, other circumstances that might lead to the non-development of a GP system, and in figure 8.1 I have already noted several other prerequisites apart from the phonological system. In other words, specific evidence is needed in order to draw the conclusion that a child who is backward in reading is truly dyslexic – which I equate here with a faulty P component. In figure 8.4, I diagram two different types of brain damage. In this theory, damage of the type br_1 affects the P component and is typical of true dyslexia. Damage of the type br_2, on the other hand, affects not only the P component but also the SAS component. This would be the case for an individual suffering from a severe learning difficulty that affects not only literacy, but also any other type of formal learning. Such an individual would suffer from a range of problems not shared by the dyslexic. These problems, including the attentional one, would be classified as *associated* with respect to the dyslexia.

A number of authors have reported that children with severe reading problems have attentional deficits to a greater extent than would be expected by chance (Taylor 1986). It remains to be seen whether or not these children would be classified as dyslexic by virtue of a faulty P component, as in the case of damage br_2 in figure 8.4. In this case, the attentional problem could be seen as being secondary so far as the

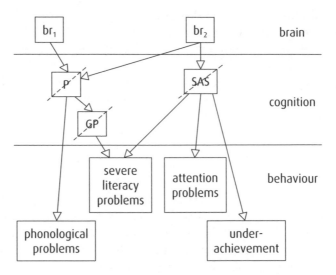

Figure 8.4 Two kinds of brain damage affecting the phonological (*P*) component. Of these, *br*₂ is a more general impairment; *br*₁ is typical of dyslexia. The first problem gives rise to a greater variety of developmental problem. SAS is the system that controls attention.

grapheme–phoneme problem is concerned. That is, the attentional problem would not be a part of the main dyslexia causal tree. In contrast is the case in which only the SAS component is directly affected by a biological malfunction. This is illustrated in figure 8.5. In this case, the absence of a GP system would result simply as a consequence of an absence of effective learning. The attentional problem would be the cause of the reading problem. In this figure, the solid box around the *P*-system indicates that it is intact.[9] Such children would not be classified as dyslexic on the purely phonological criterion and would not manifest the other signs of a missing *P*-system, such as a naming impairment or developmental speech problems.

The third possibility is that the attentional problems are *secondary* to a true dyslexia – that is, they are caused by the effects of being

---

[9] I note here that there exist other children who are hyperlexic in the presence of potentially severe SAS problems, and, indeed, general intellectual impairments. In these cases, it has been shown that a GP system is fully operative, presumably in the presence of a normal *P*-structure (Frith & Snowling 1983; Seymour & Evans 1992; Cossu et al. 1993).

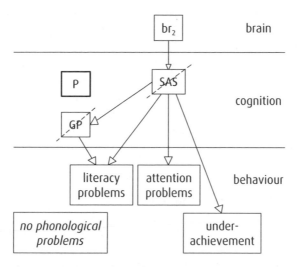

Figure 8.5 Alphabetic impairment arising in the presence of an intact phonological system. The solid box round the *P*-system indicates that it is intact and, thus, does not contribute to the dyslexia.

backwards in reading on the child's attitude to him- or herself and to the process of education (Stanovich 1986). In such a case, there would be no biological component affecting the attentional systems and the SAS component could be intact. The full causal model in this case would be very complex, possibly involving interaction with the environment. Such cases are better approached on an individual basis, using the methods developed by Frederickson and Cline (2002). An association between reading problems and conduct disorder has also long been known (Sturge 1982; Yule & Rutter 1985) and might receive one of the explanations explored above.

General and specific deficits

As maxim 4 of causal modelling demands, we must make the distinction between general and specific deficits. If a deficit is explicable in terms of the general deficit, then we need have no recourse to specific accounts. Poor reading achievement can often be explained as part and parcel of poor overall ability or general mental retardation. I would not want to talk about specific reading problems in such circumstances.

Reading tests appear to be very sensitive at certain ages compared with tests of other functions. It could therefore appear that a child has a specific reading difficulty while doing well on, say, a vocabulary test. It will turn out that, in this case, the vocabulary was a matter of rote learning and was not based on an underlying intact cognitive capacity. Several years later, this child would be revealed to have a vocabulary skill and reading skill commensurate with his or her generally low level of functioning. Before attributing specific deficits on the basis of behaviour alone, we have to be very sure of the measuring instrument.

Competing theories of dyslexia ■

There are, of course, challenges to the particular causal model of dyslexia that we have adopted. Clay (1987), for instance, argued that children learn to become learning disabled and that a biological basis may be an unsound assumption to start with. Another challenge is that we have focused on a phonological deficit when there may be others; for example, visual deficits that underlie at least one subtype of dyslexia. Our notation enables us to represent competing theories of dyslexia, and the potential to compare theories on neutral ground can be demonstrated by some examples.

In this section, I will draw extensively on the analysis carried out by the Working Party of the British Psychological Society (BPS 1999). They point out the dangers inherent in focusing on only one level of description when formulating accounts of the difficulties experienced by children. The starting point is the basic statement of the core phonological delay or deficit. This is adopted 'both because of the broad empirical support that it commands and because of the role phonology is accorded in many other hypotheses in mediating the impact of dyslexia on the acquisition of word reading and spelling skills' (p. 30). The way in which this group portrays the phonological hypothesis in a causal model is shown in figure 8.6. There are a number of things that should be noted about the approach of this group. First, they refer to 'genetic difference' and 'brain difference', rather than talking about abnormalities or damage. The clearest reason for taking this step, in relation to developmental dyslexia, is that we have no idea whether there is anything genetic in the make-up of people with dyslexia that could be thought of as abnormal. It is entirely possible that what we are seeing is the result of the coincidence of a set of normal genetic variations which,

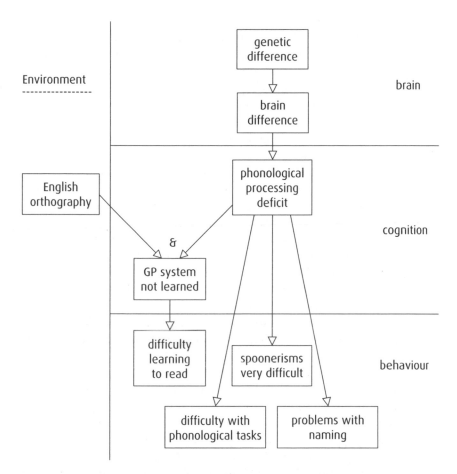

Figure 8.6 A causal model for the phonological delay/deficit hypothesis of dyslexia, adapted from BPS (1999, fig. 4.2). Of particular interest is the specification of English orthography as a causal factor in the problem with learning the GP (grapheme–phoneme) system.

outside the particular combination, would not give rise to noticeable differences. The second point is that the cognitive basis of the phonological deficit hypothesis is labelled *phonological processing deficit*. It should be remembered that this refers to a computational deficit, not to the results of any test. The computational deficit is cognitive, and its precise nature is not known. Most of the time, this phonological processing difficulty leads to the measurable behaviour called *difficulty with phonological tasks.* Implied in this model, and in contrast with the models that follow in this chapter, is that the brain difference leading to this condition has cognitive effects that are specific to and restricted to phonological processing. This is a very strong position to take and is, not surprisingly, being contested around the world. Note that if this modular hypothesis turns out not to be true, the rest of the causal model would be unaffected. Indeed, in looking at the alternative hypotheses, the BPS Working Party has in most cases been able to include the phonological deficit hypothesis as a subset of the other theories. This will become clearer in the figures that follow.

One final feature of interest in figure 8.6 is the inclusion of *English orthography* in the environment as a component of the causal model. The causal model states clearly that the behavioural sign *difficulty learning to read* depends upon the cognitive problem *GP system not learned.* It also makes it clear that the problem in learning the GP system depends on the *phonological processing deficit* in conjunction with *English orthography.* I have alluded to this earlier in the chapter, but not included it in the causal models. Why has this step been taken? The main reason is that it seems to be the case that the severe reading difficulties typical of dyslexia do not seem to be found in children learning to read in scripts that are regular. The best studied examples are Italian (see Paulesu et al. 2001) and German (Landerl et al. 1997). There are also reports of bilingual children failing at English-language schools in India because of dyslexic problems, and having no problem learning to read on transferring to an Indian-language school. Indian scripts share with Italian, and to a lesser extent German, the property that a particular written symbol is always sounded in the same way. In contrast, as you know, English is written in a very confusing way, and requires the child to learn context-sensitive rules and exceptions (see box 8.1 for further details). The implication of this is that children, and adults, who have learned to read in Italian may have the same brain condition as an English dyslexic, and so have the same basic cognitive problem, but without showing any noticeable problem in reading. They would, however, show the other behavioural problems that arise from the phonological processing deficit. All of this follows from the model shown in figure 8.6.

The temporal processing hypothesis

Tallal et al. (1997) have suggested that a crucial component of dyslexia is a difficulty in perceiving acoustic differences between speech contrasts

Box 8.1 The difference between English and Italian script

The main reasons for the particular complexity of learning to read in English are, first, the number of vowel sounds in the spoken language and, secondly, the fact that English script limits itself largely to five letters, *a e i o u*, for representing these vowel sounds, with the occasional help of other letters, particularly *r* and *y*. In English English (as opposed to American English) there are the following vowels:

Short vowels	Long vowels	Diphthongs
bat	cart	bait, bought
bet	beat	bear, beer
bit		bite, byre
cot	coot	boat, bout, boy
cut	curt	cute
foot		

This table already gives an idea of the diversity of use of individual letters; for example, the letter *a* can be found representing five different vowels.

The problem exists both ways round. Consider the following alternative ways of representing particular vowel sounds:

> beat, beet, suite, mete
> bear, bare, hair,
> bought, yawn, caught, taut, bore, boar
> boat, beau, dough, cote,
> bait, date, may,
> bite, fight,
> bet, sweat

Consider also that a particular letter combination might be pronounced in a number of ways:

> through, rough, cough, thought, dough
> foot, blood, boom,
> sweat, bear, beat
> pint, mint

Some of the pronunciations are rule-governed, such as the vowel lengthening in the pairs *bat/bate, met/mete, sit/site, cot/cote* and *cut/cute*, but even here a diphthong is sometimes produced, rather than just a vowel lengthening.

In comparison, Italian has only five vowel sounds, which are represented by the five letters.

It is not just that the English script is more difficult to learn; it is that the learning is of a different nature, requiring context-sensitive rules and a wide variety of exceptions. In the course of setting up this system, children also create generalizations that they have to abandon or qualify. I conclude that learning such correspondences requires a special kind of computational system, although researchers have not yet managed to characterize this satisfactorily.

that involve brief, rapidly changing or transient componants. An example of this would be the contrast between the syllables /ba/, /da/ and /ga/. More generally, there would be problems with any temporal processing, and this would reveal itself in the visual modality (Farmer & Klein 1993). At the biological level, differences in the magnocellular layers of the visual and auditory regions of the thalamus (see Galaburda & Livingstone 1993) have been proposed as a potential neurobiological basis. Note that this theory, diagrammed in figure 8.7, can adopt the phonological deficit hypothesis in its entirety. What it does is specify a cognitive and a biological precursor to the phonological processing difficulty that are not restricted to phonological processing, in contrast to the model in figure 8.6. In addition, it makes the prediction that certain other kinds of problems will also be found. Specifically, people with dyslexia should have weaknesses in motion detection and tone discrimination, as well as poor speech development. Ramus et al. (2003b) have addressed this question and have evidence of adult dyslexics without such sensory problems.

Tallal et al. (1997) also claim that certain remedial training, aimed at improving temporal integration skills, is effective in increasing both language and reading skills. The extent to which this claim is true, and the extent to which it is generally true, will bear on our acceptance of the underlying theory as the cause of the phonological processing deficit.

The skill automatization hypothesis

Another theory that incorporates the phonological deficit hypothesis is that of Nicolson and Fawcett (1995; see also Nicolson et al. 2001). The

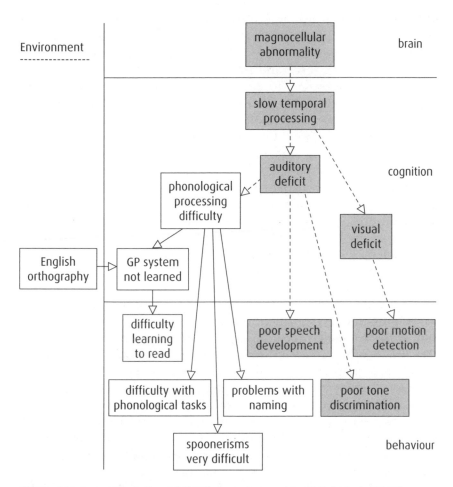

Figure 8.7 A representation of the theory proposed by Tallal et al. (1997), whereby the core deficit in dyslexia is temporal processing. This figure has been adapted from BPS (1999, fig. 4.3). The convention in this and the following diagrams is that the standard phonological deficit theory of dyslexia is presented in the clear boxes and the specific theory being modelled has shaded boxes. In this case, the phonological theory is embedded in the temporal processing theory. The model predicts that all dyslexics would show a deficit in motion detection and tone discrimination.

skill automatization hypothesis proposed by these authors claims that dyslexic children have difficulties across a range of skills. Specifically, these skills are ones that the children are required to perform at a fluent, automatic level, and so they are prevented from employing conscious compensation to overcome their difficulties. Thus, they report that dyslexic children have no problem with balancing without wobbling, unless they are blindfolded or are given a distracting task. In these two cases, they would be unable to use conscious compensation techniques. According to their position, the same problem would apply to the acquisition of phonological skills. This theory is represented in figure 8.8, with some changes derived from Nicolson et al. (2001). Note that I am not concerned here to evaluate the theory, but merely to represent it in a fashion that makes it easy to see its component parts and to see its relationship with the phonological deficit hypothesis (although for failures to replicate, see Raberger & Wimmer 2003; Ramus et al. 2003a).

At the biological level, Nicolson and Fawcett (1995) hypothesize a cerebellar abnormality that leads to problems both with phonological skills and with time estimation. It is clear that this is a full-scale competitor to the temporal processing hypothesis diagrammed in figure 8.7. The two theories agree with respect to the proximal cause of dyslexia – the phonological deficit hypothesis – however, they hypothesize different locations for the crucial brain damage involved in dyslexia, and they predict different patterns of co-morbidity. Broadly, then, the choice between them involves empirical questions that are easily conceptualized – although the direct identification of the location of brain damage is not easy. It may, of course, turn out that the two theories refer to sub-types of dyslexia. Particular genetic specifications lead to separate differences in neuroanatomy, to be found either in the magnocellular cortex or in the cerebellum. These have their own different cognitive consequences which, however, converge on a developmental problem of phonological processing difficulty. That is to say, it could be the case that the normal development of phonological processing requires particular auditory ability as well as some skill automatization. If either is missing, then there will be a phonological processing deficit. In this way, neither theory need conflict with the phonological deficit hypothesis, which is a hypothesis that deals only with the proximal cause of dyslexic signs and symptoms. This combined theory is represented in figure 8.9, in which I have replaced the entire phonological deficit hypothesis (including the environmental aspect) with a triangle.

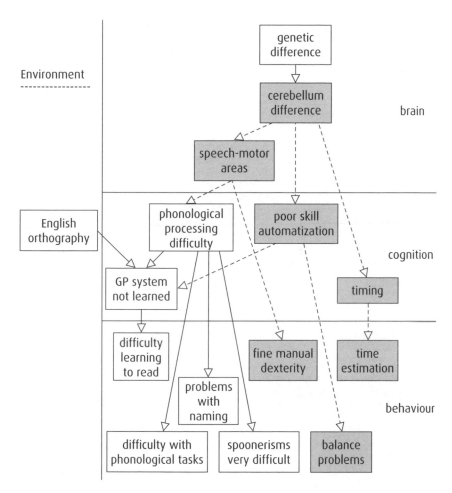

Figure 8.8 A causal model for the Nicolson and Fawcett (1990) skill automatization hypothesis. The phonological delay/deficit hypothesis still accounts for the reading difficulty and associated problems. This theory predicts that dyslexics should also have problems with balance and time. Adapted from BPS (1999, fig. 4.4), using Nicolson et al. (2001).

Skill automatization as a subset

The skill automatization hypothesis, as I have expressed it in the previous section, includes the phonological deficit hypothesis as a subset. Eamon McCrory, in a recent unpublished talk, has proposed the

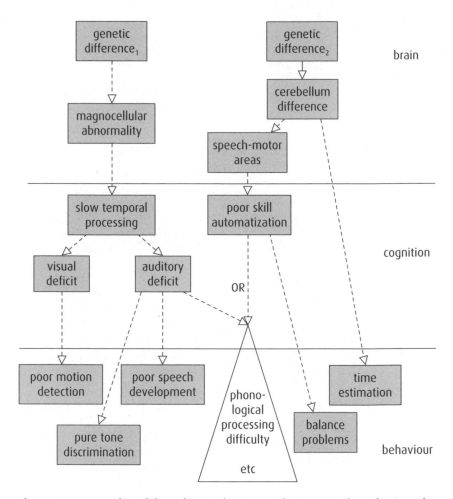

Figure 8.9 A causal model combining the temporal processing hypothesis and the skill automatization hypothesis of dyslexia. The causal subtree from the phonological processing difficulty to behaviour is represented by the solid triangle. This causal analysis reveals no conflict between the two hypotheses that could, in principle, give rise to two subsets of dyslexia. The two groups would be distinguished by the presence of particular extra specific problems, such as pure tone discrimination and poor time estimation, respectively.

reverse relationship; namely, that the skill automatization hypothesis is a subset of the phonological deficit hypothesis. His argument depends on a recasting of the tasks used in support of the skill automatization hypothesis so that, rather than performance on these tasks being

influenced directly by brain differences, as in figure 8.8, they are primarily determined by cognitive factors. According to McCrory, these
cognitive factors have to do with the role of internal speech in the
execution of a wide variety of tasks. He proposes that dyslexics are less
able to recruit these cognitive factors and so perform relatively badly on
crucial tasks. The underlying causal model is presented in figure 8.10.

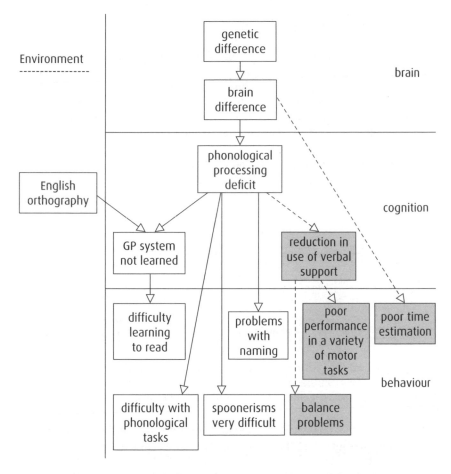

Figure 8.10 A causal model of McCrory's reinterpretation of the evidence
leading to the skill automatization hypothesis depicted in figure 8.8. According
to this theory, the problems found in balance and other motor tasks have to do
with the way in which the tasks are performed.

The evaluation of this theory compared with that of Nicolson and Fawcett (1995) will depend crucially on the design of tasks for which one theory would predict failure on the part of dyslexics and the other theory would predict success. These tasks would clearly have to do with motor skills, the two theories making identical predictions with respect to phonological skills. Another approach could be through an examination of individual differences (see box 8.2). McCrory would have to

---

Box 8.2   Individual differences

There are certain general predictions that can be made from a causal model to correlations between individual differences in performance on particular tasks. Take the two outline causal models in figure 1. They both refer to a brain difference, B, which leads to problems in a couple of cognitive processes, C_1 and C_2. These processes are the primary determinants of behaviour in tasks T_{1-3}. For both underlying theories, performance on tasks T_1 and T_3 is controlled by processes C_1 and C_2, respectively. The difference between the theories is that under theory A, task T_2 is determined by process C_1; whereas under theory B, it is controlled by process C_2.

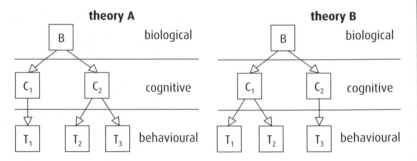

Figure 1 Two theories concerning the effects of brain difference B on a variety of tasks. On theory A, task T_2 is mediated by cognitive process C_2; on theory B, task T_2 is mediated by cognitive process C_1.

Now, it is a universal of biological systems that differences have multiple causation and that, accordingly, causal influences are variable in quantity.

As a first example, shown in figure 2, we can suppose that the formation of process C_1, or its efficiency, is determined both by B and by B_x. To give a concrete, though hypothetical, example, B could be the synaptic density in a particular brain area, and B_x could be the balance of neurotransmitters in that area. We can suppose that the effect of a particular deficit in B on the development of process C_1 will be modulated by the level of B_x. We assume here that the genetic factors controlling variation in B are completely independent from those involved in variation in B_x. In a similar way, we can consider that process C_2 is controlled by B_y as well as by B. We assume that the level of B_y is independent of either B or B_x. Within this elaborated system, we can see that while a deficit in B will give rise to deficits in both C_1 and C_2, the extent of the deficits will vary between individuals.

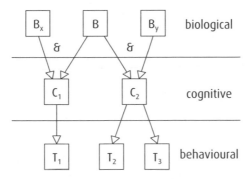

Figure 2 An extension of theory A in the previous figure. Cognitive factor C_1 is now influenced developmentally by biological factor B_x. Variations in B_x will then give rise to variations in performance in task T_1. Tasks T_2 and T_3 will likewise be affected by variations in biological factor B_y.

Now, consider how tasks are performed. The basic hypothesis is that a deficit in B leads to a decrement in tasks T_{1-3}. But there is no task that is controlled by one cognitive process only. Thus, as shown in Figure 3, we have task T_1 being controlled not only by C_1, but also by cognitive factor C_x. In most cases, C_1, the primary cognitive influence on the performance of T_1, will be a specialized process, while C_x would be a general factor. Similar elaborations can be applied to the other tasks. Candidate general cognitive factors are intelligence, language skills and motivation. Performance on any task will be a function of all the cognitive processes or factors that contribute to it. As an example, the standard account of autism says that the absence of a Theory of Mind leads to failure in the false belief task. However, the false belief task can be passed by some children with autism who have a mental age greater than ten (Frith et al. 1991). On this account of the disorder, then, performance on the false belief task is thus influenced by components related to intelligence as well as to Theory of Mind. Other accounts of autism will have to have similar accounts, though, possibly, with different cognitive factors identified. The presence of all of these sources of variation means that while all individuals with the brain difference B will show an impairment on tasks T_{1-3}, the extent of the impairment on the various tasks will differ.

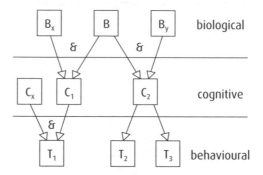

Figure 3 A further extension of theory A, indicating that the relation between the cognitive and behavioural levels is often multi-determined. In this case, performance on task T_1 will be influenced by cognitive factor C_x, as well as by C_1.

We can now return to the difference between theories A and B. It should be clear that there is a way of distinguishing between the theories on the basis on individual differences. A range of individuals with brain difference B can be given tasks T_{1-3}. Correlations can then be carried out between performance on T_1 and T_2 and between performance on T_2 and T_3. Theory A predicts that the correlation between T_2 and T_3 will be greater than the correlation between T_1 and T_2. This is because some of the variability between individuals in scores on T_2 and T_3 is provided by C_2 and so will be shared by those tasks. In the same way, theory B predicts that the correlation between T_1 and T_2 will be greater.

Note that in principle these tests could be carried out with a normal population, relying on non-clinical variation in the various controlling cognitive factors. However, it might be the case that the effects of normal variation on task performance is too small to allow a satisfactory test of this kind. For example, performance on the false belief task is not greatly affected by intelligence in the normal population, for whom the task depends overwhelmingly on the natural development of a Theory of Mind, whereas for the autistic population, which is deficient in ToM, intelligence – as estimated by mental age – is crucial for this task.

An example of the logic reviewed above is given in this chapter. The issue there is whether decrements shown by dyslexics on particular tasks are primarily due to problems with phonological processing or are due to poor skill automatization.

predict a higher correlation between phonological problems and motor tasks than between motor tasks and time estimation. For Nicolson and Fawcett (1995), the predictions are the other way round.

The co-morbidity option

There is a third possibility, which I referred to briefly in chapter 7. This is that dyslexia is co-morbid with the skill automation problem, but with no link at the cognitive level. In this case, we would have a causal model like that in figure 8.8, but with no connection from 'poor skill automatization' to 'phonological processing difficulty' and a separate genetic/ brain input into the latter. I have sketched this theory in figure 8.11. As drawn, the 'common effect' will be at the genetic level, but there are

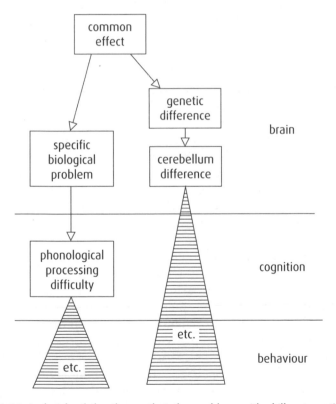

Figure 8.11 A sketch of the theory that the problem with skill automatization is co-morbid with dyslexia. Compare this with figure 4.8.

optional mechanisms further down the causal chain within the biological level.

The working memory hypothesis

The BPS (1999) report next considers the inefficiency in short-term memory (STM) associated with developmental dyslexia. Rack (1994) calls this 'one of the most reliable and often quoted characteristics of developmental dyslexia' (p. 9). This inefficiency, at the cognitive level, appears to be mediated by inefficiencies in the use of phonological codes. Stanovich et al. (1997) report that dyslexics show significantly lower working memory capacity than reading-age matched controls. Hulme and Roodenrys (1995) argue that the short-term memory problems of poor readers are not causally related to their poor reading, but are an index of other phonological deficits that are a cause of reading difficulties. The BPS report discusses the use of working memory rather than STM, but uses STM in the causal model – shown in figure 8.12. I feel that this model, and the underlying theory, is in need of some elaboration before it could be as satisfactory as the preceding ones. In particular, there would need to be some elaboration of the distinction between 'STM difficulty', notionally a cognitive problem, and 'Memory problems', which are classified as behaviour. The nature of the latter would depend upon the theory of memory being adopted. Thus, within a working memory model there might be need to specify whether the immediate cognitive deficit was related to the capacity of the phonological loop or to factors related to the functioning of the central executive. With other models of short-term memory function, the deficit would have to be expressed in terms appropriate to the particular model.

Another question that I would want to raise in the context of the causal model in figure 8.12 is the nature of the two arrows leading into 'GP system not learned'. The distinction between 'phonological processing difficulty' and 'inefficient use of phonological codes' would need to be specified, together with some indication as to why both would be necessary at the same time in order to create the problem with the GP system. This form of the causal model also prompts us to ask what would happen if either of 'phonological processing difficulty' and 'inefficient use of phonological codes' were present without the other and what other tests we might use to reveal such discrepancies.

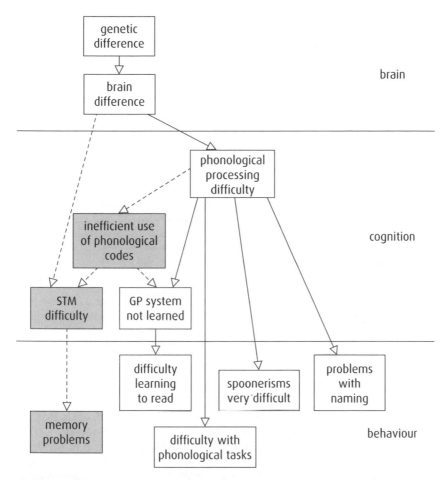

Figure 8.12 The working memory hypothesis (from BPS 1999, fig. 4.5). The unclearness of the causal model reflects that of the theories that the model represents. A stronger theory of the influence of memory weakness on the development of reading difficulties would derive a problem with phonological codes separately from the phonological processing difficulty.

Visual processing hypotheses

There are a variety of approaches to thinking about the effects of visual processing problems on reading. The BPS working party express such hypotheses in the causal model shown in figure 8.13. There are a couple of things to note about this figure. First, it is specified that there

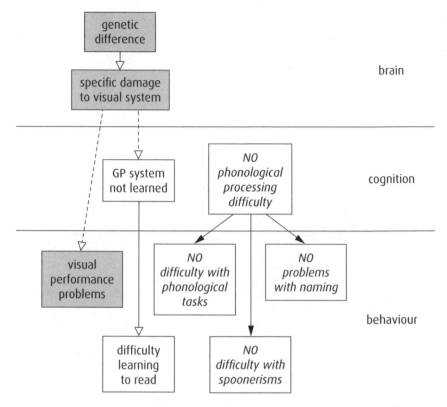

Figure 8.13 A generic causal model for hypotheses concerning dyslexia that involve visual processing (adapted from BPS 1999, fig. 4.6). The notable characteristic of such hypotheses is that we would not expect there to be any phonological processing difficulty. The difficulty in learning the GP system would be due to problems on the grapheme side rather than on the phoneme side.

is no phonological processing difficulty. This fact is then linked causally to the absence of problems in the phonological domain. Normally, we would not bother to specify the absence of problems in a causal model, but in this case it is useful for contrastive reasons, focusing us on the fact that such theories are different from the phonological deficit hypothesis in the kinds of prediction they make outside the reading domain. Secondly, note that in the figure there is no intervening cognitive factor between the specific brain difference in the visual system and the lack of learning the GP system. This is because the diagram represents the *class* of hypotheses involving the visual system rather than any

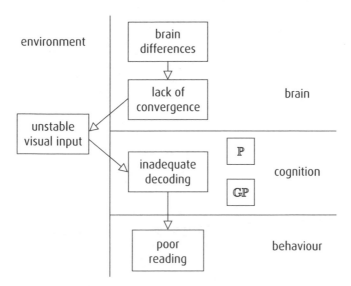

Figure 8.14 A representation of Stein's (1991, 1994) theory of the centrality of convergence problems in reading difficulties.

specific hypothesis. In fact, specific hypotheses involving the visual system are rather rare. Stein (1991, 1994) has conducted a series of studies that pointed to significant differences in binocular fixation stability and in vergence control in dyslexic and normally reading children. It is not clear how that would directly lead to problems with the setting up of a grapheme–phoneme system, other than by retarding the process of learning the set of graphemes through the unstable visual image. I would represent the correction of such factors – for example, through forcing the child to use monocular vision – as an interface with the environment. The underlying causal model is shown in figure 8.14. Note that I have represented *lack of convergence* as a biological factor rather than as behaviour, since it fits the needs of the representation better. It is possible that for other questions, we might represent *lack of convergence* as behaviour. Remember that the objective of causal modelling is to achieve representational clarity.

Morton and Frith (1993b, 1995) expanded on the theme of specific visual impairment as a cause of dyslexia by means of illustrative theories. For example, it would be possible in principle that a specific problem with *visual pattern analysis* could occur. The biological cause could be, as Livingstone et al. (1991) suggest, a particular defect within the

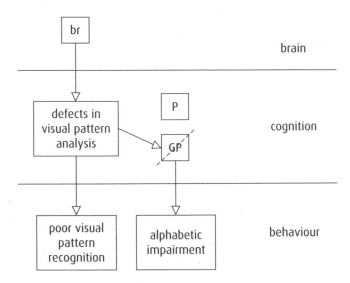

Figure 8.15 A causal model of the influence of poor visual pattern analysis on the development of reading.

magnocellular system. Note the contrast here with the *temporal processing hypothesis*, where both visual and auditory modalities are affected (figure 8.7). Cases of dissociation between phonological and visual skills exist (Seymour 1990) and strongly suggest the possibility of subgroups that can be defined at the cognitive level. In the model shown in figure 8.15, I specify a problem with visual pattern analysis, but without a problem in the phonological system. At this point I invoke maxim 6 – 'Be cognitively economical' (see p. 103). This requires that if a cognitive deficit is postulated to account for particular behaviour, then some other indicator of this deficit should be specified. In this case, I specify that there should be general problems found with visual pattern recognition.

The syndrome hypothesis

The BPS (1999) report draws on the work of Miles (1983, 1993), who pioneered, in the UK, a particular approach to the assessment of dyslexia as a syndrome – that is, as a collection of signs and symptoms that make up the syndrome and that may change over time. The items noted by Miles include uncertainty over right and left, difficulty in repeating polysyllabic words, low digit span and problems in learning the months of the year in sequence. Miles (1993) concludes that most of the manifestations of dyslexia can be attributed to difficulties in verbal labelling or working memory processes. As such, they can be seen as arising from phonological processing difficulty. Essentially, however, the syndrome approach should be seen as a clinical tool rather than as a scientific claim, and use of a causal model here would simply serve to highlight this.

Hypotheses involving intelligence

In considering the influence of intelligence on reading performance, we have to be particularly careful about the word 'reading'. While it is clear that intelligence – as represented by both knowledge and general cognitive skills – will affect the ease of comprehension of texts, it is not so clear that it has a direct effect on phonological processing. Any hypotheses involving the word 'reading' will have to specify the scope of the word that is intended.[10] This has been shown by Snowling's (1987) work with 'hyperlexic' children who can decipher texts but have few comprehension skills (also Siegel 1988, 1992). The causal model depicted by the BPS (1999), shown in figure 8.16, is fraught with problems. To start with, it claims that a particular brain difference leads both to general processing difficulty and to phonological processing difficulty. Secondly, it assumes, by default, that there is a phonological processing difficulty for low-IQ children that is the same as that for normal-IQ dyslexic groups. Thirdly, it assumes, by default, that the difficulties with phonological tasks, spoonerisms and naming found with the low-IQ groups are equivalent to those found with normal-IQ groups and are caused by the underlying phonological processing difficulty. When the underlying theory is seen through its causal model in relation to other theories, these shortcomings become obvious.

Non-biological causes ▌

Figures 8.17–8.19 show examples of externally generated causes of poor reading, such as lack of language knowledge, poor teaching/ learning environment or severe emotional resistance to school and test

---

[10] Indeed, as I have already noted, there is a good case that the term 'reading', by itself, is a pre-scientific term that has no place in any scientific discussion.

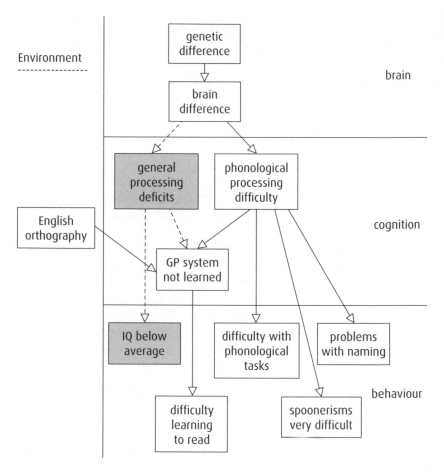

Figure 8.16 A causal model (from BPS 1999) that represents the supposed role of low intelligence in reading difficulties.

performance brought about by negative external influences. Sometimes these causes directly affect the GP component, as in figure 8.17. More often, it is the SAS component that is affected (in the form of attentional problems), as illustrated in figures 8.18 and 8.19.

We have been looking at externally motivated causes that accidentally impair reading acquisition. A 'normal' variant of this is the effect of a child being newly confronted by a different language and phonology, or simply not getting instruction because he or she grows up in a non-literate culture. In such cases, we would have no reason to suppose that

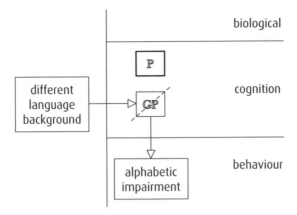

Figure 8.17 A causal model for the effects of culture on learning to read. There may be other effects that you might like to trace. Note that the phonological skills would be normal and we would expect performance on phonological tasks to be unaffected, except where differences between the child's native phonology and background have an impact. These latter have not been diagrammed.

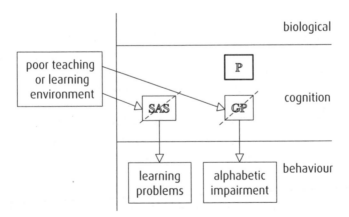

Figure 8.18 A causal model for the effects of the environment both on reading development and general learning skills.

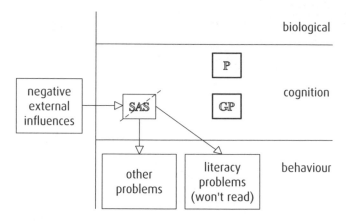

Figure 8.19 A causal model for a case in which external influences result in apparent reading backwardness in the presence of a complete GP system. This model is in need of considerable elaboration, particularly in showing exactly how the environment can affect the SAS. Some similar models are covered in chapter 10, where we look at conduct disorder.

the process P is dysfunctional; rather, there is incomplete knowledge of the phonology of the particular language that the child is still in the process of acquiring.[11] Figure 8.17 illustrates a causal model for such a cultural factor.

Figures 8.18 and 8.19, in contrast, show the effects of a different class of factors, such as a disturbed home life or a hostile relationship with the teacher or, simply, misguided teaching (all of which have been claimed to inhibit reading acquisition). These external causes may primarily affect the SAS component; that is, they have potentially more widespread effects than merely reading difficulties. I have indicated that behavioural disorders would be expected in this group. These externally caused reading problems (part of the large group of garden variety) may be mediated either through an effect on the GP system as in figure 8.18, where I would expect poor performance specifically in reading and spelling non-words, or only at the behavioural level, as in

---

[11] Strictly speaking, this is a hypothesis. When we discover what the missing phonological skill, P, is, it may be apparent that a crucial aspect of it develops only in interaction with the task of reading. In this case we would require that otherwise normal members of a pre-literate society would behave in the same way as dyslexics on crucial phonological tasks.

figure 8.19.[12] This figure presents the case of a poor reader who won't read rather than can't read. However, I am suggesting that his or her not wanting to read can and should be treated as being a cognitive link in the causal chain.

In another version of the causal theories just discussed, the damage done has its effect solely at the behavioural level. For instance, counter-productive reading strategies may have been induced by incompetent or misguided teaching. Such patterns of behaviour are established (as cognitive elements, of course) instead of the normal reading strategies, which generally function as self-teaching mechanisms. This is in con-trast to the version illustrated above in figure 8.18, where the effect occurs at the level of cognitive structures, such that the acquisition of a well functioning GP system is prevented, or in figure 8.19, where the attentional system is affected.

Other biological causes of reading failure

We can imagine the case of reading failure that is due to a cognitive deficit and yet not of biological origin. I would claim that this condi-tion, if it exists, is pseudo-dyslexia. In contrast, true dyslexia is defined by a cognitive deficit (whether in a visual or in a phonological system) and has a biological origin. The question that we now need to ask is whether all biological causes of reading failure are connected with a specific cognitive deficit and therefore all qualify as 'true' dyslexia.

The case of a blind person (who has not learned Braille) illustrates the answer to this question. Here, there would undoubtedly be a bio-logical origin that we would want to call the cause of the person being unable to read. We would not, however, want to link this through the cognitive factor, P. This is in spite of the fact that the blind person (lacking the relevant teaching) has no grapheme–phoneme system. The immediate/local cause of absence of a GP system then is not the absence of P, since P would be normal, but, merely, the absence of

---

[12]   The effect of lead in the environment has repeatedly been shown in a lowering of scores on reading tests (Fulton et al. 1987; Silva et al. 1988). I would suggest that this sort of external cause of reading impairment may act in the same way as certain psychosocial causes. Thus there would be an effect on the behavioural level (alpha-betic skills), which would be mediated through the attentional (SAS) component rather than the phonological (P) component.

Braille stimuli and a teacher. It would be more sensible to stick with the remote cause and to show the behavioural problem, lack of alphabetic skills, as being caused (remotely) by the blindness, but not by a specific cognitive problem. A similar case might be made for some types of hearing impairment. However, in the absence of a clear theory of the normal development of the P-system, I feel that such a case would have to be heavily qualified.

How do we sort among the options? ▪

It is probably clear that, so far as I am concerned, the phonological hypothesis of developmental dyslexia is the only serious contender. Three or four major issues remain, and causal modelling can help to solve them by providing a framework.

The first issue is the precise nature of the phonological deficit. In the causal models in this chapter, the deficit is referred to simply as 'phonological processing deficit' or as P (with a strike-out of some form). In practical terms, this refers to the computational problem in the child while he or she is trying to set up the grapheme–phoneme system. To be more specific, it is a problem with learning many-to-many mappings between orthographic and phonological elements. Because of the consistent pattern of other phonological deficits in people with dyslexia, I assume (with many others) that the underlying problem lies somewhere in the handling of abstract phonological symbols, but its precise nature badly needs specifying. That is, the model in figure 8.6 is the correct one. It is possible, of course, that the other phonological problems are linked to dyslexia not at the cognitive level, but biologically. In that case, the underlying causal model would look like that shown in figure 8.20. No-one has yet put forward such a model.

The second issue is whether the postulated deficit, P, *the handling of abstract phonological symbols,* can be seen as a computational primitive, in which case there would be no other cognitive precursor in the causal tree. Otherwise, we have to look for some factor that could plausibly enable the development of P in normal development, the absence of which would lead to P being absent. Such a theory is outlined in figure 8.21. According to maxim 6 of our rules of theorizing (see chapter 5), we cannot postulate a cognitive deficit to account for a behavioural problem without proposing a novel behavioural outcome, unrelated to the originating deficit. This is indicated in the figure. Note that since

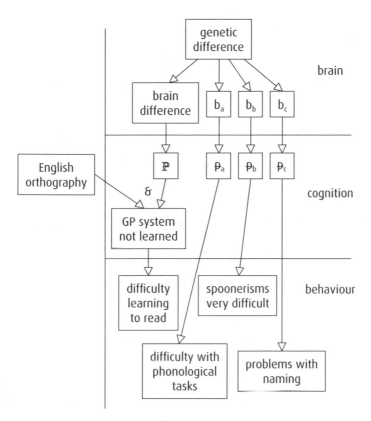

Figure 8.20 An alternative phonological hypothesis where all the other phonological problems associated with dyslexia are derived independently of the reading problem. The cognitive deficits p_a, p_b and p_c are independent of P.

the causal model is a developmental model, this deficit need not be detectible in adulthood. To start with, an early deficit may be compensated for. Alternatively, there may be developmental delay, rather than a deficit. Thus, in figure 8.22 we have a DCM, which indicates that two elements, A and B, are required for the normal development of element C, and that B is also required for the development of D. If element A is time-limited and element B is delayed, then C will not appear. The appearance of D will be delayed but could, in principle, be fully developed in adulthood. The equivalent causal model would have to be annotated as in figure 8.23. In this case, the evidence would come from studies of babies and pre-reading toddlers.

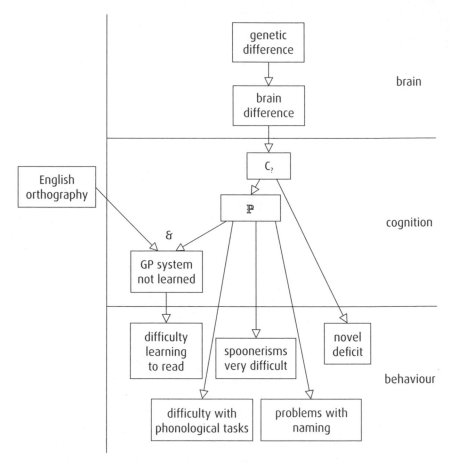

Figure 8.21 A generalized representation of the class of models wherein the deficit P – a problem handling abstract phonological symbols – is not a cognitive primitive but results developmentally from some other more basic deficit, $C_?$. This model resembles those shown in figures 8.7 or 8.8. In any case, following maxim 6 (chapter 5), the postulated deficit should be formulated in such a way as to generate predictions concerning other behavioural deficits.

The third issue is whether or not there is some other major problem that leads to the phonological deficit, as in figures 8.7 and 8.8. Note that such hypotheses usually arise from other problems actually found in the older child or in the adult dyslexic population. In such cases, as I have indicated, there are behavioural predictions that can be made

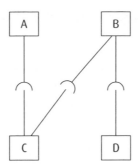

Figure 8.22 In this DCM, if element *A* is time-limited, then if *B* is delayed, there may be a deficit in *C*. *D* will also be delayed, but may be normal in adults.

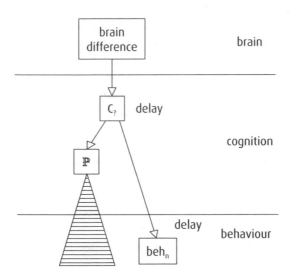

Figure 8.23 A cut-down causal model in which a delay in the development of a cognitive element gives rise to a permanent deficit *P*, without any other long-lasting problem.

to distinguish between the other problem being co-morbid with dyslexia as opposed to it being causal. Ramus et al. (2003b) have established the existence of adult dyslexics who are devoid of any detectible visual, acoustic or motor/cerebellar deficits. The presence of such deficits in other dyslexics is then taken as an indication of a disorder occurring co-morbidly with the phonological disorder.

The relationship between acquired and developmental dyslexia ▪

In the past, I have written about both kinds of disorder, and have used different methods in the two cases. The account of an acquired disorder (e.g. dyslexia caused by a stroke) will presuppose that the cognitive architecture of the patient was normal prior to the cerebral insult. Accordingly, the account will focus on disconnections between processes and destruction or damage to individual processes (e.g. Morton & Patterson 1980; Shallice 1988). The effects of such damage in individual patients will usually be widespread, and may be ameliorated by compensatory processes.

In the case of developmental disorders, the claim will usually be that some process that is a part of the normal adult architecture has not developed, has developed abnormally or has developed late. Sometimes, this architecture can be seen as 'modular' (in one of the many ways in which that term can be used). An example of this is the connectionist model of developmental dyslexia put forward by Thomas and Karmiloff-Smith (2003). This is an artificial neural network model of the grapheme–phoneme system, isolated from the rest of the reading mechanisms (and in that sense a module). Developmental dyslexia is modelled by setting some weights in the network probabilistically to zero, or by adding 'noise' to certain activation level in units in the model. This is the state of the system at the time that learning to read begins. From a developmental point of view, we still need to know what the mechanism is that leads to this disturbance. Why, for example, has this network been so affected, and not any other? The effects of the abnormality of this kind will sometimes be widespread, and may be ameliorated by compensatory processes. The difference between the acquired and the developmental disorder is that the characterization of a developmental disorder will be extended over time. What the causal modelling framework can contribute is help with the expression of such developmental theories. On the other hand, it has little or no formal contribution to make to the study of acquired disorders.

A theoretical update ▪

Ramus (in press) has made a major proposal concerning dyslexia and associated disorders, which illustrates many of the principles outlined

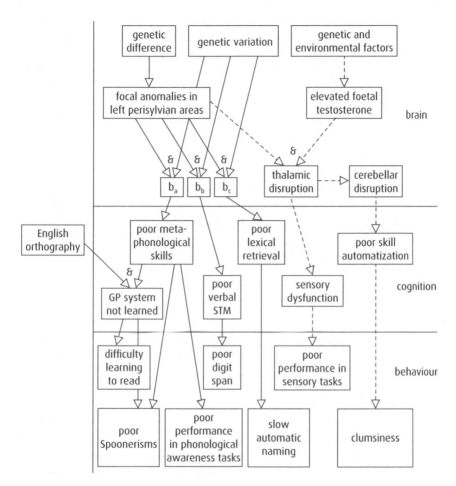

Figure 8.24 A causal model of the theory recently put forward by Franck Ramus to account for the relationships among dyslexia and various kinds of developmental sensorimotor dysfunction.

thus far in the book. A causal model of a cut-down version of his theory is shown in figure 8.24. I will not attempt to give his full argument; he has over 100 references in his article, but I will try to give a flavour. The causal chain begins with unknown genetic effects, which lead to the formation of focal anomalies in the left peri-sylvian cortex, an area known to be associated with aspects of speech and language. As a result of other genetic variation, these anomalies congregate in one or more of three brain areas, referred to in the figure as b_a, b_b and b_c. These brain areas are those that subserve meta-phonological skills, verbal (phonological) short-term memory and lexical retrieval, respectively. A lack of meta-phonological skills means that the English GP system is difficult to learn and has other behavioural consequences, as indicated in the figure.

Thus far, the model is a variation on the standard phonological theory of dyslexia, with some difference in detail. Ramus goes further. He has noted that there are cytoarchitectonic anomalies in the magnocellular layers of the thalamus of some dyslexics. Further, experiments with rats suggest that similar thalamic anomalies can be triggered by cortical anomalies in the case that foetal testosterone level is elevated. Ramus hypothesizes that the thalamic disruptions lead to auditory or visual problems depending on which part of the thalamus has been affected. Ramus further picks up on the suggestion of Stein and Walsh (1997) that the thalamic magnocellular disruption further propagates to the posterior parietal cortex and to the cerebellum. This would lead to further visuo-attentional and motor problems shown by some dyslexics (Fawcett et al. 1996; Hari et al. 2001). Only the second of those two steps have been included in the diagram at the moment, since this makes the link with the cerebellar theory already described and shown in figure 8.8. In figure 8.24, I have left the causal links associated with the main dyslexic symptoms as solid lines, and drawn the thalamic and subsequent links as dotted lines for contrast.

This theory put forward by Ramus is highly speculative and refers to a number of findings that have not yet been replicated. That should not worry those of you who are still with me. The final truth will be at least as complicated as this theory, and the important thing for the moment is to see that we can represent the theory in a way that makes predictions easy to come by. Note, of course, that parts of the theory may be wrong independently of the accuracy of other parts. Note, also, that the theory is incomplete in certain systematic ways. Let me focus on *cerebellar disruption*. First, the predictions. As the model is currently structured, there could be no cerebellar disruption unless there had been thalamic disruption. In behavioural terms, there would not be motor problems without sensory problems, allowing for the universal rules concerning the variability of causal connections. Next, the incompleteness. While, in the model, there is only one route to *cerebellar disruption*, there is no reason to rule out the possibility of other sources of disruption that would equally lead to poor skill automatization.

However, such problems would not be associated with the phonological problems. We can now refine the prediction: it is that *in the dyslexic population* there will not be motor problems without sensory problems, although there will be sensory problems without motor problems. Such predictions are relatively easily verifiable. If it turns out that in the dyslexic population there are people with motor problems without sensory problems, there are a number of options that are easy to pick out in the causal model, although they might be slightly tricky to check out. Here is a selection:

1   There is thalamic disruption, but it is insufficient to create the sensory dysfunction.
2   The dyslexia and the motor problems have a common cause, which led to a problem in brain area b_a by a route other than via the focal anomalies, together with the cerebellar problems.
3   The Stein and Walsh (1997) suggestion concerning the sequence of thalamic disruption followed by cerebellar disruption that Ramus used in his theory is wrong or incomplete.

In conclusion, figure 8.24 contrasts with figure 8.9 wherein sensorimotor problems are seen as possible causes of dyslexia. The Ramus proposals show how in principle the phonological theory of dyslexia can be combined with the observations that led to the magnocellular theory, as in figures 8.7 and 8.13, and the skill automatization hypothesis, as in figure 8.8. However, in Ramus' proposals, the sensory and motor dysfunctions do not cause the dyslexia but are the product of co-morbidity.

9 ■ The Hyperkinetic Confusions

The diagnosis of hyperactivity is contentious.[1] Not only are there major differences between North American and European practice, but there also appear to be differences within each of the communities with respect to the status of the diagnosis. Causal modelling cannot, of course, legislate in these debates. What it can do, however, is to represent the position of at least some of the protagonists and help to understand why things are the way they are.

The history of the differences between North American and European perspectives on hyperkinetic disorder is discussed by Sergeant and Steinhausen (1992). They start with a description of the treatment of hyperkinetic disorder by French psychiatrists, who have tended to associate motor instability with a disorder of personality organization. They quote one psychoanalytically oriented French psychiatrist as describing motor instability as 'not a solitary phenomenon, it provokes one's visual, auditory and tactile senses; it is a real provocation. It represents an attempt to seduce through postures'. You may care to produce a causal model for the underlying theory.

According to Sergeant and Steinhausen, in Europe there has been an emphasis on the role of organic factors, whereas in North America the socio-behavioural hypothesis has been predominant. This has led to wide differences in apparent prevalence. Thus Rutter et al. (1970), in the Isle

---

[1]   As impressive is the plethora of labels associated with the range of closely related disorders: hyperactivity, used more to describe the behaviour, hyperkinetic disorder, attention deficit disorder (ADD), attention deficit disorder – hyperactivity (ADDH) and attention deficit/hyperactivity disorder (ADHD). I will use whatever label happens to be used by the author under discussion and, otherwise, use 'hyperactivity'.

of Wight study, suggested that hyperkinetic disorder occurred in only one child in 2000. In contrast, the prevalence rate estimated by the American Psychiatric Association (1980) was of 30–40 children per 1000.

Sergeant and Steinhausen offer a number of reasons for these differences in prevalence. The first concerns the need to control for associated disorders. Most important of these is conduct disorder. They list five North American and New Zealand prevalence figures for attention deficit disorder (ADD) and conduct disorder between 1987 and 1989; the prevalence rates for ADD were between 9.5 per cent and 2.0 per cent. However, if you add the figures for the two diagnoses together, the range is only from 9.7 per cent to 11 per cent. What is constant across the prevalence estimates is behaviour and not diagnosis.

The second difference is that diagnostic schemes are designed to give single diagnoses, whereas, according to Sergeant and Steinhausen, it is a 'generally well-recognised fact that mixed cases are more the rule than the exception' (p. 37).

Thirdly, there come differences in what is termed the 'expression of the behaviour'. As an example, Sergeant and Steinhausen quote a paper by Luk et al. (1988) in which 25 per cent of their Hong Kong sample would have met criteria for hyperactivity. Sergeant and Steinhausen suggest the possibility 'that due to overcrowding in a classroom, the threshold of teachers' perception for disturbing classroom order is lower than in North America and Europe' (p. 37).

Sergeant and Steinhausen also point to the availability of long-term interventions in Europe and the need for low-cost services, including medication, in North America and the influence of such factors on diagnostic practice.

Hyperactivity is a 'pattern of restless, inattentive, and impulsive behaviour in childhood' (Schachar 1991, p. 155); such a pattern is what is called a *diagnostic entity*. There is much concern with the face validity of diagnostic entities. Rutter (1978) suggests that to be *valid*, a diagnostic entity must differ in etiology, course, characteristics or treatment response from those of other child psychiatric entities, as well as from normality.

Essentially, hyperactivity, and the associated disorders, are defined behaviourally. To start with, in DSM-III (American Psychiatric Association 1980) the diagnosis of attention deficit disorder with hyperactivity (ADDH) requires inattentiveness, impulsiveness and over-activity. These have to continue for more than six months, starting before the age of seven. If a child presents with inattentiveness and impulsiveness but without over-activity, the diagnosis of attention deficit disorder without hyperactivity (ADD/WO) is applied in the belief that this combination delineates a distinct syndrome (see Lahey et al. 1987). DSM-III-R (American Psychiatric Association 1987) introduced a further category of attention deficit hyperactivity disorder (ADHD). In order to qualify for this category, a child must exhibit eight symptoms from a menu of 14 symptoms of hyperactivity, inattention and impulsiveness. Schachar (1991) points out that this creates two new subcategories of hyperactivity, one characterized by over-activity and impulsiveness but without inattention and the other by inattention and over-activity without impulsiveness. These would be distinct, behaviourally, from the full-blown presenter of all three characteristics.

DSM-IV (American Psychiatric Association 1994) changes its viewpoint once again, requiring six out of nine symptoms of inattention that 'have persisted for at least six months to a degree that is non-adaptive and inconsistent with developmental level'. In addition, there are required six or more symptoms of hyperactivity–impulsivity, of which there are six symptoms of hyperactivity and three of impulsivity. The full ADHD diagnosis requires both sets of criteria to be met, but it is also possible to diagnose ADHD, predominantly the inattentive type, and ADHD, predominantly the hyperactive–impulsive type, although in fact, the second criteria can be fulfilled simply from hyperactivity, without any impulsivity.

The above applies mainly to the DSM criteria. The ICD-9 and -10 criteria differ in a number of ways. This is described in some detail by Schachar (1991). One feature that he focuses on is the treatment of co-morbid psychopathology. He comments:

> the syndrome of hyperactivity is viewed, for the most part, as an epiphenomenon or non-specific correlate of various forms of psychopathology that carries no particular etiological significance. Consequently, when hyperactivity occurs as part of a mixed presentation, the clinician is encouraged to diagnose the underlying condition. (p. 158)

In this case, then, the focus of diagnosis – 'the underlying condition' – would be either at the cognitive or the biological level rather than at the behavioural level. Schachar comments that 'a diagnosis of hyperkinetic syndrome is usually limited to a presentation uncomplicated by co-morbid psychopathology' (p. 158).

Hyperactivity differs, then, from the disorders covered earlier in the book, because it is specified at the behavioural level. What can we say about the rest of the causal tree? We can surmise that the intentions of the two diagnostic systems are different from each other in some respects at any rate. In particular, DSM-III permitted diagnosis of ADDH when the symptoms occurred at school but not at home, or vice versa. In contrast, the ICD-9 diagnosis of hyperkinetic syndrome requires that the behaviour is reported consistently in several situations. DSM-IV is intermediate. One might surmise that ICD-9 regards it as being more of an endogenous problem. DSM-III-R (1987), on the other hand, with its explicit 'some people . . . show signs of the disorder in only one setting, such as at home or at school' (p. 50), suggests a more temporary and exogenously caused problem. The statement clearly indicates that it is the behaviour that is important rather than the precipitating circumstances. In this classification, the notion of cause seems to be submerged under the behavioural criterion.[2]

Cantwell (1977), on the basis of studies of response to stimulant drugs, follow-up studies, neurological and neurophysiological studies, concluded that all these methods indicate that hyperactive children are a heterogeneous group. In another paper, examining the genetics of hyperactivity, Cantwell (1975) concludes that 'if there is a genetic component to the syndrome, it is operating in one sub-group of these children; or there may be several genetically distinct sub-groups' (p. 264). Further support for this comes from twin studies that show strong genetic mediation of the relationship between inattention and reading disability, but much weaker genetic mediation of the relationship between impulsivity/hyperactivity and reading disability (Willcutt et al. 2003).

Taylor (1986) also considered pharmacological effects as a means of establishing diagnostic categories. The principle behind this is the assumption that patients who respond in the same way to drugs belong to the same biologically definable category. We can illustrate this principle using the causal notation. In figure 9.1, I suppose two subgroups of children with the same signs, S. The groups differ in that they have different abnormal brain states, $br_{1,2}$, which have the same cognitive consequence, C. Whether or not the operation of a drug may be useful in helping to define subgroups will depend upon the level at which it interacts with the causal tree. If the drug operates at the biological level

---

[2] It would be more correct to talk about *reported* behaviour rather than actual behaviour, since much of the research in this area has been done with teacher-based check-lists rather than observation, and such is the basis of diagnosis in many places.

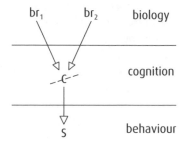

Figure 9.1 A simplified causal model that illustrates two kinds of brain condition that lead to the same cognitive dysfunction and thence to the same behavioural signs. The two groups could possibly be distinguished by their response to different drugs.

in the causal tree and the response of two patients was the same, then, according to Taylor, we would be justified in classifying the two as being in the same group. On the other hand, if two patients had different responses to such drugs, then they would be classified as coming from different subgroups. Thus, *drug$_1$* could operate selectively on *br$_1$*. Patients in this group would no longer suffer the cognitive dysfunction and would not, then, exhibit the characteristic signs. Patients with problems in *br$_2$*, on the other hand, would remain unchanged by the drug. In contrast, *drug$_2$* operates selectively on *br$_2$*, abolishing the signs in that group but not the first one. Use of these two drugs, then, will serve to distinguish the two subgroups of children. However, another drug, *drug$_3$*, might operate by suppressing the behaviour, having its operation at the output of the responsible cognitive process. In this case, the two groups of children would be responding in the same way to *drug$_3$* in spite of their underlying biological differences. The existence of a common response to *drug$_3$* would demonstrate nothing about the homogeneity of the groups. Use of such a drug would be equivalent to suppressing the signs by behaviour modification techniques or even simple physical restraint.

Drugs as diagnostic refinement

The success and failure of particular drugs in treatment of various conditions manifesting hyperactivity has illuminated the diagnostic issues. Thus the use of Ritalin has become standard. The paradox is that Ritalin is a stimulant. However, it stimulates a brain centre that is

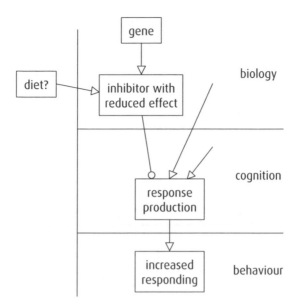

Figure 9.2 A schematic causal model for ADHD, assuming that the cause is reduced response inhibition. Response production is shown as being influenced by unspecified biological and cognitive elements. The circle terminating the connection on response production is inhibitory. It is small compared with normal and is shown corrected in figure 9.3.

responsible for or participates in the inhibition of responses. The causal theory underlying such interventions is that some developmental abnormality either accelerates response production (effectively by increasing the level of endogenous stimulation) or reduces the inhibition of response production. Ritalin thus either acts to raise the level of response inhibition sufficiently to compensate for the overstimulation or restores it back to the normal level. Causal models for the underlying theory and for the effect of Ritalin are shown in figures 9.2 and 9.3.

Ritalin, however, does not act successfully on all children who satisfy the behavioural requirements for a hyperactive (or ADHD) diagnosis. For example, there are children whose hyperactivity is driven by anxiety states. Such children respond very badly to Ritalin, their hyperactivity in fact increasing. Instead, the appropriate drug in these cases has been found to be Imiprimine. In trying to represent what is going on here, we straight away expose the lack of underlying theory. Anxiety states could be represented at both the biological and the cognitive levels. An

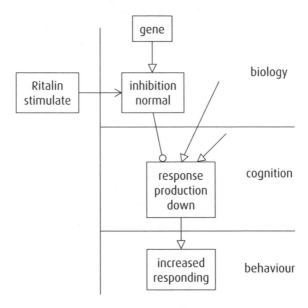

Figure 9.3 The causal model for the effect of Ritalin as stimulating response inhibition. Other factors remain unchanged. The small circle indicates an inhibitory relationship.

example at the cognitive level would be an anxiety state maintained by a belief (that the parents' marriage was about to break up, for example), where the anxiety could be relieved or abolished by suitable therapeutic intervention. The underlying model is shown in figure 9.4. Note also that the relationship between the anxiety state and the hyperactivity needs to be specified. Clinically, the effect of Ritalin is to increase anxiety in such children. One theory is that the drug stimulates the brain centre that contributes to anxiety more than it stimulates the behavioural inhibitor. This is shown in figure 9.5. The simplest assumption is that the appropriate drug, Imiprimine, has the opposite effect on that same brain centre. This is left for you to diagram.

Another group for whom Ritalin is ineffectual is the manic depressive group with large mood swings. These are more readily diagnosed, since the hyperactive behaviour comes only in the manic part of the cycle, and is highly aggressive as well as being impulsive. Ritalin has been tried on such children and does nothing to control their behaviour in the hyperactive phase. The response production in this phase, then, can be seen to be unconnected with either the brain or cognitive

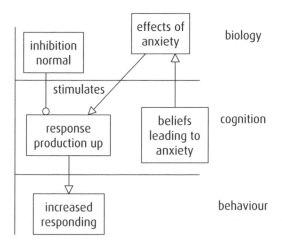

Figure 9.4 A model for hyperactivity caused by anxiety states.

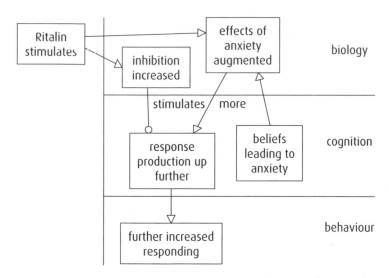

Figure 9.5 A model that represents a particular theory of how Ritalin has an adverse effect on children with anxiety states.

centres involved in hyperactivity. In fact, such children respond to anti-epileptic drugs, which happen also to be psychotropic. The situation is summarized in figure 9.6. The aggressive–impulsive component has been omitted.

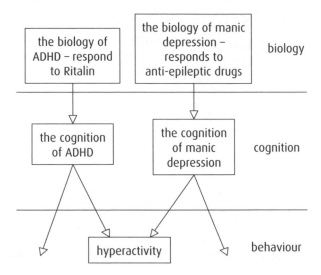

Figure 9.6   The outline of a couple of causal models that converge on hyperactive behaviour. Other behaviours have been indicated without being specified.

There is another group of children for whom Prosac and SSRI anti-depressants are the best way of controlling hyperactivity. These tend to be children with multiple deficits, including severe mental retardation. Finally, at least one case has been described of an 11-year-old child with Asperger's syndrome whose hyperactive behaviour was driven by obsessionality and anxiety. This child also became worse on Ritalin. Such findings reinforce Schachar's (1991) strictures on co-morbidity, already quoted, concerning the advisability of diagnosing the underlying condition and treating ADHD as secondary.

Types of theory ■

We can show in simplified causal diagrams how various causal theories can be represented (figure 9.7, A–E). With respect to the role of biological factors, Taylor (1986) suggests two possibilities, namely that such factors may affect activity levels directly (figure 9.7, A) or that they are mediated through cognitive factors (figure 9.7, B). In either case, the condition could be exacerbated by psychosocial factors, which, for example, increase levels of stress. In figure 9.7C, I have indicated

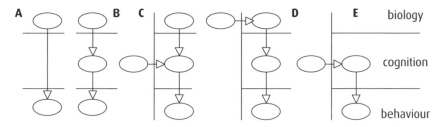

Figure 9.7 Five possible ways of producing disordered behaviour. Three of these, C, D and E, involve the environment in some form.

the environmental factors as interacting with some genetic factor to precipitate a state that cannot be described at the biological level. The theory that hyperactivity is caused by an environmental toxin of sorts (suggestions include lead intake and dietary additives) is illustrated in figure 9.7D. In this figure, I diagram the possibility of an external cause operating at the biological level. A factor originating in the environment need not operate at the biological level in the causal chain. It may affect general attitudes to schooling, while interacting with other factors. This is represented in figure 9.7E.

At the behavioural level, all of these diagrams refer to the same behavioural complex. Thus, we can put them all together into a single causal diagram, as shown in figure 9.8. This is an example of the V-shaped theory that I discussed in chapter 7. In all of the alternative pathways, some degree of freedom is left for specification of the involvement of alternative constructs at the cognitive level.

The studies of hyperactivity over the past 20–30 years give some very interesting illustrations of the kinds of confounding possible. Several studies have provided evidence of relationships between particular environmental circumstances and hyperactivity. For example, hyperactivity was found to be associated with low socio-economic status (Schachar et al. 1981), overcrowding (Sandberg et al. 1978) and critical controlling parents (Hartsough & Lambert 1982). Hyperactivity was also found to be more common in children who grew up in institutions (Tizard & Hodges 1978) and in adopted children (Deutsch et al. 1982). However, as researchers from the Institute of Psychiatry remarked in an unpublished manuscript: 'children may be referred because of stress in family life rather than due to extreme deviance'. Sometimes, studies of hyperactivity refer to the possibility of biological factors (as in figure 9.7, C), sometimes not (figure 9.7, E), and there do not seem to be

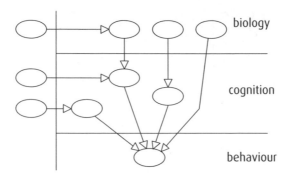

Figure 9.8 A composite diagram that summarizes the alternative aetiologies of the disordered behaviour.

well articulated theories tracing the causal path from environment to behaviour.

Population studies, on the other hand, have often included conduct-disordered children among the hyperactive, which means that the known, strong relationship between conduct disorder and family adversity (Wolkind & Rutter 1985) may have confounded the results.

The problem of co-morbidity: conduct disorder and ADHD ▨

Silberg et al. (1996) say that

> the classification of behaviours into discrete diagnostic classes of categories represents an important goal for understanding the underlying causes of psychiatric problems and for devising effective preventative and emulative interventions from the disabling psychological conditions. (p. 803)

However, numerous epidemiological and clinical studies have demonstrated the high frequency with which supposedly separate child psychiatric disorders co-occur (Biederman et al. 1991; Caron & Rutter 1991). Co-occurrence of conduct disorders and hyperkinetic/attention deficit disorders and their symptoms is so strong that commentators have questioned the reality of distinction between them (see Hinshaw 1987). However, as Silberg et al. say, the distinctiveness of separate diagnostic conditions needs to be determined, not by the degree of overlap between the symptoms but rather by the extent to which they differ in their patterns of associations with correlates external to the symptoms that comprise them, such as psychosocial factors, responsiveness to treatment, and long-term outcome. (Silberg et al. 1996, p. 804)

Thus, a longitudinal study has shown that early conduct problems serve as a major precursor for future offending, whereas early attentional problems are a precursor for poor scholastic performance (Fergusson & Horwood 1993). Hyperkinetic disorders are more likely to be associated with cognitive impairment and developmental delay and more likely to be responsive to stimulant medication (Taylor et al. 1987; Szatmari et al. 1989).

Can something be decided about the causal relationships by looking at gender differences? ADHD and CD are much less frequent in girls than boys. It is also the case that the effects of stressors such as marital discord on parents have less effect on daughters than on sons in terms of the likelihood of breakdown of their own marriage. As we also know that environmental lead has more effect on boys than girls (Smith et al. 1983), we should beware of general effects masquerading as specific ones – boys may be more vulnerable to everything. Taylor et al. (1991) contrast a couple of theories. In one of them, the stressors are influenced by biology or cognition in the same way for girls and boys, but girls have means of controlling their outcome. This is shown in figure 9.9. The alternative theory is that the gender effect (unspecified in nature) acts directly on the stressor, reducing its effect on the cognitive effective systems of girls. This is shown in figure 9.10.

The cognitive level ▮

A number of cognitive theories of the attention deficit have been put forward (these have been discussed at some length by Sandberg 1996):

1   A deficit in executive control (Schachar et al. 1995; Barkley 1997). The proposal is of a generalized deficit of the 'executive cognitive functions'. This results in inattentiveness when a flexible shifting from one response to another is required, and in impulsiveness

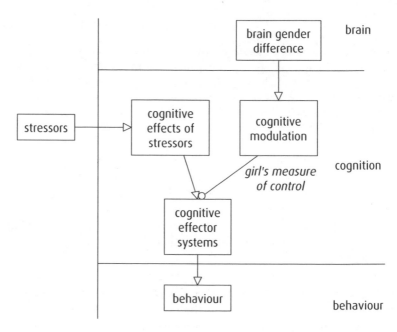

Figure 9.9 One theory of the origins of gender differences in the effects of stressors.

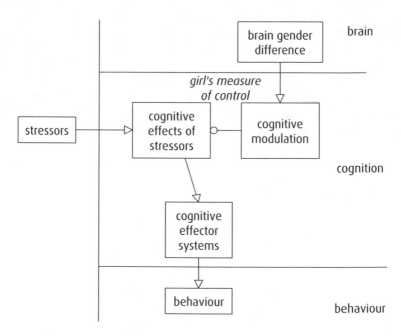

Figure 9.10 An alternative to the model shown in figure 9.9.

when inhibition of responses demanded. Both of these contribute to impaired sustained attention. This kind of theory has all the weaknesses of executive dysfunction theories of practically every other developmental disorder, as I have noted in chapter 6.

2   Abnormal sensitivity to reward (Sonuga-Barke et al. 1992a,b; Douglas & Parry 1994). Here, the immediacy of a reward, rather than its size, is of importance. Thus the hyperactive child will not wait for a delayed reward. It is also postulated that waiting is perceived as particularly aversive.

3   Defect of motivation (Barkley 1997). According to this theory, a hyperactive child does not pay attention in particular tasks because there is insufficient inherent motivational value in either the tasks or their outcome.

4   State regulation defect (van der Meere et al. 1995). Here, the primary fault is in output-related processes such as response decision and response organization. Problems of orientation focusing are seen as secondary to this, and the defect is responsive to manipulations of external control, rewards and motivation.

The general assumption has always been that the fundamental defect in hyperactivity is an inability to concentrate. This is enshrined in DSM-III, -III-R and -IV, which all name the condition 'attention deficit disorder'. Indeed, children with 'ADD' get poor scores on tests that are supposed to measure attention, such as the continuous performance test and the matching familiar figures test, visual memory tests, repetitive reaction time and speeded classification tests, and so on (see Taylor 1985).

A number of other precautions are necessary. First of all, it is clear that the 'attention' tests can be influenced by many factors other than attention. One possibility is IQ, and indeed the IQ is lower in hyperactive children in most studies. However, some abnormalities are still found after IQ has been controlled by analysis of covariance (and we have no idea whether the reduced IQ is caused by the hyperactivity or by effects at the behavioural, cognitive or biological levels).

The second issue is whether impairments can be seen in other tests that do not involve attention. These include the digit span (Taylor et al. 1991), serial and choice reaction times (Sykes et al. 1973), and paired associate learning (Swanson & Kinsbourne 1976). These studies failed to find deficits in encoding, search or decision, although there is some evidence of abnormalities in response selection. There is no particular problem with extensively sustained attention, nor with selective attention, since the addition of irrelevant information has the same effect on hyperactive children as on other children (Douglas & Peters 1979; Sergent & Scholten 1985a,b). Such considerations indicate that the area is in need of careful models of the underlying information processing, as well as of the causal relations.

The approach followed by Sonuga-Barke et al. (1992a) and Sonuga-Barke et al. (1992b) suggests that it would be fruitful now to consider an X-shape of causal modelling with a hypothesized underlying cognitive deficit, labelled as *impulsiveness* or *inability to delay reward.* This approach is possible because of the convergence of clinical, epidemiological and neuropsychological studies, which (just as in the case of autism) together strongly point to hyperactivity as a valid diagnostic entity, not in terms of behaviour but in terms of underlying causes. Like autism, hyperactivity is likely to be defined as a cognitively based and biologically caused developmental disorder. As the first step, twin studies show that hyperactivity–impulsivity has a very high heritability (see Castellanos et al. 2003). If it were possible to have a biological/cognitive definition of a subset of ADHD, it would be essential to create a separate diagnostic category for children with the same behaviour patterns but with different cognitive causes; otherwise, there would be confusion of diagnosis. This would be particularly crucial if different treatment regimes were required.

Other people have looked for early psychological or social precursors. Sandberg (1996) considers the idea that intrusive care-giving interferes with early modulation of arousal. Optimal qualities of early care-giving may also stimulate the development of cognitive and linguistic competencies. This could constitute an important link, as cognitive and linguistic problems appear to precede hyperactivity (Olson et al. 1990; Taylor et al. 1991). The associated problems of non-compliance may in turn arise in the context of care-giver directiveness and be maintained by inept parental control techniques, thus placing the child at risk for escalating cycles of coercive interactions. Where there is maternal depression, for example, the effect is likely to be via inconsistent emotional feedback, lack of mutual contingencies, less cognitive stimulation and absence of rewarding experiences (Olson et al. 1990).

These suggestions, corresponding to figure 9.7E or possibly figure 9.7C, are very like some accounts of conduct disorder that are reviewed in chapter 10.

Sonuga-Barke's dual pathway model ▓

The conflict between AD/HD (to use Sonuga-Barke's notation) as a problem of motivational style (delay aversion) as opposed to a neurocognitive disorder of regulation (poor inhibitory control) has been attacked by Solanto et al. (2001), who carried out a 'head-to-head' study of the two accounts. The conclusion was that delay aversion and poor inhibitory control are independent coexisting characteristics of AD/HD (combined type).

Sonuga-Barke (2002) turns this empirical result into a theoretical advance with a dual pathway model. He points out that AD/HD has been reified 'as an ontological and psychological reality (rather than just a useful clinical construct)' (p. 29) and that 'The heterogeneity of its clinical expression and its multifactorially determined aetiology makes achieving the sort of theoretical unity required by [single neuropsychological] models of AD/HD unlikely' (p. 29).

The dual model that he comes up with is shown in figure 9.11. Into this model are packed a few quite complicated ideas. The simple aspects of the model from a causal point of view include the initial separation of the two pathways. There is a core dysfunction of inhibitory control, which contrasts with an acquired delay aversion. The latter requires both a weakness in limbic reward circuits, leading to an impulsive behaviour pattern, together with a particular kind of environment.

The inhibitory dysfunction has two distinct consequences, what Sonuga-Barke calls 'Cognitive Dysregulation' and 'Behavioural Dysregulation'. The latter leads directly to the AD/HD symptoms of impulsiveness, inattention and over-activity. Cognitive dysregulation is seen 'in the pattern of difficulties displayed by AD/HD children on tasks requiring attentional flexibility, behavioural monitoring, planning and working memory' (p. 32). Such 'executive functions' are not directly connected to the AD/HD symptoms. Instead, they affect what Sonuga-Barke calls 'Task Engagement', which is divided into two parts. '*Quality*' refers to performance on the tasks, while '*Quantity*' refers to the problem that the AD/HD children spend less time on task. One consequence of this is a reduction in the time available to develop higher-order skills associated with the provision, protection and utilization of time. This is shown by the feedback arrow from '*Quantity*' to 'Cognitive Dysregulation'.

Sonuga-Barke starts the other pathway off with a 'shortened delay of reward gradient', which means that AD/HD children 'discount the value

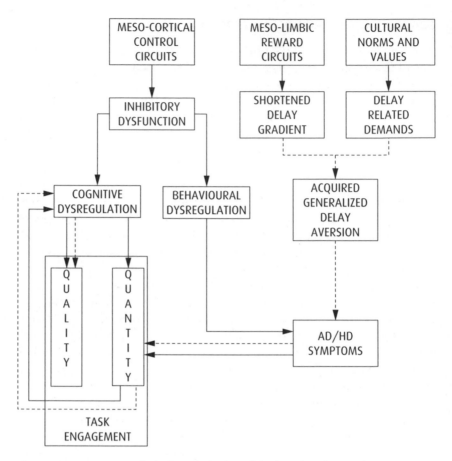

Figure 9.11 Sonuga-Barke's (2002) dual model of AD/HD (copyright © 2002 Elsevier; reproduced with permission).

of future events at a higher rate than other children' (p. 32). This leads to a preference for immediacy – behavioural impulsivity. Through a simple associative conditioning mechanism within a particular social context, there comes to be a generalized delay aversion, leading to the occurrence of inattention and over-activity in no choice delay settings and impulsiveness in choice settings. The resulting behaviour will impact on task engagement, and thence to Cognitive Dysregulation, as shown in the figure.

I have scarcely given justice to Sonuga-Barke's complex ideas in the above summary. In his figure, the arrows are sometimes causal and sometimes not. In figure 9.12, I have attempted to represent his model

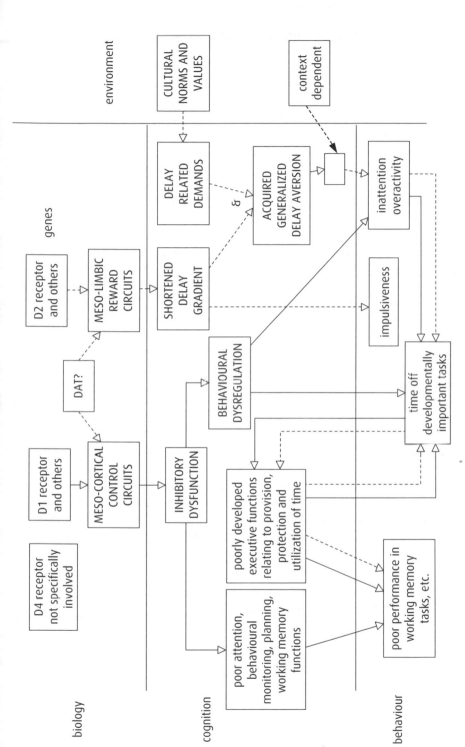

Figure 9.12 A reconfiguration of Sonuga-Barke's dual process model.

in the causal modelling framework. In doing this, I have redescribed his element 'Task Engagement' with a couple of sets of higher-order cognitive functions, derived from the text of the article. One of these, described as 'poor attention, behavioural monitoring, planning, working memory functions', is a part of the inhibitory dysfunction pathway and would not be affected by the motivational style pathway. The other cognitive function, labelled as 'poorly developed executive functions relating to provision, protection and utilization of time', would be affected, but only secondarily, through both routes, as a result of a reduction in the time spent on development of these time management skills.

Other changes from figure 9.11 include linking *impulsiveness* solely to *shortened delay gradient*. If it is thought that impulsivity is a characteristic of the inhibitory dysfunction route as well, then the model would have to be made more complicated. There would be a couple of options at least. One would be to specify two kinds of impulsive behaviour with different causal mechanisms; while the other would be to specify a cognitive mechanism of the production of normal (non-impulsive) behaviour, which could be caused to malfunction in two different ways. You may care to sketch the two causal models corresponding to these theories.

Summary ■

It will be clear to you that a lot of work remains to be done in the formalization of theories of the various kinds of hyperactivity. Sonuga-Barke's is the only theory that I have been able to find of any scope, and that will only apply to a subset of the people diagnosed as having some form of the disorder. One of the most important advances in the future will be the creation of well motivated sub-types. Causal modelling should provide a framework for the formulation of such work.

10 ■ THEORIES OF CONDUCT DISORDER

The special interest for us in conduct disorder is in the substantial causal role that environmental factors are supposed to play. The work in this chapter has been adapted from a paper I wrote with Nicole Krol and Eric de Bruyn from Nijmegen (Krol et al. 2004). Conduct disorder (CD) is a term used to describe a group of symptoms or problematic behaviours. The term as used in DSM-IV (American Psychiatric Association 1994) includes four types of behaviour: (1) aggression to people or animals; (2) destruction of property; (3) deceitfulness or theft; and (4) serious violations of rules. It is a very heterogeneous disorder both in its occurrence and in its etiology. To emphasize this heterogeneity, Frick (1998) started using the plural term 'conduct disorders'. Two different types of CD are nowadays distinguished – 'the childhood onset type' (DSM-IV) or 'the life-course persistent type' (Caspi & Moffitt 1995), and 'the adolescent onset' (DSM-IV) or the 'adolescence limited type' (Caspi & Moffitt 1995), each with a different etiology. The spectrum of conduct disorder also includes more extreme forms such as psychopathic behaviour. It has been acknowledged that the distinction between these two types of conduct disorders is of importance for its causal accounts and treatment decisions (Caspi & Moffitt 1995; Frick 1998). In this chapter, the focus is on the 'childhood onset' or 'life-course persistent type'.

The following theories were selected for modelling: the social information theory of Dodge (1991; see also Crick & Dodge 1994), the coercive parenting theory of Patterson (Patterson et al. 1992), the theory of life-course persistent antisocial behaviour by Moffitt (Moffitt 1993; Caspi & Moffitt 1995) and the violence inhibition theory of Blair (1995). One can question whether this latter theory can be used as a causal model for conduct disorder, since the theory is very specific to psychopathy.

Classifications of psychopathy are not synonymous with diagnoses of CD, but represent an extension (Blair 2001). An absence of moral emotions is reported in the clinical description of psychopathy. In the DSM-IV manual we find that 'little empathy', 'little concern for feelings, wishes, well-being of others' and 'callous and lack of appropriate feelings of guilt or remorse' are described as associated descriptive features of conduct disorder. So this model can be seen as an explanation for a specific subtype of CD, a subtype that may develop to psychopathy. This subtype has as yet not been defined in the DSM manual, but parallels the childhood-onset type with severe symptoms; that is, symptoms that cause considerable harm to others.

It was not the intention of any of the authors we will be looking at, apart from Blair, to produce a causal model for conduct disorder. They were interested in a variety of other aspects of the topic, such as preconditions, risk factors, current circumstances, taxonomy and treatment. All of the theories have been enormously successful in their different ways. This is largely ignored here. Instead, I will only look at what the authors have said or implied with respect to the causes of conduct disorder. I start with Blair's violence inhibition theory, because this theory used the causal model framework for its representation.

The violence inhibition mechanism (VIM) model ▪

The VIM model is a developmental model. Mitchell and Blair (2000) summarize the approach as follows:

> ... it is biological make-up that determines whether individuals show emotional difficulties. However, these emotional difficulties are only risk factors for the development of the disorder. It is the individual's adverse social environment that creates the conditions necessary for the development of psychopathy. (p. 357)

Blair's model was prompted by ethologists who proposed that most social animals possess mechanisms for control of aggression. These ethologists noted that a conspecific aggressor stops fighting if the opponent displays submission cues. For example, an aggressor dog ceases fighting if its opponent bares his throat. According to Blair, humans might have a functionally similar mechanism, which he called a **violence inhibition mechanism** (**VIM**). Blair considers VIM to be:

a cognitive mechanism which, when activated by non-verbal communications of distress (i.e., sad facial expression, the sight and sound of tears), initiates a withdrawal response: a schema will be activated predisposing the individual to withdraw from the attack. (Blair 1995, p. 3)

Blair et al. (2001) suggest that the 'representations that are current at the time of VIM activation will become triggers for the activation of VIM through a process of classical conditioning' (p. 800). Blair (1995) gives a developmental account for psychopathic behaviour as a causal model in which VIM is conceptualized as a basic emotion mechanism that, when impaired, would act as a risk factor for the development of psychopathy. The model is given in figure 10.1. Elements that are

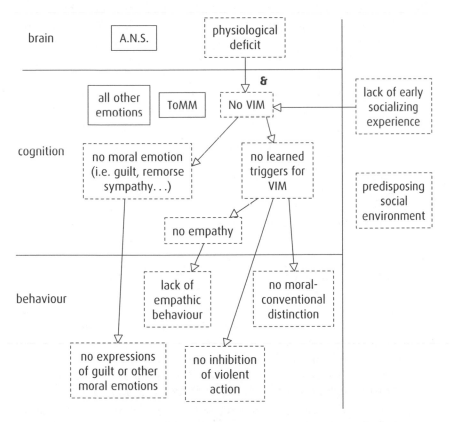

Figure 10.1 A causal model of the developmental consequences of an absence of VIM (Blair 1995). Elements in solid boxes are supposed to be operating normally (copyright © 1995 Elsevier; reproduced with permission).

not affected by an absence of VIM are 'protected' within boxes. Blair (1995) reports that psychopaths are not impoverished on 'Theory of Mind' tasks and that they showed arousal to threat stimuli. There is thus a contrast with autism, in which the Theory of Mind Mechanism (ToMM) is damaged or absent, resulting in impairment in Theory of Mind tasks such as the false belief task (see chapter 4). There is also a contrast with conditions in which the autonomic nervous system (ANS) is damaged, resulting in a reduced response to all emotions (Hohmann 1962; reported in Atkinson et al. 1985).

In figure 10.1, the absence of VIM is conceptualized as a consequence of either a physiological deficit or the absence of early socialization experiences, or a combination of these factors. Such claims are hypotheses which are to be tested. In effect, this causal model can be seen as Blair's research programme. In the model, the lack of VIM will result in the absence of moral emotions and, as a result, no expressions of moral emotions such as guilt. According to Blair, the child without VIM would not be negatively reinforced by distress cues and would therefore be much more likely to show violent tendencies from an early age. He states that

the core features of the behavioural description of the psychopath – the early onset of extremely aggressive behaviour that is not tempered by any sense of guilt or empathy with the victim – are all direct causal predictions of a lack of VIM . . . A lack of VIM does not of itself motivate an individual to commit aggressive acts. A lack of VIM just means that one source of the interruption of violent action is lost. (Blair 1995, p. 11)

In figure 10.1, we have reference to a 'predisposing social environment' without explicit connections. Blair (1995, fig. 2) linked this element straight to behaviour. However, the idea is that the environment fosters motive and motivation is necessary for the development of psychopathy. The environment must, therefore, influence some cognitive factor – although, in the paper, Blair doesn't specify such an interaction. This detail remains to be elaborated. The relation of lack of early socialization experience to VIM is not specified either, but can be deduced from the following note in the text: '. . . if the child is rewarded for his attacks, particularly during the attack, either by material gain or by peer/parental praise, the child is likely to overrule VIM and continue the attack' (Blair 1995, note, p. 5).

Blair describes how the lack of VIM makes an individual fail to make the distinction between moral and conventional rules. VIM may be a prerequisite for the internal generation of moral meta-knowledge; that is, explicit theories held by a person as to why moral transgressions are bad to do. According to Blair, people without VIM will judge an act as bad only because they have been told that it is bad and they will not make a reference to the victim's welfare. Empirical data (Blair 1995, 1999; Blair et al. 2001) have been produced in support of the existence of the VIM mechanism.

Blair's model describes factors on all three levels, together with environmental factors. In later publications, Blair makes specific proposals concerning the biological level and its relation to the cognitive level (Blair 2001). He also refers to the different types of behaviour that are distinguished by the Psychopathy Checklist: (1) the emotion dysfunction behaviours defined by emotional shallowness and lack of guilt; and (2) the antisocial behaviours such as impulsive aggression and different types of offences. According to Blair, the emotion dysfunctional behaviours are to a certain extent more determined by different influences than are the antisocial behaviours. The persistence of emotion dysfunction behaviours may more closely reflect neurocognitive impairments that are thought to result in the development of psychopathy. These developments in Blair's thinking would result in a slightly different causal model from that shown in figure 10.1, but such additions and extensions are easy to do. Causal modelling readily allows the depiction of such alternative formulations and directly indicates where these formulations make divergent predictions.

The social information processing model for aggressive children ▮

Dodge (1991) makes the distinction between reactive and proactive aggression, and hypothesizes that these types of aggression have different neural and cognitive mechanisms and different etiologies and developmental courses:

> Reactive aggression is displayed as anger or temper tantrums, with an appearance of being out of control. Proactive aggression occurs usually in the form of object acquisition, bullying, or dominance of a peer. (Dodge 1991, p. 205)

Dodge has associated a range of social information processing biases and deficits with aggressive behaviour. In order to understand how these biases can lead to aggression, he gives a description of the steps that an individual passes through in order to respond to social cues. These include encoding the cues, representing them as threatening or benign, searching for possible responses and then evaluating these before selecting one.

Aggressive children demonstrate biased attention and encoding of hostile stimuli, intention-cue detection errors, hostile-attributional bias, inadequate response search and problem-solving, and 'biassed response evaluation in the form of expectations of favourable outcomes for aggression' (p. 211):

> Problems at early stages of processing, such as hypervigilance to hostile cues, hostile attributions regarding minor provocations, and unwarranted fear responses, are hypothesized to lead to over reactive, defensive aggressive responses. On the other hand, a child who accurately perceives others' intentions but has a limited and biassed response repertoire, and who evaluates the outcomes of behaving aggressively in positive ways may be likely to employ aggressive tactics proactively in instrumental ways. (Dodge 1991, p. 211)

Dodge has found experimental support for these hypotheses. The form of development is influenced by the environment in particular ways. According to Dodge:

> a history of trauma, abuse, deprivation, and insecure attachment relations will lead to hypervigilance and active aggressive behavior; on the other hand, a history of coercive training (in Patterson's terms) and observation of and experience with successful aggressive tactics will lead a child to access aggressive responses and to evaluate them favorably, resulting in proactive aggression. (pp. 213–14)

When we describe Dodge's theory in the causal modelling framework, as in figure 10.2, it becomes clear that Dodge focuses on the cognitive level and that no causal factors are specified at the biological level. Dodge does refer to the importance of neural mechanisms, but he doesn't explicitly relate them to the social information processing. Dodge does not assign any causal role to these neural mechanisms, either developmentally or currently. He focuses, rather, on how the

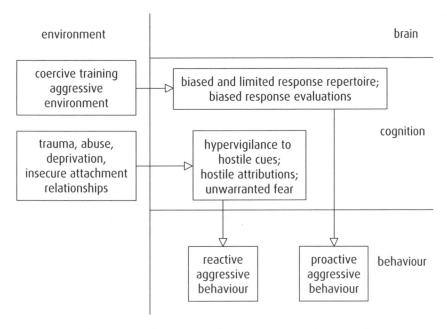

Figure 10.2 The origins of reactive and proactive aggression according to Dodge (1991).

development of social information processing biases is causally influenced by environmental factors (Dodge 1991).

Note that the general category of 'social information processing biases and deficits', which played a role in Dodge's description of his theories, would not normally be a component in a causal model. The three factors used at the cognitive level in figure 10.2 are all related to social information processing, but this relationship has to do with (on-line) information processing and not with cause. In fact, underlying Dodge's causal claims is a theory of response production. This can readily be expressed in an information flow model, shown in figure 10.3. Crick and Dodge (1994) also produce such a model.

The cognitive factors that Dodge implicates in reactive aggressive behaviour are all concerned with the perception of the environment. On the other hand, the response repertoire and particular response evaluations lead to proactive aggressive behaviour.

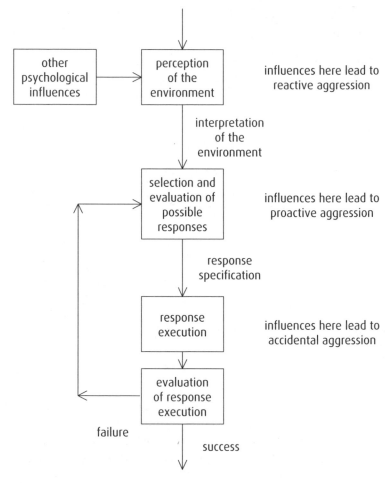

Figure 10.3 An information flow model of the influence of various cognitive factors on the production of aggressive behaviour (based on Dodge 1991). Since this is not a causal model, the arrows are different.

Dodge's model has proved to be successful in predicting patterns of behaviour on the basis of risk factors, and his emphasis on such factors together with the ongoing cognitive processing involved in aggression provides an interesting contrast with Blair on the one hand and the ideas of Patterson and Moffitt that follow.

The coercive parenting model of Patterson ▊

The work of Patterson (e.g. Patterson et al. 1992; Dishion et al. 1995) has focused on the contributions of the parent–child interaction to antisocial behaviour. Their social interactional model, referred to as a coercion model, implies 'an emphasis on parent–child exchanges as the proximal cause of antisocial behaviour throughout the life span' (Dishion et al. 1995, p. 438).[1] The model focuses on the process by which the child learns antisocial behaviour within parent–child exchanges and describes how families train children to be antisocial through repeated coercive exchanges:

> The child learns to avoid parent demands through a process of negative reinforcement. . . . These patterns become overlearned and automatic, and operate without conscious, cognitive control. In the absence of countervailing forces, the child may progress from displaying these trivial aversive behaviors in the family to exhibiting similar patterns with other people in other settings, to engaging in other social behaviors, including physical aggression, lying, or stealing. (Dishion et al. 1995, p. 439)

These coercion patterns consist of well rehearsed action–reaction sequences that are performed without conscious awareness of the people involved. Patterson et al. (1992) refer to the coercion model theory as a micro-social reinforcement theory. They refer to the concept of 'overlearned behavior', and note that this concept highlights the difference between the social cognitive perspective (see Dodge) and their social interactional perspective. The events in the coercive patterns are 'performed too quickly to be mediated by cognitive processes' (Patterson et al. 1992, p. 56). By 'cognitive', Patterson means 'conscious', so there is no contradiction in our representing these processes at the cognitive level in the three-level framework. (But do remember that, elsewhere in this book, cognitive is not equivalent to conscious.)

The causal model representation of Patterson's ideas is rather limited. Indeed, the only possible causal claim seems to be that conduct disorder is caused by coercive parenting, through the mediation of certain mental

[1]   In fact, in most causal models the proximal cause would be some factor at the cognitive level that led to particular behavioural consequences. Early parent–child interaction seems pretty distal to me, though proximal compared with genetic influences on neurodevelopment.

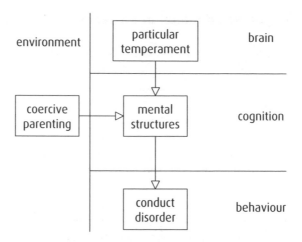

Figure 10.4 The causal content of Patterson's theory.

structures that are created through these parent–child interactions. This claim is shown in figure 10.4. There are a number of factors specified that predispose the setting up of coercive parenting – contextual variables such as stressors, socio-economic status and parental personality traits – but they do not seem to have the status of causal factors. The growth of the mental structures depends upon the microstructure of reinforcement and punishment of behaviours under a wide variety of contexts. This would be inappropriate for causal modelling. The way in which the mental structures operate is specified by Patterson as being 'automatic' – that is, not consciously mediated – and its operation would probably be most easily specified by a listing of the kinds of situation in which particular kinds of behaviour emerge. Again, causal modelling would not be an appropriate tool. However, there would probably be a causal model in a theory that specified how the parents came to be coercive in the first place.

The theory of life-course persistent antisocial behaviour ■

Moffitt (1993) and Caspi and Moffitt (1995) develop their account of the roots of lifelong persistent antisocial behaviour along two lines. In the first, they expand on the cognitive consequences of various neurodevelopmental problems, and in the second they discuss at length various kinds of maladaptive interaction between the growing child and their parents. The latter presents some rather acute problems of representation in a causal model and further discussion will be postponed. For the moment I will focus on the former issue, what Caspi and Moffitt (1995) term 'neuropsychological' problems. The theoretical force of the term 'neuropsychological' is that the problems are supposed to arise as a result of biological problems. This would be captured in a causal model by the causal link from the biological level to any specified cognitive deficit.

Moffitt (1993) expands along these lines as follows:

> One possible source of neuropsychological variation that is linked with problem behaviour is disruption in the ontogenesis of the fetal brain. Minor physical anomalies ... are thought to be observable markers for hidden anomalies in neural development ... Neural development may be disrupted by maternal drug abuse, poor prenatal nutrition, or pre- or postnatal exposure to toxic agents ... some individual differences in neuropsychological health are heritable in origin ... After birth, neural development may be disrupted by neonatal deprivation of nutrition, stimulation and even affection ... Some studies have pointed to child abuse and neglect as possible sources of brain injury in the histories of delinquents with neuropsychological impairments. (p. 680)

These quotations make it clear that there is a substantial role for the biological level in the causal model underlying Moffitt's theory, both through the role of genetic factors and through environmental influence on neural development. Caspi and Moffitt (1995) state that the link between neuropsychological deficits and antisocial outcomes has been repeatedly documented in studies of children's aggression, adolescents' delinquency and adults' criminality, and is one of the most robust effects in the study of antisocial behaviour. They report that two deficits are empirically associated with antisocial behaviour, verbal deficits and executive function deficits. In attempting to summarize their position in terms of a causal model, there is a problem as to how to express the deficit at the cognitive level. In figure 10.5, the associations between neuropsychological deficits and antisocial outcomes are treated as being causal, although Caspi and Moffitt do not make that connection explicitly. I will point to some limitations of making the connection in the form of figure 10.5, in the interests of illustrating the requirements of causal modelling.

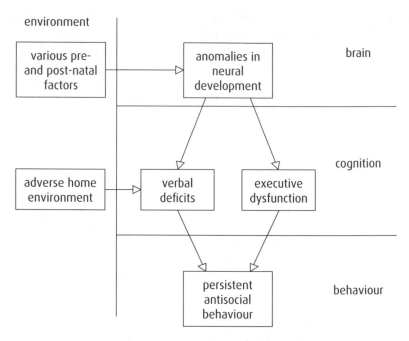

Figure 10.5 Possible causal interpretations of Moffitt's position.

Caspi and Moffitt spend some time exploring the relationship between the neuropsychological deficits and antisocial behaviour. In respect to the verbal deficit, they refer to the fact that many studies found that performance IQ (PIQ) was greater than verbal IQ (VIQ) in delinquents, and they state that 'This verbal deficit is pervasive, affecting receptive listening and reading, problem solving, expressive speech, writing and memory for verbal material' (Caspi & Moffitt 1995, p. 478).

They also report evidence suggesting that this verbal deficit interacts with an adverse home environment (Moffitt 1990). However, as it stands, there is no satisfactory way to include such a raw finding in a causal model without knowing the nature of the crucial verbal deficit, the particular aspect of the adverse home environment, or possible mechanisms of interaction.

Caspi and Moffitt (1995) refer to several authors who have proposed that verbal neurological deficits may contribute to children's antisocial behaviour. They include connections made by Luria (1961) between verbal reasoning and the socialization process, and a study by Kaler and

Kopp (1990) that demonstrated that much of toddler non-compliance can be explained by poor verbal comprehension.

This set of speculations have in common some chain of events starting with some problem in the verbal domain and ending with unsocial behaviour. Caspi and Moffitt (1995) repeatedly call the verbal deficits 'neuropsychological', implying that they have a biological rather than an environmental origin. They make no attempt to specify what the nature of the verbal deficit might be – apart from noting that it appears to be 'pervasive' – nor is any link made to any of the literature on developmental language disorders. This theoretical incompleteness does not detract from the value of Moffitt's work (e.g. Moffitt et al. 2002). Indeed, it is the productivity of the Moffitt approach that makes it worth analysing its incompleteness from a causal modelling point of view.

Why cannot we just accept the causal model in figure 10.5 as being incomplete? Well, it is a feature of causal modelling that it enables us to address differential diagnosis from a developmental viewpoint. It becomes relevant to ask, then, about other groups of children with pervasive language problems. Let us be clear why this is so. Any element of a causal model stands on its own. If I make a bald claim that $\langle A$ causes $B \rangle$, then A should cause B in all circumstances within the limits of normal variability. Let us take an example from the causal model of autism. The initial causal claim is that, with young children, if the Theory of Mind (ToM) is missing (A), there will be failure in the false belief task (B). But this will be so irrespective of the reason for the lack of Theory of Mind Mechanism (ToMM). It is not, as it stands, just a claim about autism. Thus we find that young blind children, who are delayed in the establishment of a ToM since they miss the important clues given by eye fixation, also have problems with false belief compared with sighted children (Hobson 1993; Minter et al. 1998). As we explore the situation, the bald causal claim will usually need to be modified. For example, we may discover that a particular task can be solved in a way that avoids the use of the target mechanism. Thus, we find that many higher-functioning autistic children, aged ten or more, have worked out a way of solving the first-order false belief task (Frith et al. 1991). The causal claim concerning the relation between the ToMM and behaviour on the false belief task will have to be refined to specify 'young children' – or some such modification.

With this background, we can explore a little further those claims of Caspi and Moffitt (1995) concerning the contribution of verbal deficits to the development of antisocial behaviour. It becomes relevant to ask, then, about other groups of children with pervasive language problems. If, as Wilson and Herrnstein (1985) claim, 'low verbal intelligence contributes to a present-oriented cognitive style, which in turn, fosters irresponsible and exploitative behaviour', then this relation should hold for any group with low verbal intelligence; otherwise, the claim has very limited explanatory force. It then becomes relevant to ask whether 'irresponsible and exploitative behaviour' is typical of groups with specific language impairment (SLI). I suspect that such behaviour will not be found endemically in such groups, and conclude that the simple claim of a causal relation between verbal deficits and antisocial behaviour is seriously incomplete.

Caspi and Moffitt refer to two kinds of neuropsychological deficit, verbal and executive. The problems that I have identified above, concerning the role of verbal deficits in the cause of maladaptive behaviour, do not apply to the same extent to executive deficits. Caspi and Moffitt begin by talking about:

> deficiencies in the brain's self-control functions ... commonly referred to as 'executive' functions ... According to neuropsychological theory, executive dysfunctions should interfere with children's ability to control their own behavior, producing inattentive, impulsive children who are handicapped in considering the future implications of their acts. Such children have difficulty in understanding the negative impact of their behavior on others, fail to hold in mind abstract ideas of ethical values and future rewards, and fail to inhibit inappropriate behavior or adapt their behavior to changing social circumstances. (p. 479)

I do not find such general language very helpful. There are two main reasons for this. The first, as already spelled out in chapter 6 (p. 128), is that many other diagnostic types fail on one or more 'executive' task. This creates problems for differential diagnosis and for the specification of the causal model. As I have said before, one cannot have pairs of causal elements such as

▓ ⟨executive dysfunction causes conduct disorder⟩

and

▓ ⟨executive dysfunction causes autism⟩

because operation of the one should be accompanied by operation of the other. If this is not what is intended – and it surely isn't – then one has to say that 'executive dysfunction' is not the same as 'executive dysfunction', and it is clear that one is not in a theoretical mode of discourse, let alone a causal mode of discourse.

The second reason for dissatisfaction with the use of the term 'executive dysfunction' is the impression that it gives of a single, well defined functional problem. In fact, it covers a variety of functions, ranging from perception to response production by way of every central cognitive function. Caspi and Moffitt are well aware of this, and give the following list:

> sustaining attention and concentration, abstract reasoning and concept formation, goal formulation, anticipation and planning, programming and initiating purposive sequences of behaviour, self-monitoring and self-awareness, inhibition of unsuccessful, inappropriate or impulsive behavior. (p. 479)

Given this diversity of function, it should come as no surprise that 'executive dysfunction' is not a unitary concept and that most patient groups fail only on some executive tests. Any causal model, then, will need to specify the nature of the executive deficit. Caspi and Moffitt do this, drawing attention to the connection between deficits in self-control of attention and long-term antisocial behaviour. They refer to studies by Moffitt of boys in New Zealand (e.g. Moffitt 1990) where boys who exhibited co-morbidity of conduct disorder and ADD scored poorly on neuropsychological tests of attentional function, as well as having continuity of extreme antisocial behaviour from age three to age 15. Boys with conduct disorder without ADD had no neuropsychological deficits; nor were their behaviour problems stable. Caspi and Moffitt speculate about the possible genetic origins of the condition, as well as pointing to possible 'perinatal sources of cognitive deficit to the development of antisocial behaviour' (p. 480), such as maternal drug abuse. Although these ideas are only briefly alluded to by Caspi and Moffitt, in terms of work that remains to be done, we can see that they are working towards a causal model such as that shown in figure 10.6.

The question also arises as to whether the environmental and neuropsychological factors have separate effects or are both factors necessary to generate the antisocial behaviours. In fact, Caspi and Moffitt (1995) lay great stress on the interaction between the individual

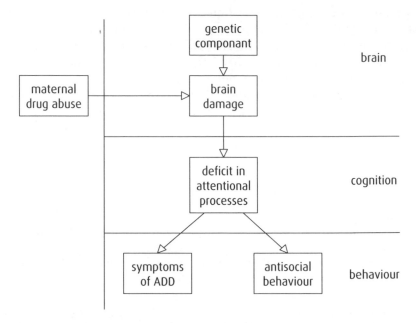

Figure 10.6 A causal model of the relation between an executive dysfunction – self-control of attention – and antisocial behaviour.

and the environment, distinguishing among three kinds of person–environment interaction: reactive interaction, evocative interaction and proactive interaction. These interactions result in the build-up of knowledge structures and schemas that will serve to interpret the environment and guide the choice of response. In effect, they are the mechanisms that build up the structures specified in Dodge's social processing model. The interactions need to be maintained by both sides, and while it is not within the scope of a causal model to chart the micro-detail of these interactions, it is clear causally that the child must possess certain properties, and that the environment must possess certain properties for these interactions to take place.

As an example of a micro-social mechanism, Caspi and Moffitt (1995) mention that 'children with poor verbal communication skills may elicit less positive interaction and more physical punishment from parents, especially if the family is stressed' (p. 478). So 'poor verbal abilities thus may hinder the development of healthy parent–child attachment bonds that might forestall and deter later delinquency' (p. 478).

From examples of this kind, we see that Caspi and Moffitt (1995), then, are implying a causal model that has both biological and environmental input to the cognitive level. The complexity of the kinds of interaction makes it possible that, in the history of the creation of the adult conduct disorder, both verbal and attentional deficit are implicated.

Is the causal model framework a proper way to represent causal accounts for conduct disorder? In this discussion I will evaluate our exercise to apply causal modelling to theories of conduct disorder, and discuss the theories and the framework.

We have seen that the causal model framework has been able to capture parts of the theories of conduct disorder described. It seems that the theories that I have described focus on different descriptive levels of the framework. Only Blair's theory could be expressed in terms of a full causal model, with the biological, cognitive and behavioural elements, as well as the environmental elements, described. However, the environmental elements do need further specification in this theory. Although it seems almost self-evident that Dodge's cognitive information processing (SIP) theory of conduct disorder relates to the cognitive level of the causal model, it is best described in terms of an information flow model of cognitive processing. There is a developmental component, in that particular control parameters have been learned by the child in interaction with the environment, but these are simply described as they exist at the time of the conduct disorder, rather than being derived as the consequence of particular developmental phenomena. In particular, the examples of verbal deficits that are given as illustrations are not given a developmental justification. There is nothing which could be used as a causal model for any of these deficits. In Patterson's work, the focus is on the microstructure of the process whereby environmental influences mould automatic behaviour. If we were trying to create a causal model to represent Dodge's ideas, we might want to specify that certain environmental conditions play a causal role in the development of conduct disorder. However, the boundary between causal elements and predisposing conditions is reasonably clear: (a) in the absence of any mechanism linking predisposing condition to outcome; and (b) given that these predisposing conditions apply to a number of different outcomes, and that, as previously discussed, our clinical interest is in differential diagnosis.

Moffitt's views can be clarified to a certain extent through a causal modelling treatment. There are both environmental and biological elements specified. However, the specification at the cognitive level is either too broad – as in the general appeal to verbal deficits – or not demonstrably differentiating – as with the mention of deficits in self-control of attention. However, we have not been able to encompass everything in the framework, and we are left with the belief that a multi-model approach is necessary. Examples of the other kinds of model needed are the information flow model needed to describe some of Dodge's thinking and some state transition models necessary to describe the detail of the child–parent interactions in Patterson's theory. I do wish to emphasize that causal modelling is only one way of expressing theories about disorders. Specifically, it is about cause, and about historical cause. If specifying cause is not the primary aim of a body of work, then causal modelling, while not central to such work, will still be able to illuminate the developmental trajectory.

What does the application of the framework tell us about the theories? ▧

The application of the framework has helped us see the relationships among the various theories of conduct disorder. To start with, it is clear that the approaches of Blair and Dodge are complementary. Blair is primarily concerned with the possible biological origins of the psycho-pathic personality and with the mechanisms of inhibition of aggressive responses in normal people. The causal model concerns the detail of the establishment of this inhibition for the normal child over the course of development and the way in which the development of this inhibitory process breaks down with the psychopathic individual. On the other hand, we have not been able to create a causal model for Dodge, who is more concerned with what is happening at the time of the aggressive behaviour. In creating his causal model, Blair indicated that the environment had some role, but did not specify how it would have an effect. The coercive parenting theory of Patterson does just that, describing the way in which the environment trains the child to become antisocial. In figure 10.7, I indicate how Patterson's ideas would interface with Blair's in a causal model. I have also added a frontal/executive dysfunction to show how Caspi and Moffitt's conjectures might be fitted in to the same framework. As I have already indicated, these would require some further specification before they could take their place in a developed causal model. This model is to be interpreted in terms of the development of three kinds of cognitive dysfunction that combine

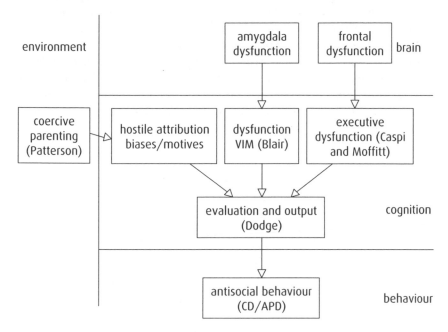

Figure 10.7 An attempt to produce an integrated causal model of conduct disorder/antisocial personality disorder.

to create the 'particular cognitive processing' of an idealized individual with conduct disorder. The detail of this processing is outside the scope of a causal model, and requires an information processing model such as that of Dodge. This idea is developed further in Krol et al. (2004), where the causal/developmental theories of Blair on the one hand and Caspi and Moffitt on the other hand can be used to flesh out Dodge's theory.

It is clear that conduct disorder is very different from such disorders as autism and dyslexia, where there is a strong, limited and relatively well specified disorder. Given their biological beginnings, the environment can serve to mitigate these disorders but cannot remove them; nor can it play a major role in creating them. Although experience is necessary for a child to build a Theory of Mind, almost any kind of human interaction will serve, and the role of knowledge is minimal. Thus, the specification of the interactions that lead to the construction of a Theory of Mind has not played any significant role in the development of the current theories of autism and related studies on normal children. The differences between competing theories of autism can readily be captured in a series of causal models. The development and continuation of conduct disorder, on the other hand, requires the creation of complex knowledge structures that presuppose particular kinds of environmental interactions. Specification of the dynamic of these interactions requires other theoretical techniques. However, by use of causal modelling we have been able to see the relationships among the various theories that I have described.

11 ■ TYING IN BIOLOGY

Relations between the cognitive and biological levels ■

Throughout this book, I have given examples of causal models in which there are causal arrows that remain within a descriptive level, and causal arrows that appear to go from one descriptive level to another. Within the biological level, there are a number of different sub-levels that might need to be specified in a causal chain that started from the gene and ended up with a cognitive change. But cognitive neuroscience has produced examples in which brain states have already been defined in some detail. For example, Gallese (1999) has made distinctions among a number of levels in the biological domain within which he embeds his work, which is anchored in brain physiology. These levels are as follows:

- membrane proteins
- receptors
- neurons and synapses
- neural assemblies
- cortical circuits
- behaviour/cognition.

He discusses the possible independence of these levels, pointing out that while complexity at the receptor level is not relevant for behaviour/cognition, action potentials, which arise from activity in neurons, can have such meaning. Assemblies of neurons are even more likely to have meaning. Functional imaging studies currently relate to cortical circuits. We can note that a full causal model of developmental disorder could

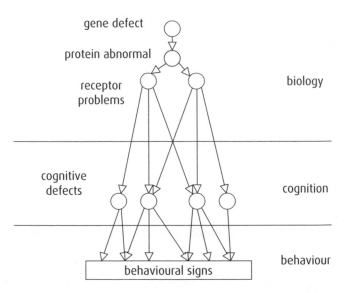

gene defect

protein abnormal

receptor
problems

biology

cognitive
defects

cognition

behavioural signs

behaviour

Figure 11.1 A sketch of a generic causal model of a developmental disorder with a biological origin. For reasons of simplicity, the environmental factors are omitted.

start with a problem at the membrane protein level (preceded by a genetic disorder, perhaps) and move down through the five biological levels before leading to a cognitive problem.

Let us now take a look at the shift of level from brain to cognition in the causal chain. Closer examination reveals a particular relationship between the levels. To appreciate this, we can start with the causal model sketched in figure 11.1. We have no problem in saying that the gene defect *causes* the various cognitive defects and behavioural signs. This is a very common type of claim in the area of developmental disorder. Equally, it is straightforward to say that receptor problems (assuming that they are specified) *cause* a cognitive defect – such as, in autism, the lack of a Theory of Mind Mechanism (Frith et al. 1991). However, it is clear that there is an explanatory gap between these two elements that would have to be filled before the theory could be considered satisfactory. To start with, using Gallese's scheme outlined above, the receptor problem could lead to a defect at the level of neurons and synapses, which could, in turn, lead developmentally to an abnormality best described in terms of neural assemblies, *n*. All of this could be specified causally. However, given that we have the specification of a deficit described in terms of n, it could be that there is no further causal statement that could be made at the level of brain physiology.

Let us now look at the cognitive level, still using the example of autism. The lack of a Theory of Mind Mechanism, in the case of autism, has been attributed in one version of the theory to the absence of a computational device called an Expression Raiser (or EXPRAIS) (Leslie 1987). Morton (1986) supposed EXPRAIS to be a cognitive primitive – that is, EXPRAIS is supposed to be irreducible. What this means is that there is no other *cognitive* element above it in the causal chain that accounts for its absence in this particular theory of autism.[1]

In figure 11.2, I have brought together the considerations of the previous two paragraphs. In this figure, x represents EXPRAIS and n is the deficit described in terms of neural assemblies. The cognitive element t represents the Theory of Mind Mechanism. From this figure, we might say that the neural deficit (n) causes a deficit in the Theory of Mind Mechanism (ToMM). Equally, we might say that a deficit in x causes the deficit in the t – in other words, the deficit in EXPRAIS causes the deficit in ToMM. The odd relationship is that between n and x. To start with, the deficit in n, in the context of this model, is *defined* by the deficit in x. If n was abnormal from the point of view of neuroanatomy, it would still only count as a relevant deficit in the theory if it no longer performed the function x. Secondly, the only way in which there can be a deficit in x is if there is a deficit in n.[2] This is the claim of the theory that underlies the model. Otherwise, there would be other elements in the biological level with connections to x. Because of these factors, we would not want to say that the neural

---

[1] Note, as I pointed out in chapter 4, among other places, that you do not have to agree with the specific illustrative theory in order to appreciate the logic of the point being made. It could turn out that EXPRAIS was analysable into two parts, Y and Z, each of which would either be a primitive or analysable – and so on. Equally, if you don't like EXPRAIS, substitute your own theory – of equal specificity, of course. Then apply the same logic. Note that if you postulate a primitive that is the result of learning, then its absence could be caused through a problem in some learning mechanism. The argument with respect to the relation between biology and cognition will remain the same.

[2] There remains the tricky possibility that n is normal but disconnected from other neural assemblies that support the function x; for example, by transmitting the results of some computation. I will leave it to others to discuss whether, under these circumstances, we would want to talk about a deficit in x.

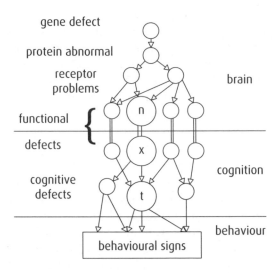

Figure 11.2 An expansion of the model in figure 11.1, showing the equivalence relation between elements at the biological and cognitive levels. *n* is the neural equivalent to *x* (EXPRAIS), while *t* represents the Theory of Mind Mechanism.

deficit *causes* the deficit in EXPRAIS. A deficit in one is *equivalent to* a deficit in the other. The two claims are identical and so cannot have a causal relationship, at least in the sense used elsewhere.[3]

I have shown above that, on our interpretation of the Leslie theory, EXPRAIS, as a cognitive primitive, will have a simple equivalent in neural circuitry, and there will be a one-to-one mapping between the two. The neural assembly would be equivalent to EXPRAIS because it would refer to the identical element. A further and stronger step that could be made in the argument is to suppose that such cognitive primitives are invariably instantiated in the brain in the same way. So, a particular cognitive primitive, *C*, is always instantiated by a particular, identifiable neuron, type of synapse or assembly of neurons, *N*. Further, each occurrence of activity in *N* can be taken as evidence for the operation of *C*. I suspect that theories that require what might be loosely called 'innate' structures might require strong cognitive primitives of this form.[4]

---

[3] Barry Smith (personal communication) has suggested that the relationship between the deficit in *n* and the deficit in *x* is one of '*causally necessary*'.

[4] It has been suggested to me that this strong relationship between a cognitive primitive and its neural equivalent can be characterized as what some philosophers

Equivalence: brain to cognition ▊

In the previous section, the starting point for the discussion was a cognitive primitive, EXPRAIS, which, at the moment, lacks a neural instantiation. Next, we can take as our starting point a structure identified on the biological side. One candidate as a biological primitive (in the sense that I am developing) is 'mirror neurons' (Gallese et al. 1996; Rizzolatti et al. 1996). These are neurons in the prefrontal lobe of the monkey cortex, which respond selectively both when the animal sees another animal pick up an object in a particular way and when the animal picks up an object itself in the same way. The observed actions that most commonly activate mirror neurons are grasping, placing and manipulating. Other mirror neurons are even more specific, responding to seeing another animal or human use a particular grip – such as a precision grip or a power grip – as well as to the animal itself picking up an object using the same kind of grip.

It is important to understand what these neurons are *not* for. To start with, they cannot be interpreted in terms of the preparation for an impending movement, since the neurons still fire when the monkey sees a specific movement while it is engaged in an action that is unrelated to the observed movement. Neither can the response be interpreted in terms of the anticipation of a reward, since there is no response from the neuron when the experimenter picks up a piece of food with a pair of pliers prior to the monkey picking it up; whereas if the experimenter picks the food up with his fingers, the target neuron does fire (Rizzolatti & Fadiga 1998). According to Rizzolatti and Fadiga, the most likely interpretation of the mirror neurons is that their discharge generates an internal representation of the observed action. Since there are a number of neurons that specialize in the same action, we can assume that, in respect of 'generating an internal representation', these collections can be considered as functional units. What Morton and Frith (2002) proposed was that these collections can be seen as *equivalent to* cognitive elements. To understand this, let us take two collections of these mirror

call a 'type–type' relationship. However, Barry Smith (personal communication) has pointed out that the type–type relationship refers to such identities as the mean molecular energy and temperature. Since it is clear that any well defined cognitive function (computation) can be carried out in a variety of substrates, one cannot claim that there is a type–type relationship with any one of those substrates, except (in the case of EXPRAIS) in the restricted context of the human brain.

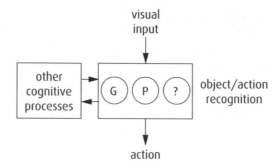

Figure 11.3 A cognitive model of grasping action meanings. Whether an action follows output of the units will depend on other factors.

neurons, one specializing in grasping – *MNg* – and one specializing in placing – *MNp*.[5]

Let us now consider a possible *cognitive* theory about the recognition of actions, which could be seen as equivalent to the biological theory outlined above. This model, illustrated in figure 11.3, is based on the early **logogen model** (Morton 1969). The basic computational unit in this model, the logogen, corresponded to a word. A logogen responded when sensory information was detected that matched a description of the associated word. This could be from a written or a spoken stimulus. The word in question would then be available as a response. In addition, this element would respond when central processes produced relevant information – such as a semantic description or a context. Information from stimulus and context interacted in a logogen. In this way, context could facilitate perception.

Now, it turned out that this theory of word recognition was not entirely correct (see Morton 1979). However, the construct of a logogen, operating in that way, serves our purpose here. The theory illustrated

[5] Let us further note that while these collections of neurons could, in principle, play a role in imitation, their activation cannot be seen as being equivalent to imitation. The reason for this is that, while apes and humans imitate the actions of others, it seems that monkeys do not. According to Rizzolatti and Fadiga (1998), 'monkeys, although endowed of a mechanism that generates internal copies of actions made by others, are unable to use them for replicating those actions' (p. 91). We might hypothesize that the neural circuits involved in the imitation of action in the apes included collections of neurons such as *MNg* and *MNp*.

in figure 11.3 considers that there are units, equivalent to logogens, that fire when there is enough evidence in the input to conclude that a grasping action, G, or a placing action, P, and so on, is occurring. Such firing would have the effect of 'generating an internal representation' of that action, which would be interpreted by cognitive processes. In addition, such units could be stimulated by inputs from other cognitive processes (an internal action goal), as a result of which instructions would be sent to the effector systems to use the specified action on an object of current attention. Under this, or a similar theory, the unit labelled G would be equivalent to the neural collection MNg, and the unit labelled P would be equivalent to the neural collection MNp. In either a brain theory or a cognitive theory, the sets of terms could be used interchangeably without any change in meaning. That is, a statement about MNg would be identical to a statement about G, and vice versa. Equally, any deficit in MNg at the biological level would be equivalent to a deficit in G at the cognitive level.

To summarize, then, I am claiming that in some cases there will be equivalence between biological and cognitive descriptions of functional entities, and that the relation between the two is to be contrasted with the causal relationship, which is the primary concern of causal modelling.[6]

Causal influences from cognition to brain

In all but one of the causal models in the book thus far, causal arrows have gone from the biological/brain level to the cognitive level. This is because the developmental disorders that I wish to explain are known to have a biological origin before birth. There could be other disorders that may be best explained by postulating a *causal* influence from the cognitive to the biological level. I don't know of any such disorders, but I can illustrate the methodology in relation to acquired disorders.

Consider someone involved in a traumatic event such as a traffic accident. According to some theories (e.g. Metcalf & Jacobs 1998), the fear (cognitively mediated) engendered by the event leads to the memory record being stored without the involvement of the hippocampus. The

---

[6] In considering the lack of constraints from biological facts on to cognitive theory, Jacques Mehler, Peter Jusczyk and I (Mehler et al. 1984) made an exception of cases of a one-to-one relationship between the levels – effectively what is meant by 'equivalence' here.

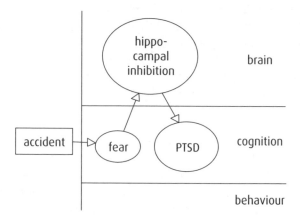

Figure 11.4 A model for PTSD, in which a cognitive change leads to a change in brain state with further cognitive consequences.

consequence of this is that the memory becomes intrusive and the person suffers from flashbacks in the condition known as post traumatic stress disorder (PTSD). This sequence can be seen as a cognitive state having brain consequences that lead to further cognitive outcomes, and is illustrated in figure 11.4.

A further example is in relation to pain. The traditional theory of pain, as proposed by Descartes, was that pain fibres relay information to a 'pain centre' in the brain. Activity in the pain centre is then experienced as pain. This is the usual brain-to-cognition causal relationship. However, as Derbyshire (1997) points out, it has become clear that there is no direct relationship between the amount of stimulation of pain fibres and the experience of pain. Rather, with something like dental pain, psychological factors such as the circumstances of an operation, the patient's understanding of and attention to the trauma, and levels of experienced anxiety intervene to produce the final perception of pain. Even for the apparently simple case of dental pain, then, a model is required in which the social context, and psychological factors, mediate at the biological level in the perception of pain. Derbyshire also summarizes current work on the experience of pain by sufferers of rheumatoid arthritis. The theory specifies feedback from the cognitive to the biological level, such that some aspects of a 'negative coping strategy' can lead to an increase in inflammation.

Causal feedback from the cognitive to the brain level should be contrasted with a further kind of relation between the two, which philosophers term 'token–token correspondence'. This refers to the way in which cognitive elements (such as processes or beliefs) are matched (embodied, represented) in the brain in cases other than those covered by the definition of equivalence. To illustrate, consider that any change at the cognitive level leads to a change at the brain level. However, such changes are not usually part of a causal model. When you change from believing that B is the case to believing that B is not the case, there is a change in the brain. The change is not systematic, however; the identity relation is not consistent, since if the belief changes back to B there will be a further change in the brain – but it will not change back to where it was before. Furthermore, for every individual, the brain state change that accompanies the shift in belief from B to not-B will be different. Thus, take the case that I came to believe something new: that this book had to be completed by the end of 2003, for example, rather than by the beginning of 2003. This welcome change in belief would, of course, have been accompanied by some change in brain state. However, the causal consequences of the change of belief cannot be traced or predicted from the change in brain state. We have to consider the cognitive (meaning) representation in order to trace the causal consequences. Indeed, although the change in belief may have been identical for me and for my editor, and the causal consequences were similar, the accompanying changes in our brains are very unlikely to have had any relationship. The accompanying changes in brain states would not normally enter into any causal chain and so can be ignored for the purposes of the causal model.

Genes and cause: the end of behaviour genetics ▊

As I have noted from time to time, the idea that a developmental disorder can be accounted for by the operation of a single gene is likely to be the case only in a few, very rare, disorders. The same is true for types of mental breakdown that occur later in life. True, there are still some overenthusiastic scientists hunting for a scientific crock of gold, and journalists who believe them when they claim that they have found the gene for love, anorexia, homosexuality or dyscalculia, but the rest of us sigh and wait. What are the problems? They are fourfold – at least.

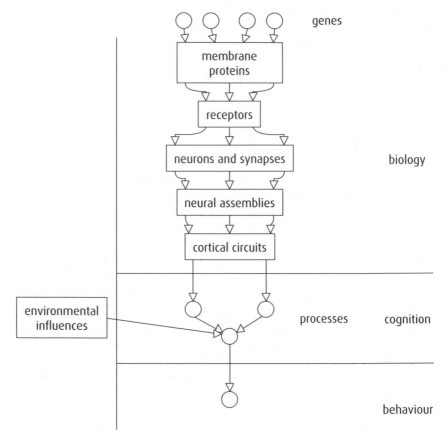

Figure 11.5 A generic causal model with the biological component expanded.

Genes are too low level

Genes code for proteins; not for cell assemblies, not for cognitive processes and even more remotely for behaviour. This is illustrated in figure 11.5, where a number of genes are shown as contributing to the causal chain. At each of the levels and sub-levels, one can envisage a number of different contributing elements. There may be a few cases in which the link between gene and behaviour is more direct, but they seem to be rare (see box 11.1). Marcus (2004) considers ways in which genes can interact in the creation of complexity.

There are other influences every step of the way

A causal chain from gene to target behaviour may be possible. However, as indicated in figure 11.5, at every step of the causal chain what actually happens will be influenced by the products of other genes or aspects of the environment. In this way, identical twins can end up different from each other in significant ways. In the figure, the environment is shown as acting only at the latter stages of cognition. In fact, there

---

Box 11.1 The power of a single gene in causing deafness

Some years ago, there was a report of a family in Costa Rica in which, over many generations, about half the members developed deafness (Leon et al. 1992). The gene responsible was identified in chromosome 5. It turns out that the mutated gene operates not only in the inner ear, but also in the brain, lungs, kidney and many other tissues. However, the only symptom appears to be the late-developing deafness. Some clues as to why this might be were given when a homologous gene was found in the fruit fly, and another in the mouse. Studies of these genes indicated that they produced proteins that helped other molecules to form filaments of yet another protein, called *actin*. The actin filaments produce a dynamic skeleton for cells and are likely to be vital for hair cells in the inner ear, to provide the stiffness that enables them to respond to sound. In other tissues, either the actin is not so important or there might be some other protein that can substitute.

No doubt there were journalists who dubbed the gene 'the hearing gene'. The reason why I went into so much detail describing the causal chain was to show how far away such a description would be. In addition, another family with inherited deafness, this time in Israel, was shown to have a problem in a different gene, also found in chromosome 5, but with a very different function. Members of a third family with specific deafness, in a village on the north shore of Bali, have a mutated gene localized to chromosome 17. In this way, we obtain a picture of a complex chain of events. It is possible for a mutation in a single gene to have a very specific effect. In addition, there are a number of genes that can produce the same effect.

In figure 1, I give a sketch of a DCM for the need for actin in the production of hair cells. The equivalent causal model is shown in figure 2, where if there is a problem with any one of genes G_a, G_b or G_c, the hair cells will be faulty. This contrasts with what we believe to be the case

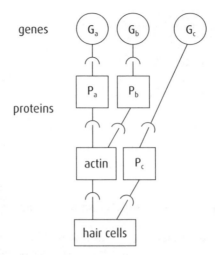

Figure 1 A DCM representation of the interactions among genes and proteins in the formation of hair cells, such as is described in the text.

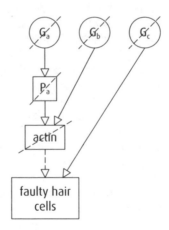

Figure 2 A causal model for a variety of hearing disorders, based on the DCM in figure 1. Problems in any of genes G_a, G_b or G_c will give rise to a hearing disorder. As previously, a line through an element means that it is missing or faulty in some way.

with most developmental psychopathological disorders, where there have to be a number of genes all with abnormal properties before the syndrome is found. The relevant causal model is given in figure 3.

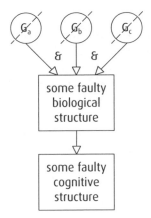

Figure 3 A contrasting causal model to that in Figure 2, in which faults in one of the three genes would lead to problems. In this case, all three genes would have to be faulty to get the effect.

will be aspects of the environment that act at most, if not all, of the levels. All of this makes the route between gene and behaviour even more complex. An alternative way of thinking about the relationship is to make statements of the kind:

■ without gene *G*, behaviour *B* will not be found

However, since people can exhibit episodes of behaviour typical of various pathologies under particular environmental conditions, even statements such as the one above are easily falsified. Claims of the kind:

■ without gene *G*, element *E* will not be found

would be stronger, where *E* is a positive or negative characteristic at either the cognitive or the biological level.

Note the paradox: in spite of our putting some causal distance between genes and cognitive processes, it still could be the case that cognitive processes might be the direct cause of evolutionary selection. For example, it seems possible that the ability to use language conferred an advantage for survival on our remote ancestors over other members of the species *Homo* who lacked this ability. Possible mechanisms for such an advantage are easy to imagine – for example, the ability to plan and coordinate co-operative hunting would give a appreciable edge over a group of a lesser species. However, even if the evolutionary claim was accepted in its most literal fashion – language good, no language bad – it would be a mistake to expect there to be a gene for language. There will be a number of genes in which abnormalities will lead to problems with language learning or use. One of these may have more widespread effects within the language domain than the rest and would thus have survival value. But it will still not be 'the language gene' in the tabloid sense.

Genes are promiscuous

One of the objectives of pairing up genes with disorders has to be that of being able to predict a disorder from the presence of the gene. However, many of the genes implicated in particular disorders as a result of standard behaviour genetic techniques turn out to be implicated in a variety of disorders. Thus, the 7-repeat allele of DRD-4 has been variously associated with attention deficit, Tourette's syndrome, hyper-activity and dyslexia, at least. In this case, it does not make sense to regard DRD-4 as being the gene for any of them. Let me spell this out in a little more detail. The strong causal claim concerning the relation-ship between the DRD-4 gene and attention deficit is represented in figure 11.6. What the model says is that the presence of the 7-repeat allele of DRD-4 causes a dopamine-related problem, which leads even-tually to behaviour that is classified as attention deficit. Some intervening stages will, of course, be required. The problem is the same one as we have met earlier, in chapter 6 (p. 128), in relation to the use of 'executive dysfunction' as a causal element: it doesn't discriminate. In figure 11.6, there is no indication as to why *attention deficit* is the resulting behaviour, rather than *Tourette's syndrome*. In fact, there have to be two overlapping causal models, one for each syndrome. The first is shown in figure 11.7. In this, I have added another cognitive element and supposed that it, together with the first cognitive deficit, combine to give the attention deficit. This is the very simplest that the model could be and is intended to be only for illustrative purposes. The expert will want to create a much more complex model. In contrast to the model relating DRD-4 and attention deficit is one linking the same gene with Tourette's syndrome. This is shown in figure 11.8. Here, it is the presence of a third cognitive deficit operating in conjunction with the dopamine

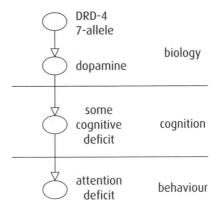

Figure 11.6 An overly simple causal model of behaviour genetics.

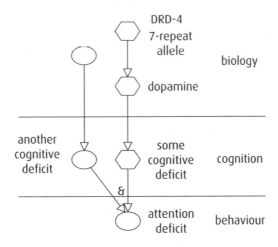

Figure 11.7 An extension of the model in figure 11.6, which allows for the need for differential diagnosis. At its simplest, the cognitive deficit arising from the DRD-4 7-repeat allele must operate in conjunction with other cognitive deficit, with some biological (genetic?) origin. This contrasts with figure 11.8, with which it has the hexagonal elements in common.

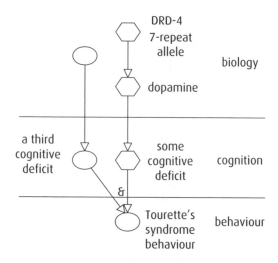

Figure 11.8 A causal model for the effects of the DRD-4, 7-repeat allele in creating Tourette's syndrome. This model contrasts with that in figure 11.7, with which it has the hexagonal components in common. They differ crucially in the accompanying deficit. It is, of course, possible that the interaction leading to Tourette's syndrome takes place at the biological or cognitive levels, as illustrated in figure 11.9.

associated deficit that gives rise to the target syndrome. The existence of the two models involving the DRD-4 allele allows the relationship between gene and behaviour to be expressed differentially.

Now, it may seem that it is unlikely that attention deficit and Tourette's syndrome should be distinguished by interactions at the cognitive level that create the observed behaviour. Instead, it might be preferable to think about more complex variations either at the cognitive or at the biological levels. The kinds of models that might result for expressing the causal relation between DRD-4 and Tourette's syndrome are illustrated in figure 11.9. In both cases, the effect of the variation in the DRD-4 gene is shared in the two conditions up to a particular point. In the figure, you will see the symbols G_t and G_a. These indicate, in a sketchy way, the differences between the diseases. These differences probably start with genetic differences, which could be different variations on the same gene, but could include environmental factors and interactions between genes and the environment. The notation is ultimately neutral with respect to such decisions – although if an

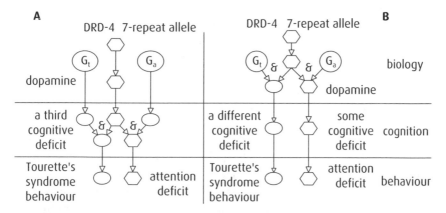

Figure 11.9 Alternative models to that in figure 11.8 for the relation between the DRD-4 variation and Tourette's syndrome. The hexagonal elements are those that the models have in common with the account of attention deficit given in figure 11.7. The symbols G_t and G_a indicate factors that differentiate the two conditions. They could be genetic variations (the two could be different variations of the same gene), environmental factors or combinations of these. The claims of the two alternatives are clear. In version A, the DRD variation is shared between the two conditions as far as the cognitive level. In version B, the split comes at the biological level. As always, the notation is neutral. See the text for further discussion.

environmental factor was being hypothesized, it would be notated explicitly. The two models in figure 11.9 differ in respect of the level of the interaction of the variations brought about by G_t and G_a with those due to DRD-4. In version A, the model represents a theory that says that the consequences of the DRD-4 variation are shared between the diseases down to the level of cognition. It is at the cognitive level that the differences between the diseases would be manifest – for example, by effecting differences in decision-making in two different domains. In version B, the difference between the diseases interacts with the DRD-4 causal pathway at the biological level. This would include developmental effects. Such a model would be consistent with the notion of the DRD-4, 7-repeat allele being related to some generalized developmental susceptibility.

The above analysis illustrates how causal arrows in a causal model can either refer to what happened in the course of development, possibly very early development, or to on-line effects. Theories of developmental disorders include both kinds of component, and since the objective of causal modelling is to be able to represent other people's theories, both kinds are allowed. Usually, there is no ambiguity.

Genes create disorder spectrums

Simple statements about genes causing disorders would not be able to account for the phenomena that members of the families of affected individuals can have minor indications of the same syndrome. One example of this is that some relatives of individuals with dyslexia have particular difficulties with the spoonerism task. What this suggests is that we think about a gene as having *influence* over a whole spectrum of behaviour in a causal model of the A-type. This is illustrated in figure 11.10. Such a diagram could be used to map individuals with a wide range of specifications. In the figure, one such example has been given of an individual with the gene defect that has only resulted in one cognitive defect and a mild behavioural manifestation. In this case it has been assumed that most of the cognitive defects require two or more functional defects. The diagrammatic form of the model allows such factors to be specified as they are needed in order to enable consistency to be achieved. There are no obvious limits to the complexity that can be easily expressed in this format in terms of the interactions among genes and their products. Environmental factors can also be inserted into the model, as we have seen in many places in this book.

Endophenotypes ▪

In the previous section, I outlined a number of reasons for dissatisfaction with attempts to relate genes directly with behaviour or with disease entities as usually defined. A similar move has been made recently by a number of people, under the heading of *endophenotypes*. Almasy and Blangero (2001) point out how diagnosis of psychiatric disorder is complicated by factors such as the presence of milder forms of disease in relatives and co-morbidity with other disorders or with substance abuse. They talk about the interest in 'traits that directly index the underlying pathology, or liability to disease, and can be measured in both affected and unaffected individuals' (p. 42). It is hoped that endophenotypes involve the same biological pathways as the disease and so are closer to the relevant gene action than are diagnostic categories.

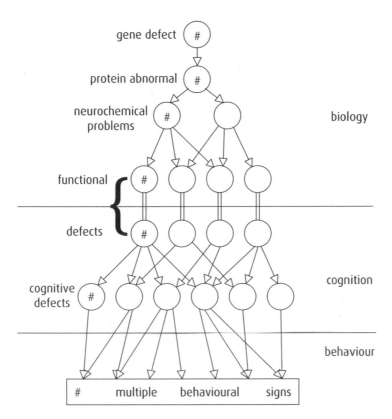

Figure 11.10 A schematic causal model of a gene's influence over a wide range of behaviour. The causal arrows are all to be seen as contingent and multiple influences from one level to the next might be disjunctive or conjunctive (& or OR). In any individual, which of the causal connections are potentiated will depend on other genes and their influence. For example, a mildly affected individual might only have the abnormal elements marked with an '#' in the figure.

Examples of endophenotypes cited by Almasy and Blangero (2001) include characteristic variations in the amplitude of the P300 evoked brain potential in alcoholic individuals and in their alcohol-naïve sons. They also point to a characteristic profile of neurocognitive deficits in schizophrenic individuals, together with a milder pattern in unaffected first-degree relatives. These examples, and the way in which endopheno-types are referred to, makes it quite easy to relate the work to causal modelling. If you look at figure 11.10 again, you can see that any of the elements marked '#' could be associated with an endophenotype. In addition, the idea of an endophenotype indexing *liability* can be seen as the same as the claim

■ without gene *G*, element *E* will not be found

noted above in the context of causal models. The search for an endophenotype and the search for a causal model are parts of the same enterprise.

The emphasis in the work on endophenotypes is towards genetic analysis. Because of this, Almasy and Blangero (2001) stress that endophenotypes must be quantifiable rather than dichotomous. This means that some elements of a causal model might not be suitable candidates as an endophenotype.

Castellanos and Tannock (2002) discuss endophenotypes in the context of ADHD. They note that research into ADHD has been hampered by confusion over diagnostic criteria. More generally, they state: 'Nearly two decades of unsuccessful efforts in psychiatric genetics have led to the conclusion that symptom-based diagnostic classification systems do not facilitate (and can actively obstruct) mapping between susceptibility genes and behavioural outcomes' (p. 619). They discuss three candidate endophenotypes for ADHD: shortened delay gradient, temporal processing and working memory. In all three cases, they produce a causal model with the endophenotype effectively at the cognitive level, located between putative brain abnormalities and behaviours. In every case, the behaviours specified in the model are only a subset of those in the full ADHD specification. The underlying idea is that the endophenotypes each represent a dimension on each of which a quantitative measure can be assigned to anyone with a starting diagnosis of ADHD. It is believed that working with these measures, which are experimentally obtainable, will be more tractable than the ungainly, subjective classifications typical of DSM-IV and other systems.

Mouse (and other) models for human disorders ■

There is an increasing use of other species, in particular the mouse, in an attempt to understand psychiatric disorders and other kinds of developmental disorders. There are a number of ways in which this can be done. First of all, if you suspect that a particular gene is implicated in a disorder and a similar or homologous gene is found in the mouse, the role of this gene in the mouse could be traced. This could lead to hypotheses concerning the biological basis of the disorder in humans. This sort of process is described in box 11.1, in the context of hearing disorders. This limited objective seems straightforward. However, often, the objective is more ambitious – to provide a model for the entire disorder. There would be a number of problems with this. We have already learned that human developmental disorders involve an extended phenotype. It is unlikely that a lesser species would display the same complexity. This would certainly be the case where the human disorder included specifically human abilities – language, mentalizing or meta-cognitive abilities. Possibly the best case one could hope for is where there are equivalent genes that are part of similar biological paths that control equivalent behaviour. With a causal model, this would be rep-resented as in figure 11.11. I have omitted any cognitive component

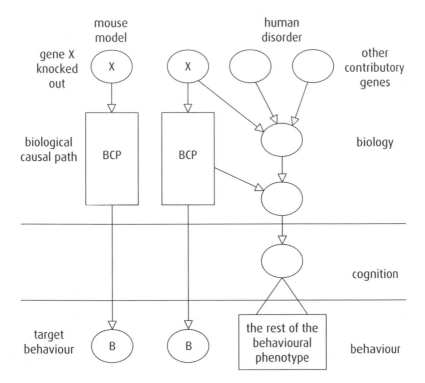

Figure 11.11 A best case scenario for the use of a mouse model for a developmental disorder. The links between the mouse path and the rest of the human phenotype path are optional.

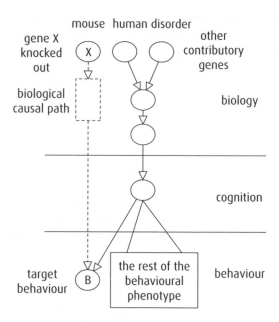

Figure 11.12 A worst case scenario for the use of a mouse model for a developmental disorder. There is nothing in common between mouse and human paths except for the element of behaviour. There is nothing to be learned that is relevant to the human disorder.

in the *X–B* chain on the grounds that there would then be bound to be differences introduced between mouse and human, even for the simplest behaviour. However, investigations of the biological causal path in the mouse would be relevant to the human case. In particular, the effects of drugs in the mouse pathway could give strong leads to human treatment. Note that if there were no connections in the human causal chain between the *X–B* path and the rest of the model, then the *X–B* path might be an example of co-morbidity.

A worst case scenario is shown in figure 11.12. In this, we can imagine that someone has identified a target behaviour in the human disorder and found an equivalent in a mouse mutation. As can be seen in the causal model, there is nothing else in common between the paths. The researcher would be extremely lucky if anything useful came out of the mouse research.

This analysis of mouse modelling has been very shallow. I have included it in order to show another use of causal models. When the mouse and the human disorders are modelled in this way, one can have a clearer idea as to the extent of application of results from the other species.

12 ■ To Conclude

I have not included everything that I intended to include in this book. I have notes on other developmental disorders; I have used causal modelling to interpret experimental findings in the remediation of clumsiness (Sims & Morton 1998); I have large numbers of press cuttings showing governmental misuse of causal reasoning; and members of Uta Frith's group at the Institute of Cognitive Neuroscience in London routinely use causal modelling in planning future research, and I could have told you about that. But I have more than run out of time, and I think I have done enough to make the points that I want to make. Let me try to sum up.

Cause is not an easy word. Its popular use would be laughable if it was not so dangerous, informing, as it does, government policy on matters that affect us all. I have only touched on such issues, and only in the context of developmental disorders.

What I have tried to do in the book is provide a tool for thinking. It is a graphical tool with all the advantages of pictures. In particular, it gives more freedom to the expression of complex ideas. For me, language can be a strait-jacket, getting in the way of thought and communication as it forces me into a linear stream. This has been something of a problem in any case in the book, as I found it necessary to refer to particular ideas in a number of different places and never knew what order to put things in. Next time, I will use more advanced technology and put the whole thing on disk, moving you around with hyperlinks. The figures are not bad, though. Imagine how long it would take to express Franck Ramus' theory of dyslexia, shown in figure 8.24, if you only had words with which to do it. The other thing that the figures do for me is act as a memory aid, and that gets more important with every year that passes.

Throughout the development of causal modelling over the past ten years, Uta Frith and I have tried to keep the theory neutral with respect to the content of the theories that could be represented. I have talked about theories whose development I have been involved in, particularly with respect to autism and dyslexia, but there is nothing about the techniques of causal modelling that favoured the expression of those theories over any others. The major theoretical point that I have tried to put across has been the essential role of cognition as a mediator between biological and behavioural matters. But the causal modelling method itself can be used just as well within biology, to keep track of gene interactions, for example, and if you want to have causal theories of human development that exclude cognition, then the format is easily adaptable. Just omit the middle layer. I will be interested to see how far you get.

From time to time, I have laid down the law about the proper way to go about things. Chapter 5, with its ten maxims, is the place where most of this has been gathered together. Uta and I assembled this list partly as a result of our own mistakes in theory development, and partly in response to the irritation that we experienced seeing how progress was slowed down by, for example, people mistaking correlation for cause. Some other maxims will doubtless appear, perhaps out of errors that I have made in this book. Some of the existing ones have gained strength as I have proceeded. The best example is the need for differential diagnosis. I have found myself working up quite a head of steam against the use of general terms such as 'executive dysfunction' in explanatory contexts, since it is clear that we ought to be doing much better than that. I have called it 'pre-scientific'; it gives the illusion of progress without the substance.

Throughout my scientific life, I have drawn models of processes. The results sometimes look trivial, but there is scarcely a model that I have developed that has not resulted in a wastepaper basket or two filled with rejects. The moral here is that when you try to create a causal model of your favourite theory, don't expect to get things right first time. On the other hand, don't be afraid to adapt the method to suit yourself. You don't have to have boxes round the descriptions of the elements that you use; you don't have to have hollow arrows; and you may want to label each causal link with a time frame. You certainly will not want to write 'Biology', 'Cognition' and 'Behaviour' every time you sketch out a causal model.

The other thing is not to be surprised if you cannot get everything into the causal framework. Cause is only one way of thinking about development. In this book, I have used DCMs as well as causal models, and we saw in chapter 10 on conduct disorder that there were a number of aspects of the explanations proposed for which other kinds of model – information processing and information flow models – had to be used.

If you find causal modelling useful, I hope you will let me know. And if problems arise on which you would like to consult me, I will be happy to hear from you. Science has to be a global co-operative enterprise.

References

Aarkrog, T. 1968: Organic factors in infantile psychoses and borderline psychoses. A retrospective study of 46 cases subjected to pneumoencephalography. *Danish Medical Bulletin*, 15, 283–8.

Almasy, L. & Blangero, J. 2001: Endophenotypes as quantitative risk factors for psychiatric disease: rationale and study design. *American Journal of Medical Genetics*, 105, 42–4.

American Psychiatric Association 1980: *The Diagnostic and Statistical Manual of Mental Disorders*, 3rd edn (DSM-III). Washington, DC: APA.

American Psychiatric Association 1987: *The Diagnostic and Statistical Manual of Mental Disorders*, 3rd edn – revised (DSM-III-R). Washington, DC: APA.

American Psychiatric Association 1994: *The Diagnostic and Statistical Manual of Mental Disorders*, 4th edn (DSM-IV). Washington, DC: APA.

Anderson, M. 1992: *Intelligence and Development: a Cognitive Theory*. Oxford: Blackwell.

Annett, M. 1992: Phonological processing and right minus left hand skill. *Quarterly Journal of Experimental Psychology*, 44A, 33–46.

Annett, M. & Kilshaw, D. 1984: Lateral preference and skill in dyslexics: implications of the right shift theory. *Journal of Child Psychology and Psychiatry*, 25, 357–77.

Astington, J., Harris, P. & Olson, D. (eds) 1988: *Developing Theories of Mind*. Cambridge: Cambridge University Press.

Atkinson, R. L., Atkinson, R. C., Smith, E. E., Bem, D. J. & Hilgard, E. R. 1985: *Introduction to Psychology*, 10th edn. San Diego: Harcourt Brace Jovanovich.

Bailey, A., Phillips, W. & Rutter, M. 1996: Autism: towards an integration of clinical, genetic, neuropsychological, and neurobiological perspectives. *Journal of Child Psychology and Psychiatry*, 37, 89–126.

Barkley, R. A. 1997: Advancing age, declining ADHD. *American Journal of Psychiatry*, 154, 1323–5.

Baron-Cohen, S. 1991: Precursors to a theory of mind: understding attention in others. In A. Whiten (ed.), *Natural Theories of Mind: Evolution, Development and Simulation of Everyday Mindreading.* Oxford: Blackwell, 233–51.

Baron-Cohen, S. 1997: *Mindblindness: an Essay on Autism and Theory of Mind.* Cambridge, MA: The MIT Press.

Baron-Cohen, S., Leslie, A. M. & Frith, U. 1985: Does the autistic child have a 'theory of mind'? *Cognition,* 21, 37–46.

Bauman, M. & Kemper, T. L. 1985: Histoanatomic observations of the brain in early infant autism. *Neurology,* 35, 866–74.

Belsky, J., Spritz, B. & Crnic, K. 1996: Infant attachment, security and affective-cognitive information processing at age 3. *Psychological Science,* 7, 111–4.

Bettelheim, B. 1967: *The Empty Fortress: Infantile Autism and the Birth of the Self.* New York: The Free Press.

Biederman, J., Newcorn, J. & Sprich, S. 1991: Comorbidity of attention deficit hyperactivity disorder with conduct, depressive, anxiety, and other disorders. *American Journal of Psychiatry,* 148, 564–77.

Bíro, S. & Russell, J. 2001: The execution of arbitrary procedures by children with autism. *Development & Psychopathology,* 13, 97–110.

Bishop, D. V. M. 1990: *Handedness and Developmental Disorder.* London: Mac Keith Press; Oxford: Blackwell Scientific.

Blair, R. J. R. 1995: A cognitive developmental approach to morality: investigating the psychopath. *Cognition,* 57, 1–29.

Blair, R. J. R. 1999: Responsiveness to distress cues in the child with psychopathic tendencies. *Personality and Individual Differences,* 27, 135–45.

Blair, R. J. R. 2001: Neurocognitive models of aggression, the antisocial personality disorders, and psychopathy. *Journal of Neurology, Neurosurgery and Psychiatry,* 71, 727–31.

Blair, R. J. R., Monson, J. & Frederickson, N. 2001: Moral reasoning and conduct problems in children with emotional and behavioural difficulties. *Personality and Individual Differences,* 31, 799–811.

Bolton, P. & Rutter, M. 1990: Genetic influences in autism. *International Review of Psychiatry,* 2, 67–80.

Bornstein, R. A. 1990: Neuropsychological performance in children with Tourette's syndrome. *Psychiatry Research,* 33, 73–81.

Bowlby, J. 1969: *Attachment.* London: Hogarth Press.

Bradley, L. L. & Bryant, P. E. 1983: Categorizing sounds and learning to read: a causal connection. *Nature,* 301, 419.

British Psychological Society 1999: *Dyslexia, Literacy and Psychological Assessment: Report by a Working Party of the Division of Educational and Child Psychology.* Leicester: BPS.

Bryant, P. E. & Impey, L. 1986: The similarities between normal children and dyslexic adults and children. *Cognition,* 24, 121–37.

Bryant, P. E., Maclean, M., Bradley, L. L. & Crossland, J. 1990: Rhyme and alliteration, phoneme detection and learning to read. *Developmental Psychology*, 26, 429–38.

Bryson, S. E. 1983: Interference effects in autistic children: evidence for the comprehension of single stimuli. *Journal of Abnormal Psychology*, 92, 250–4.

Butterworth, G., Harris, P., Leslie, A. M. & Wellman, H. (eds) 1991: *The Child's Theory of Mind.* Oxford: Oxford University Press.

Byrne, B. & Fielding-Barnsley, R. 1989: Phonemic awareness and letter knowledge in the child's acquisition of the alphabetic principle. *Journal of Educational Psychology*, 81, 313–21.

Campbell, M., Rosenbloom, S., Perry, R., George, A. E., Kricheff, I. I., Anderson, L., Small, A. M. & Jennings, S. J. 1982: Computerized axial tomography in young autistic children. *American Journal of Psychiatry*, 139, 510–12.

Cantwell, D. 1975: Genetics of hyperactivity. *Journal of Child Psychology and Psychiatry*, 16, 261–4.

Cantwell, D. 1977: Hyperkinetic syndrome. In K. F. Rutter & L. Hersov (eds), *Child Psychiatry: Modern Approaches.* Oxford: Blackwell, 524–55.

Caron, C. & Rutter, M. 1991: Comorbidity in childhood psychopathology: concepts, issues and research strategies. *Journal of Child Psychology and Psychiatry*, 32, 1063–80.

Caspi, A. 2002: Social selection and social causation: empirical strategies for disentangling sources of influence on development across the life course. In L. Pulkinnen & A. Caspi (eds), *Paths to Successful Development: Personality in the Life Course.* Cambridge: Cambridge University Press, 281–301.

Caspi, A. & Moffitt, T. E. 1995: The continuity of maladaptive behavior: From description to understanding in the study of antisocial behavior. In D. Cicchetti & D. J. Cohen (eds), *Developmental Psychopathology*, vol. 2: *Risk, Disorder and Adaptation.* New York: Wiley, 472–511.

Castellanos, F. X. & Tannock, R. 2002: Neuroscience of attention-deficit/ hyperactivity disorder: the search for endophenotypes. *Nature Reviews Neuroscience*, 3, 617–28.

Castellanos, F. X., Sharp, W. S., Gottesman, R. F., Greenstein, D. K., Giedd, J. N. & Rapoport, J. L. 2003: Anatomic brain abnormalities in monozygotic twins discordant for attention deficit hyperactivity disorder. *American Journal of Psychiatry*, 160, 1693–6.

Cataldo, S. & Ellis, N. 1990: Learning to spell, learning to read. In P. D. Pumfrey & C. D. Elliott (eds), *Children's Difficulties in Reading, Spelling and Writing.* London: The Falmer Press, 101–25.

Catts, H. W. 1989: Defining dyslexia as a developmental language disorder. *Annals of Dyslexia*, 39, 50–64. The Orton Dyslexia Society.

Chelune, G., Ferguson, W., Koon, R. & Dickey, T. O. 1986: Frontal lobe disinhibition in Attention Deficit Disorder. *Child Psychiatry and Human Development*, 16, 221–34.

Clarke, A. & Clarke, A. 1999: Early experience and the life path. In S. J. Ceci & W. M. Williams (eds), *The Nature–Nurture Debate*. Oxford: Blackwell.

Clay, M. M. 1979: *The Early Detection of Reading Difficulties*. London: Heinemann.

Clay, M. M. 1987: Learning to be learning disabled. *New Zealand Journal of Educational Studies*, 22, 155–72.

Cossu, G., Rossini, F. & Marshall, J. C. 1993: When reading is acquired but phonemic awareness is not: a study of literacy in Down's syndrome. *Cognition*, 46, 129–38.

Courchesne, E., Yeung-Courchesne, R., Press, G. A., Hesselink, J. R. & Jernigan, T. L. 1988: Hypoplasia of cerebellar vermal lobules VI and VII in autism. *New England Journal of Medicine*, 318, 1349–54.

Creasey, H., Rumsey, J. M., Schwartz, M., Duara, R., Rapoport, J. L. & Rapoport, S. I. 1986: Brain morphometry in autistic men as measured by volumetric computed tomography. *Archives of Neurology*, 43, 669–72.

Crick, N. R. & Dodge, K. A. 1994: A review and reformulation of social information-processing mechanisms in children's social adjustment. *Psychological Bulletin*, 115, 74–101.

Critchley, M. 1970: *The Dyslexic Child*. London: Heinemann.

Damasio, H., Maurer, R. G., Damasio, A. R. & Chui, H. C. 1980: Computerized tomographic scan findings in patients with autistic behavior. *Archives of Neurology*, 37, 504–10.

Dawson, G. & Levy, A. 1989: In G. Dawson (ed.), *Autism: Nature, Diagnosis and Treatment*. New York: Guilford Press, 144–73.

Derbyshire, S. W. G. 1997: Sources of variation in assessing male and female responses to pain. *New Ideas in Psychology*, 15, 83–95.

Deutsch, C. K., Swanson, J. M., Bruell, J. H., Cantwell, D. P., Weinberg, F. & Baren, M. 1982: Overrepresentation of adoptees in children with the attention deficit disorder. *Behavioural Genetics*, 12, 231–8.

Dishion, T. J., French, D. C. & Patterson, G. R. 1995: The development and ecology of antisocial behavior. In D. Cicchetti & D. J. Cohen (eds), *Developmental Psychopathology, vol. 2: Risk, Disorder and Adaptation*. New York: Wiley, 421–71.

Dodge, K. A. 1991: The structure and function of reactive and proactive aggression. In D. J. Pepler & K. H. Rubin (eds), *The Development and Treatment of Childhood Aggression*. Hillsdale, NJ: Lawrence Erlbaum Associates, 201–18.

Donnai, D. & Karmiloff-Smith, A. 2000: Williams syndrome: from genotype through to the cognitive phenotype. *American Journal of Medical Genetics*, 97, 164–71.

Douglas, V. I. & Parry, P. A. 1994: Effects of reward and nonreward on frustration and attention in attention deficit disorder. *Journal of Abnormal Child Psychology*, 22, 281–302.

Douglas, V. I. & Peters, K. G. 1979: Toward a clearer definition of the attentional deficit of hyperactive children. In G. A. Hale & M. Lewis (eds), *Attention and the Development of Cognitive Skills*. New York: Plenum Press, 173–247.

Duncan, J. 1986: Consistent and varied training in the theory of automatic and controlled information processing. *Cognition*, 23, 279–84.

Ehri, L. C. 1984: How orthography alters spoken language competencies in children learning to read and spell. In J. Downing & R. Valtin (eds), *Language Awareness and Learning to Read*. New York: Springer-Verlag, 119–47.

Eskes, G. A., Bryson, S. E. & McCormick, T. A. 1990: Comprehension of concrete and abstract words in autistic children. *Journal of Autism and Developmental Disorders*, 20, 61–73.

Farmer, M. E. & Klein, R. 1993: Auditory and visual temporal processing in dyslexic and normal readers. *Annals of the New York Academy of Sciences*, 682, 339–41.

Fawcett, A., Nicolson, R. & Dean, P. 1996: Impaired performance of children with dyslexia on a range of cerebellar tasks. *Annals of Dyslexia*, 46, 259–83.

Fergusson, D. M. & Horwood, L. J. 1992: Attention deficit and reading achievement. *Journal of Child Psychology and Psychiatry*, 33, 375–85.

Fife-Shaw, C. 2000: Introduction to structural equation modelling. In G. M. Breakwell, S. Hammond & C. Fife-Shaw (eds), *Research Methods in Psychology*, 2nd edn. London: Sage, 397–413.

Fisher, S. E. & DeFries, J. C. 2002: Developmental dyslexia: genetic dissection of a complex cognitive trait. *Nature Reviews Neuroscience*, 3, 767–80.

Fowler, L. N. 1895: *Fowler's Self Instructor in Phrenology and Physiology*, 20th edn. London: Fowler.

Frederickson, N. & Cline, T. 2002: *Special Educational Needs, Inclusion and Diversity: a Textbook*. Buckingham: Open University Press.

Frick, P. J. 1998: *Conduct Disorders and Severe Antisocial Behavior*. New York: Plenum Press.

Frith, U. 1985: Beneath the surface of developmental dyslexia. In K. Patterson, M. Coltheart & J. Marshall (eds), *Surface Dyslexia*. London: Lawrence Erlbaum Associates, 301–30.

Frith, U. 1989: *Autism: Explaining the Enigma*. Oxford: Blackwell.

Frith, U. 2003: *Autism: Explaining the Enigma*, 2nd edn. Oxford: Blackwell.

Frith, U. & Snowling, M. 1983: Reading for meaning and reading for sound in autistic and dyslexic children. *British Journal of Developmental Psychology*, 1, 329–42.

Frith, U., Morton, J. & Leslie, A. M. 1991: The cognitive basis of a biological disorder: autism. *Trends in Neurosciences*, 14, 433–8.

Fulton, M., Raab, G., Thomson, G., Laxen, D., Hunter, R. & Hepburn, W. 1987: Influence of blood lead on the ability and attainment of children in Edinburgh. *The Lancet*, 1, 1221–6.

Gaffney, G. R., Kuperman, S., Tsai, L. Y. & Minchin, S. 1989: Forebrain structure in infantile autism. *Journal of the American Academy of Child and Adolescent Psychiatry*, 28, 534–7.

Galaburda, A. M. 1989: Ordinary and extraordinary brain development: anatomical variation in developmental dyslexia. *Annals of Dyslexia*, 39, 67–80. The Orton Dyslexia Society.

Galaburda, A. M. & Livingstone, M. 1993: Evidence for a magnocellular defect in developmental dyslexia. *Annals of the New York Academy of Sciences*, 682, 70–82.

Galaburda, A. M., Rosen, G. D. & Sherman, G. F. 1989: The neural origin of developmental dyslexia: implications for medicine, neurology and cognition. In A. M. Galaburda (ed.), *From Reading to Neurons*. Cambridge, MA: The MIT Press, 377–88.

Gallese, V. 1999: Actions, faces, objects and space: how to build a neurobiological account of the self. In *Proceedings of the III Conference of the Association for the Scientific Study of Consciousness (ASSC)*.

Gallese, V., Fadiga, L., Fogassi, L. & Rizzolatti, G. 1996: Action recognition in the premotor cortex. *Brain*, 119, 593–609.

Geschwind, N. & Galaburda, A. 1985: Cerebral lateralization: biological mechanisms, associations and pathology, part I: a hypothesis and programme for research. *Archives of Neurology*, 42, 428–59.

Gilbertson, M. W., Shenton, M. E., Ciszewski, A., Kasai, K., Lasko, N. B., Orr, S. P. & Pitman, R. K. 2002: Smaller hippocampal volume predicts pathologic vulnerability to psychological trauma. *Nature Neuroscience*, 5, 1242–7.

Gillberg, C. 1992: Autism and autistic-like conditions: subclasses among disorders of empathy. *Journal of Child Psychology and Psychiatry*, 33, 813–42.

Goswami, U. 1986: Children's use of analogy in learning to read: a developmental study. *Journal of Experimental Child Psychology*, 42, 73–83.

Goswami, U. 1990: A special link between rhyming skills and the use of orthographic analogies by beginning readers. *Journal of Child Psychology and Psychiatry*, 31, 301–11.

Gough, P. B. & Tunmer, W. E. 1986: Decoding, reading and reading disability. *Remedial and Special Education*, 7, 6–10.

Gray, G., Smith, A. & Rutter, M. 1980: School attendance and the first year of employment. In L. Hersov & I. Berg (eds), *Out of School: Modern Perspectives in Truancy and School Refusal*. Chichester: Wiley, 343–70.

Happé, F. G. 1995: The role of age and verbal ability in the theory of mind task performance of subjects with autism. *Child Development*, 66, 843–55.

Happé, F. 2000: Parts and wholes, meanings and minds: Central Coherence and its relation to theory of mind. In S. Baron-Cohen, H. Tager-Flusberg & D. Cohen (eds), *Understanding Other Minds: Perspectives from Autism and Developmental Cognitive Neuroscience*, 2nd edn. Oxford: Oxford University Press, 203–21.

Happé, F. 2001: Social and non-social development in autism: Where are the links? In Burack, J. A., Charman, T., Yirmia, N. & Zelazo, P. R. (eds), *Development in Autism: Perspectives from Theory and Research*. Mahwah, NJ: Lawrence Erlbaum Associates.

Happé, F. & Frith, U. 1995: Theory of mind in autism. In E. Schopler & G. B. Mesibov (ed.), *Learning and Cognition in Autism*. New York: Plenum Press, 177–97.

Happé, F. & Frith, U. 1996: The neuropsychology of autism. *Brain*, 119, 137–400.

Harcherik, D. F., Cohen, D. J., Ort, S., Paul, R., Shaywitz, B. A., Volkmar, F. R., Rothman, S. L. & Leckman, J. F. 1985: Computed tomographic brain scanning in four neuropsychiatric disorders of childhood. *American Journal of Psychiatry*, 142, 731–4.

Hari, R., Renvall, H. & Tanskanen, T. 2001: Left minineglect in dyslexic adults. *Brain*, 124, 1373–80.

Hartsough, C. S. & Lambert, N. M. 1982: Some environmental and familial correlates and antecedents of hyperactivity. *American Journal of Orthopsychiatry*, 52, 272–87.

Hauser, S. L., DeLong, G. R. & Rosman, N. P. 1975: Pneumographic findings in the infantile autism syndrome. A correlation with temporal lobe disease. *Brain*, 98, 667–88.

Hermelin, B. & O'Connor, N. 1970: *Psychological Experiments with Autistic Children*. Oxford: Pergamon Press.

Herold, S., Frackowiak, R. S., Le Couteur, A., Rutter, M. & Howlin, P. 1988: Cerebral blood flow and metabolism of oxygen and glucose in young autistic adults. *Psychological Medicine*, 18, 823–31.

Hinshaw, S. P. 1987: On the distinction between attention deficits/hyperactivity and conduct problems/aggression in child psychopathology. *Psychological Bulletin*, 101, 443–63.

Hobson, R. P. 1989: Beyond cognition: a theory of autism. In G. Dawson (ed.), *Autism: Nature, Diagnosis and Treatment*. New York: Guilford Press, 22–48.

Hobson, R. P. 1990: On acquiring knowledge about people, and the capacity to pretend: a response to Leslie 1987: *Psychological Review*, 97, 114–21.

Hobson, R. P. 1993: *Autism and the Development of Mind*. Hove, UK: Lawrence Erlbaum Associates.

Hobson, R. P. & Bishop, M. 2003: The pathogenesis of autism: insights from congenital blindness. *Philosophical Transactions of the Royal Society*, 358, 335–44.

Hobson, R. P., Lee, A. & Brown, R. 1999: Autism and congenital blindness. *Journal of Autism and Developmental Disorders*, 29, 45–56.

Hohmann, G. W. 1962: Some effects of spinal chord lesions on experienced emotions. *Psychophysiology*, 3, 143–56.

Horwitz, B., Rumsey, J. M., Grady, C. L. & Rapoport, S. I. 1988: The cerebral metabolic landscape in autism. Intercorrelations of regional glucose utilization. *Archives of Neurology*, 45, 749–55.

Hughes, C. & Russell, J. 1993: Autistic children's difficulty with mental disengagement from an object: its implications for theories of autism. *Developmental Psychology*, 29, 498–510.

Hughes, C., Russell, J. & Robbins, T. W. 1994: Evidence for executive dysfunction in autism. *Neuropsychologia*, 32, 477–92.

Hulme, C. & Roodenrys, S. 1995: Practitioner review: verbal working memory development and its disorders. *Journal of Child Psychology and Psychiatry*, 36, 373–98.

Hynd, G. W. & Semrud-Clikeman, M. 1989: Dyslexia and brain morphology. *Psychological Bulletin*, 106, 447–82.

Jackson, N. & Coltheart, M. 2001: *Routes to Reading Success and Failure*. Hove: Psychology Press.

Johnson, M. & Morton, J. 1991: *Biology and Cognitive Development: the Case of Face Recognition*. Oxford: Blackwell.

Johnson, M., Siddons, F., Frith, U. & Morton, J. 1992: Can autism be predicted on the basis of infant screening tests? *Developmental Medicine and Child Neurology*, 34, 314–20.

Johnston, R. S. 1982: Phonological coding in dyslexic readers. *British Journal of Psychology*, 73, 455–60.

Kaler, S. R., & Kopp, C. B. 1990: Compliance and comprehension in very young toddlers. *Child Development*, 61, 1997–2003.

Kanner, L. 1943: Autistic disturbances of affective contact. *Nervous Child*, 2, 217–50.

Karmiloff-Smith, A., Tyler, L. K., Voice, K., Sims, K., Udwin, O., Howlin, P. & Davies, M. 1998: Linguistic dissociations in Williams syndrome: evaluating receptive syntax in on-line and off-line tasks. *Neuropsychologia*, 36, 343–51.

Kolvin, I., Miller, F. J. W., Scott, D. M., Gatzanis, S. R. M. & Fleeting, M. 1990: *Continuities of Deprivation?* Aldershot: Avebury.

Kraemer, H. C., Kazdin, A. E., Offord, D. R., Kessler, R. C., Jensen, P. S. & Kupfer, D. J. 1997: Coming to terms with the terms of risk. *Archives of General Psychiatry*, 54, 337–43.

Krol, N., Morton, J. & De Bruyn, E. 2004: Theories of conduct disorder: a Causal Modelling analysis. *Journal of Child Psychology and Psychiatry*, 45, 727–42.

Lahey, B. B., Schaughency, E. A., Hynd, G. W., Carlson, C. L. & Nieves, N. 1987: Attention deficit disorder with and without hyperactivity: comparison of behavioral characteristics of clinic-referred children. *Journal of the American Academy of Child and Adolescent Psychiatry*, 26, 718–23.

Landerl, K., Wimmer, H. & Frith, U. 1997: The impact of orthographic constancy on dyslexia: a German–English comparison. *Cognition*, 63, 315–34.

Lenel, J. C. & Cantor, J. H. 1981: Rhyme recognition and phonemic perception in young children. *Journal of Psycholinguistic Research*, 10, 57–68.

Leon, P. E., Raventos, H., Lynch, E., Morrow, J. & King, M. C. 1992: The gene for an inherited form of deafness maps to chromosome 5q31. *Proceedings of the National Academy of Science, USA*, 89, 5181–4.

Leslie, A. M. 1987: Pretense and representation: the origins of 'theory of mind'. *Psychological Review*, 94, 412–26.

Leslie, A. M. & Frith, U. 1987: Metarepresentation and autism: how not to lose one's marbles. *Cognition*, 27, 291–4.

Leslie, A. M. & Frith, U. 1990: Prospects for a cognitive neuropsychology of autism: Hobson's choice. *Psychological Review*, 97, 122–31.

Leslie, A. M. & Happé, F. 1989: Autism and ostensive communication: the relevance of metarepresentation. *Development and Psychopathology*, 1, 205–12.

Liberman, I., Liberman, A. M., Mattingley, I. & Shankweiler, D. 1980: Orthography and the beginning reader. In J. F. Kavanagh & R. I. Venezky (eds), *Orthography, Reading and Dyslexia*. Baltimore, MD: University Park Press, 137–53.

Livingstone, M. S., Rosen, G. D., Drislane, F. W. & Galaburda, A. M. 1991: Physiological and anatomical evidence for a magnocellular deficit in developmental dyslexia. *Proceedings of the National Academy of Science, USA*, 88, 7943–7.

Lovegrove, W., Garzia, R. P. & Nicholson, S. B. 1990: Experimental evidence for a transient system deficit in specific reading disability. *Journal of the American Optometric Association*, 61, 137–46.

Lueger, R. J. & Gill, K. J. 1990: Frontal lobe cognitive dysfunction in conduct disorder adolescents. *Journal of Clinical Psychology*, 46, 696–706.

Luk, S. L., Leung, P. W. & Lee, P. L. 1988: Conners' Teacher Rating Scale in Chinese children in Hong Kong. *Journal of Child Psychology and Psychiatry*, 29, 165–74.

Lundberg, I., Frost, J. & Peterson, O. 1988: Effects of an extensive program for stimulating phonological awareness in preschool children. *Reading Research Quarterly*, 23, 263–84.

Luria, A. R. 1961: *The Role of Speech in the Regulation of Normal and Abnormal Behavior*. New York: Basic Books.

Marcus, G. 2004: *The Birth of the Mind: How a Tiny Number of Genes Creates the Complexity of the Human Mind*. New York: Basic Books.

McCrory, E., Mechillo, A., Frith, U. & Price, C. J. in press: More than words: the neurocognitive basis of naming deficits in developmental dyslexia.

Mehler, J., Morton, J. & Jusczyk, P. W. 1984: On reducing language to biology. *Cognitive Neuropsychology*, 1, 83–116.

Meltzoff, A. & Gopnik, A. 1993: The role of imitation in understanding persons and developing a theory of mind. In S. Baron-Cohen, H. Tager-Flusberg & D. Cohen (eds), *Understanding Other Minds: Perspectives from Autism*. Oxford: Oxford University Press, 335–66.

Metcalf, J. & Jacobs, W. J. 1998: Emotional memory: the effects of stress on cool and hot memory systems. In D. L. Medin (ed.), *The Psychology of Learning and Motivation*. Advances in Research and Theory, 38. New York: Academic Press, 187–222.

Miles, T. R. 1983: *Dyslexia: the Pattern of Difficulties*. London: Granada.

Miles, T. R. 1993: *Dyslexia: the Pattern of Difficulties*, 2nd edn. London: Whurr.

Miles, T. & Haslum, M. 1986: Dyslexia: anomaly or normal variation. *Annals of Dyslexia*, 36, 103–17.

Minter, M., Hobson, R. P., & Bishop, M. 1998: Congenital visual impairment and 'theory of mind'. *British Journal of Developmental Psychology*, 16, 183–96.

Mitchell, D. & Blair, R. J. R. 2000: State of the art: psychopathy. *Psychologist*, 13, 356–60.

Moffitt, T. E. 1990: Juvenile delinquency and attention-deficit disorder: developmental trajectories from age three to fifteen. *Child Development*, 61, 893–910.

Moffitt, T. E. 1993: Adolescence-limited and life-course-persistent antisocial behavior: a developmental taxonomy. *Psychological Review*, 100, 674–701.

Moffitt, T. E., Caspi, A., Harrington, H. & Milne, B. J. 2002: Males on the life-course-persistent and adolescence-limited antisocial pathways: follow-up at age 26 years. *Developmental Psychopathology*, 14, 179–207.

Monsell, S. 1987: On the relation between lexical input and output pathways for speech. In A. Allport, D. G. Mackay, W. Prinz & E. Scheerer (eds), *Language Perception and Production: Relationships between Listening, Speaking, Reading, and Writing*. London: Academic Press, 273–311.

Morais, J. 1991: Metaphonological abilities and literacy. In M. J. Snowling & M. Thompson (eds), *Dyslexia: Integrating Theory and Practice*. London: Whurr, 95–107.

Morais, J., Cary, L., Alegria, J. & Bertelson, P. 1979: Does awareness of speech as a sequence of phones arise spontaneously? *Cognition*, 7, 323–31.

Morris, R. G., Downes, J. J., Sahakian, B. J., Evenden, J. L., Heald, A. & Robbins, T. W. 1988: Planning and spatial working memory in Parkinson's disease. *Journal of Neurology, Neurosurgury and Psychiatry*, 51, 757–66.

Morton, J. 1961: *Reading, Context and the Perception of Words*. PhD thesis, University of Reading.

Morton, J. 1964a: The effects of context on the visual duration threshold for words. *British Journal of Psychology*, 55, 165–80.

Morton, J. 1964b: A preliminary functional model for language behaviour. *International Audiology*, 3, 216–25.

Morton, J. 1969: Interaction of information in word recognition. *Psychological Review*, 76, 165–78.

Morton, J. 1979: Facilitation in word recognition: experiments causing change in the logogen model. In P. A. Kolers, M. E. Wrolstad & H. Bouma (eds), *Processing of Visible Language*. New York: Plenum Press.

Morton, J. 1981: Will cognition survive? *Cognition*, 10, 227–34.

Morton, J. 1986: Developmental contingency modelling: a framework for discussing the processes of change and the consequence of deficiency. In P. L. C. van Geert (ed.), *Theory Building in Developmental Psychology*. Amsterdam: North Holland–Elsevier, 141–65.

Morton, J. 1989: An information-processing account of reading acquisition. In A. M. Galaburda (ed.), *From Reading to Neurons*. Cambridge, MA: The MIT Press, 43–65.

Morton, J. & Bekerian, D. A. 1986: Three ways of looking at memory. In N. E. Sharkey (ed.), *Advances in Cognitive Science*, vol. I. Chichester: Ellis Horwood, 43–71.

Morton, J. & Frith, U. 1993a: What lesson for dyslexia from Down's syndrome? Comments on Cossu, Rossini and Marshall. *Cognition*, 48, 289–96.

Morton, J. & Frith, U. 1993b: Approche de la dyslexie developpementale par la modelisation causale. In J.-P. Jaffré (ed.), *Les Actes de la Villette*. Paris: Nathan.

Morton, J. & Frith, U. 1995: Causal modelling: A structural approach to developmental psychopathology. In D. Cicchetti & D. J. Cohen (eds), *Developmental Psychopathology*, vol. 1: *Theory and Methods*. New York: Wiley, 357–90.

Morton, J. & Frith, U. 2002: Why we need cognition: cause and developmental disorder. In E. Dupoux, S. Dehane & L. Cohen (eds), *Cognition: a Critical Look. Advances, Questions and Controversies in Honour of J. Mehler*. Cambridge, MA: The MIT Press, 263–78.

Morton, J. & Patterson, K. 1980: A new attempt at an interpretation, or, an attempt at a new interpretation. In M. Coltheart, K. Patterson & J. C. Marshall (eds), *Deep Dyslexia*. London: Routledge and Kegan Paul, 91–118.

Morton, J., Hammersley, R. H. & Bekerian, D. A. 1985: Headed records: a model for memory and its failures. *Cognition*, 20, 1–23.

Mundy, P., Sigman, M. & Kasari, C. 1990: A longitudinal study of joint attention and language development in autistic children. *Journal of Autism and Developmental Disorders*, 20, 115–28.

Mundy, P., Sigman, M., Ungerer, J. & Sherman, T. 1986: Defining the social deficit of autism: the contribution of non-verbal communication measures. *Journal of Child Psychology and Psychiatry*, 27, 657–69.

Nicolson, R. & Fawcett, A. 1995: Dyslexia is more than a phonological disability. *Dyslexia*, 1, 19–36.

Nicolson, R., Fawcett, A. & Dean, P. 2001: Developmental dyslexia: the cerebellar deficit hypothesis. *Trends in Neurosciences*, 24, 508–11.

Nunn, K. P., Lask, B. & Cohen, M. 1986: Viruses, neurodevelopmental disorder and childhood psychosis. *Journal of Child Psychology and Psychiatry*, 27, 55–64.

Olson, R. K., Wise, B., Conners, F. & Rack, J. 1990: Organization, heritability and remediation of component word recognition and language skills in disabled readers. In T. H. Carr & B. A. Levy (eds), *Reading and its Development: Component Skills Approaches*. New York: Academic Press, 261–322.

Olson, R. K., Wise, B., Conners, F., Rack, J. & Fulker, D. 1989: Specific deficits in component reading and language skills: genetic and environmental influences. *Journal of Learning Disabilities*, 22, 339–48.

Ozonoff, S. & Jensen, J. 1999: Brief report: specific executive function profiles in three neurodevelopmental disorders. *Journal of Autism and Developmental Disorders*, 29, 171–7.

Ozonoff, S., Pennington, B. F. & Rogers, S. J. 1991: Executive function deficits in high-functioning autistic individuals: relationship to theory of mind. *Journal of Child Psychology and Psychiatry*, 32, 1081–105.

Pantelis, C., Nelson, H. E. & Barnes, T. R. E. (eds) 1996: *Schizophrenia: a Neuropsychological Perspective*. London: Wiley.

Patterson, G., Reid, J. & Dishion, T. 1992: *Antisocial Boys*. Eugene, OR: Castalia.

Patterson, K. E. 1981: Neuropsychological approaches to the study of reading. *British Journal of Psychology*, 72, 151–74.

Paulesu, E., Démonet, J.-F., Fazio, F., McCrory, E., Chanoine, V., Brunswick, N., Cappa, S. F., Cossu, G., Habib, M., Frith, C. D. & Frith, U. 2001: Dyslexia: cultural diversity and biological unity, *Science*, 291, 2165–7.

Pennington, B. F. 1989: Using genetics to understand dyslexia. *Annals of Dyslexia*, 39, 81–93. The Orton Dyslexia Society.

Pennington, B. F., Rogers, S. J., Bennetto, L., Griffith, E. M., Reed, D. T. & Shyu, V. 1997: Validity tests of the executive dysfunction hypothesis of autism. In J. Russell (ed.), *Autism as an Executive Disorder*. Oxford: Oxford University Press, 143–78.

Perfetti, C. A. 1991: Representations and awareness. In L. Rieben & C. A. Perfetti (eds), *Learning to Read: Basic Research and its Implications*. Hillsdale, NJ: Lawrence Erlbaum Associates, 33–44.

Piven, J. 1990: The biological basis of autism. *Current Opinion in Neurobiology*, 7, 708–12.

Plomin, R., DeFries, J. C., McClearn, G. E. & McGuffin, P. 2000: *Behavioural Genetics*, 4th edn. New York: Wiley.

Plomin, R., Hill, L., Craig, I. W., McGuffin, P., Purcell, S., Sham, P., Lubinski, D., Thompson, L. A., Fisher, P. J., Turic, D. & Owen, M. J. 2001: A genome-wide scan of 1842 DNA markers for allelic associations with general cognitive ability: a five-stage design using DNA pooling and extreme selected groups. *Behavioural Genetics*, 31, 497–509.

Poeck, K., De Bleser, R. & von Keyserlingk, D. G. 1984: Neurolinguistic status and localization of lesion in aphasic patients with exclusively consonant-vowel recurring utterances. *Brain*, 107, 199–217.

Posner, M. I. & Carr, T. H. 1992: Lexical access and the brain: anatomical constraints on cognitive models of word recognition. *American Journal of Psychology*, 105, 1–26.

Premack, D. & Woodruff, G. 1978: Does the chimpanzee have a theory of mind? *Behavioral and Brain Sciences*, 4, 515–26.

Prior, M. R. 1989: Reading disability: 'normative' or 'pathological'. *Australian Journal of Psychology*, 41, 135–58.

Prior, M. R. & Hoffmann, W. 1990: Brief report: neuropsychological testing of autistic children through an exploration with frontal lobe tests. *Journal of Autism and Developmental Disorders*, 20, 581–90.

Quinton, R. & Rutter, M. 1988: *Parental Breakdown: the Making and Breaking of Intergenerational Links*. Aldershot: Gower.

Raberger, T. & Wimmer, H. 2003: On the automaticity/cerebellar deficit hypothesis of dyslexia: Balancing and continuous rapid naming in dyslexic and ADHD children. *Neuropsychologia*, 41, 1493–7.

Rack, J. P. 1994: Dyslexia: the phonological deficit hypothesis. In Fawcett, A. & Nicolson, N. (eds), *Dyslexia in Children: Multi-disciplinary Perspectives*. London: Harvester Wheatsheaf.

Rack, J. P., Snowling, M. & Olson, R. K. 1992: The nonword reading deficit in developmental dyslexia: a review. *Reading Research Quarterly*, 27, 29–53.

Ramus, F. 2001: Outstanding questions about phonological processing in dyslexia. *Dyslexia*, 7, 197–216.

Ramus, F. 2003: Developmental dyslexia: specific phonological deficit or general sensorimotor dysfunction? *Current Opinion in Neurobiology*, 13, 212–18.

Ramus, F. in press: A neurological model of dyslexia and other domain-specific developmental disorders with an associated sensorimotor syndrome. In G. D. Rosen (ed.), *Developing New Pathways in the Study of the Dyslexic Brain*. Baltimore, MD: York Press.

Ramus, F., Pidgeon, E. & Frith, U. 2003a: The relationship between motor control and phonology in dyslexic children. *Journal of Child Psychology and Psychiatry*, 44, 712–22.

Ramus, F., Rosen, S., Dakin, S. C., Day, B. L., Castellote, J. M., White, S. & Frith, U. 2003b: Theories of developmental dyslexia: insights from a multiple case study of dyslexic adults. *Brain*, 126, 841–65.

Reddy, V. 1991: Playing with others' expectations: teasing and mucking about in the first year. In A. Whiten (ed.), *Natural Theories of Mind: Evolution, Development and Simulation of Everyday Mindreading*. Oxford: Blackwell, 143–58.

Ritvo, E. R., Freeman, B. J., Scheibel, A. B., Duong, T., Robinson, H., Guthrie, D. & Ritvo, A. 1986: Lower Purkinje cell counts in the cerebella of four autistic subjects: initial findings of the UCLA–NSAC Autopsy Research Report. *American Journal of Psychiatry*, 143, 862–6.

Rizzolatti, G., Fadiga, L., Fogassi, L. & Gallese, V. 1996: Premotor cortex and the recognition of motor actions. *Cognition & Brain Research*, 3, 131–41.

Rizzolatti, G. & Fadiga, L. 1998: Grasping objects and grasping action meanings: the dual role of monkey rostroventral premotor cortex (area F5). In *Novatis Foundation Symposium 218: Sensory Guidance of Movement*. Chichester: Wiley, 81–103.

Rogers, S. J. & Pennington, B. F. 1991: A theoretical approach to the deficits in infantile autism. *Development and Psychopathology*, 3, 137–62.

Ruffman, T., Perner, J. & Parkin, L. 1999: How parenting style affects false belief understanding. *Social Development*, 8, 395–411.

Rumsey, J. M. & Hamburger, S. D. 1988: Neuropsychological findings in high-functioning men with infantile autism, residual state. *Journal of Clinical and Experimental Neuropsychology*, 10, 201–21.

Russell, J. 1996: *Agency: its Role in Mental Development*. Hove, UK: Lawrence Erlbaum Associates/London: Taylor & Francis.

Russell, J. 1997: How executive disorders can bring about an adequate 'theory of mind'. In J. Russell (ed.), *Autism as an Executive Disorder*. Oxford: Oxford University Press, 250–304.

Russell, J. 2002: Cognitive theories of autism. In J. E. Harrison & A. M. Owen (eds), *Cognitive Deficits in Brain Disorders*. London: Martin Dunitz, 295–323.

Rutter, M. 1978: Diagnostic validity in child psychiatry. *Advances in Biological Psychiatry*, 2, 2–22.

Rutter, M. 1989: Pathways from childhood to adult life. *Journal of Child Psychology and Psychiatry*, 30, 23–51.

Rutter, M. 2000: Genetic studies of autism: from the 1970s into the millennium. *American Journal of Psychiatry*, 157, 2043–5.

Rutter, M. & Yule, W. 1975: The concept of specific reading retardation. *Journal of Child Psychology and Psychiatry*, 16, 181–97.

Rutter, M., Graham, P. & Yule, W. 1970: *A Neuropsychiatric Study in Childhood*. Clinics in Developmental Medicine, nos. 35/36. London: SIMP with Heinemann.

Rutter, M., Shaffer, D. & Sturge, C. 1975: *A Guide to a Multi-axial Classification Scheme for Psychiatric Disorders in Childhood and Adolescence*. London: Institute of Psychiatry.

Rutter, M., Tizard, J. & Whitmore, K. (eds) 1970: *Education, Health and Behaviour*. London: Longman.

Rutter, M., Tizard, J., Yule, W., Graham, P. & Whitmore, K. 1976: Research report: Isle of Wight studies 1964–1976. *Psychological Medicine*, 6, 313–32.

Rutter, M., Macdonald, H., Le Couteur, A., Harrington, R., Bolton, P. & Bailey, A. 1990: Genetic factors in child psychiatric disorders – II. Empirical findings. *Journal of Child Psychology and Psychiatry*, 31, 39–83.

Sandberg, S. T. 1996: Hyperkinetic or attention deficit disorder. *British Journal of Psychiatry*, 169, 10–17.

Sandberg, S. T., Rutter, M. & Taylor, E. 1978: Hyperkinetic disorder in psychiatric clinic attenders. *Developmental Medicine and Child Neurology*, 20, 279–99.

Scarborough, H. S. 1990: Very early language deficits in dyslexic children. *Child Development*, 61, 1728–43.

Schachar, R. 1991: Childhood hyperactivity. *Journal of Child Psychology and Psychiatry*, 32, 155–91.

Schachar, R., Rutter, M. & Smith, A. 1981: The characteristics of situationally and pervasively hyperactive children: implications for syndrome definition. *Journal of Child Psychology and Psychiatry*, 22, 375–92.

Schachar, R., Tannock, R., Marriott, M. & Logan, G. D. 1995: Deficient inhibitory control and attention deficit hyperactivity disorder. *Journal of Abnormal Child Psychology*, 23, 411–37.

Schulte-Korne, G. 2001: Annotation: genetics of reading and spelling disorder. *Journal of Child Psychology and Psychiatry*, 42, 985–97. Sergeant, J. A. & Scholten, C. A. 1985a: On data limitations in hyperactivity. *Journal of Child Psychology and Psychiatry*, 26, 111–24.

Sergeant, J. A. & Scholten, C. A. 1985b: On resource strategy limitations in hyperactivity: cognitive impulsivity reconsidered. *Journal of Child Psychology and Psychiatry*, 26, 97–109.

Sergeant, J. A. & Steinhausen, H. C. 1992: European perspectives on hyperkinetic disorder. *European Child and Adolescent Psychiatry*, 1, 34–41.

Seymour, P. H. K. 1990: Developmental dyslexia. In M. W. Eysenck (ed.), *Cognitive Psychology: an International Review*. Chichester: Wiley, 135–96.

Seymour, P. H. K. & Evans, H. M. 1992: Beginning reading without semantics: a cognitive study of hyperlexia. *Cognitive Neuropsychology*, 9, 89–122.

Shah, A. & Frith, U. 1983: An islet of ability in autistic children: a research note. *Journal of Child Psychology and Psychiatry*, 24, 613–20.

Shallice, T. 1981: Neurological impairment of cognitive processes. *British Medical Journal*, 37, 187–92.

Shallice, T. 1988: *From Neuropsychology to Mental Structure*. Cambridge: Cambridge University Press.

Shankweiler, D., Liberman, I. Y., Mark, L. S., Fowler, C. & Fischer, F. W. 1979: The speech code and learning to read. *Journal of Experimental Psychology: Human Learning and Memory*, 5, 531–45.

Siegel, L. S. 1988: Evidence that IQ scores are irrelevant to the definition and analysis of reading disability. *Canadian Journal of Psychology*, 42, 201–15.

Siegel, L. S. 1989: IQ is irrelevant to the definition of learning disabilities. *Journal of Learning Disabilities*, 22, 469–86.

Siegel, L. S. 1992: An evaluation of the discrepancy definition of dyslexia. *Journal of Learning Disabilities*, 25, 618–29.

Sigman, M. & Mundy, P. 1989: Social attachments in autistic children. *Journal of the American Academy of Child and Adolescent Psychiatry*, 28, 74–81.

Silberg, J., Rutter, M., Meyer, J., Maes, H., Hewitt, J., Simonoff, E., Pickles, A., Loeber, R. & Eaves, L. 1996: Genetic and environmental influences on the covariation between hyperactivity and conduct disturbance in juvenile twins. *Journal of Child Psychology and Psychiatry*, 37, 803–16.

Silva, P. A., Hughes, P., Williams, S. & Faed, J. M. 1988: Blood lead, intelligence, reading attainment and behaviour in eleven year old children in Dunedin, New Zealand. *Journal of Child Psychology and Psychiatry*, 29, 43–52.

Sims, K. & Morton, J. 1998: Modelling the training effects of kinaesthetic acuity measurement in children. *Journal of Child Psychology and Psychiatry*, 39, 731–46.

Smith, S. D., Kimberling, W. J., Pennington, B. F. & Lubs, H. A. 1983: Specific reading disability: identification of an inherited form through linkage analysis. *Science*, 219, 1345–7.

Snowling, M. 1987: *Dyslexia: a Cognitive Developmental Perspective.* Oxford: Blackwell.

Snowling, M. 1991: Developmental reading disorders. *Journal of Child Psychology and Psychiatry*, 32, 49–77.

Snowling, M., Stackhouse, J. & Rack, J. 1986: Phonological dyslexia and dysgraphia – a developmental analysis. *Cognitive Neuropsychology*, 34, 309–39.

Solanto, M. V., Abikoff, H., Sonuga-Barke, E., Schachar, R., Logan, G. D., Wigal, T., Hechtman, L., Hinshaw, S. & Turkel, E. 2001: The ecological validity of delay aversion and response inhibition as measures of impulsivity in AD/HD: a supplement to the NIMH multimodal treatment study of AD/HD. *Journal of Abnormal Child Psychology*, 29, 215–28.

Sonuga-Barke, E. J. S. 2002: Psychological heterogeneity in AD/HD: a dual pathway model of behaviour and cognition. *Behavioural Brain Research*, 130, 29–36.

Sonuga-Barke, E. J. S., Taylor, E. & Heptinstall, E. 1992a: Hyperactivity and delay aversion – II. The effect of self versus externally imposed stimulus presentation periods on memory. *Journal of Child Psychology and Psychiatry*, 33, 399–409.

Sonuga-Barke, E. J. S., Taylor, E., Sembi, S. & Smith, J. 1992b: Hyperactivity and delay aversion – I. The effect of delay on choice. *Journal of Child Psychology and Psychiatry*, 33, 387–98.

Stanovich, K. E. 1986: Matthew effects in reading: some consequences of individual differences in the acquisition of literacy. *Reading Research Quarterly*, 21, 360–407.

Stanovich, K. E. 1988: Explaining the differences between the dyslexic and the garden-variety poor reader: the phonological-core variable-difference model. *Journal of Learning Disabilities*, 21, 590–612.

Stanovich, K. E., Siegel, L. S., & Gottardo, A. 1997: Converging evidence for phonological and surface subtypes of reading disability. *Journal of Educational Psychology*, 89, 114–27.

Steffenburg, S. 1991: Neuropsychiatric assessment of children with autism: a population-based study. *Developmental Medicine and Child Neurology*, 33, 495–511.

Stein, J. F. 1991: Vision and language. In M. J. Snowling. & M. Thomson (eds), *Dyslexia: Integrating Theory and Practice.* London: Whurr, 31–43.

Stein, J. F. 1994: Developmental dyslexia, neural timing and hemispheric lateralisation. *International Journal of Psychophysiology*, 18, 241–9.

Stein, J. F. & Walsh, V. 1997: To see but not to read; the magnocellular theory of dyslexia. *Trends in Neurosciences*, 20, 147–52.

Stevenson, J., Graham, P., Fredman, G. & McLoughlin, V. 1987: A twin study of genetic influences on reading and spelling ability and disability. *Journal of Child Psychology and Psychiatry*, 28, 229–47.

Stevenson, J., Pennington, B. F., Gilger, J. W., DeFries, J. C. & Gillis, J. J. 1993: Hyperactivity and spelling disability: testing for shared genetic aetiology. *Journal of Child Psychology and Psychiatry*, 34, 1137–52.

Stuart, M. & Coltheart, M. 1988: Does reading develop in a sequence of stages? *Cognition*, 30, 139–81.

Sturge, C. 1982: Reading retardation and antisocial behaviour. *Journal of Child Psychology and Psychiatry*, 23, 21–31.

Swanson, J. M. & Kinsbourne, M. 1976: Stimulant-related state-dependent learning in hyperactive children. *Science*, 192, 1354–7.

Sykes, D. H., Douglas, V. I. & Morgenstern, G. 1973: Sustained attention in hyperactive children. *Journal of Child Psychology and Psychiatry*, 14, 213–20.

Szatmari, P. & Jones, M. B. 1991: IQ and the genetics of autism. *Journal of Child Psychology and Psychiatry*, 32, 897–908.

Szatmari, P., Boyle, M. & Offord, D. R. 1989: ADDH and conduct disorder: degree of diagnostic overlap and differences among correlates. *Journal of the American Academy of Child and Adolescent Psychiatry*, 28, 865–72.

Tallal, P. 1988: Developmental language disorders. In J. Kavanagh & T. Truss (eds), *Learning Disabilities: Proceedings from the National Conference*. Tarkton, MD: York Press, 181–272.

Tallal, P., Miller, S., Jenkins, B. & Merzenich, M. 1997: The role of temporal processing in developmental language-based learning disorders: research and clinical implications. In B. Blachman (ed.), *Foundations of Reading Acquisition and Dyslexia*. Mahwah, NJ: Lawrence Erlbaum Associates, 49–66.

Taylor, E. 1985: Syndromes of overactivity and attention deficit. In M. Rutter & L. Hersov (eds), *Child and Adolescent Psychiatry: Modern Approaches*, 2nd edn. Oxford: Blackwell Scientific, 424–43.

Taylor, E. 1986: Childhood hyperactivity. *British Journal of Psychiatry*, 149, 562–73.

Taylor, E. 1991: Developmental neuropsychiatry. *Journal of Child Psychology and Psychiatry*, 32, 3–47.

Taylor, E., Sandberg, S., Thorley, G. & Giles, S. 1991: *The Epidemiology of Childhood Hyperactivity*. Institute of Psychiatry, Maudsley Monograph. London: Oxford University Press.

Taylor, E., Schachar, R., Thorley, G., Wieselberg, H. M., Everitt, B. & Rutter, M. 1987: Which boys respond to stimulant medication? A controlled trial of methylphenidate in boys with disruptive behaviour. *Psychological Medicine*, 17, 121–43.

Thomas, M. S. & Karmiloff-Smith, A. 2002: Are developmental disorders like cases of adult brain damage? Implications from connectionist modelling. *Behavioural Brain Sciences*, 25, 727–50; discussion 750–87.

Thomas, M. S. & Karmiloff-Smith, A. 2003: Modeling language acquisition in atypical phenotypes. *Psychological Review*, 110, 647–82.

Thompson, R. A. 1999: Early attachment and later development. In J. Cassidy & P. Shaver (eds), *Handbook of Attachment: Theory, Research and Clinical Implications.* New York: Guilford Press, 265–86.

Tinbergen, N. & Tinbergen, E. A. 1983: *'Autistic' Children: New Hope for a Cure.* London: George Allen & Unwin.

Tizard, B. & Hodges, J. 1978: The effect of early institutional rearing on the development of eight year old children. *Journal of Child Psychology and Psychiatry,* 19, 99–118.

Treiman, R. & Hirsh-Pasek, K. 1985: Are there qualitative differences in reading behaviour between dyslexics and normal readers? *Memory and Cognition,* 13, 357–64.

Tsai, L. Y. 1989: Recent neurobiological findings in autism. In C. Gillberg (ed.), *Diagnosis and Treatment of Autism.* New York: Plenum Press, 83–104.

Tustin, F. 1981: *Autistic States in Children.* London: Routledge and Kegan Paul.

van der Meere, J., Stemerdink, N. & Gunning, B. 1995: Effects of presentation rate of stimuli on response inhibition in ADHD children with and without tics. *Perceptual and Motor Skills,* 81, 259–62.

Wellman, H. M. 1991: From desires to beliefs: acquisition of a theory of mind. In A. Whiten (ed.), *Natural Theories of Mind: Evolution, Development and Simulation of Everyday Mindreading.* Oxford: Blackwell, 19–38.

Welsh, M., Pennington, B. F., Ozonoff, S., Rouse, B. & McCabe, E. R. B. 1990: Neuropsychology of early-treated phenylketonuria: specific executive function deficits. *Child Development,* 61, 1697–713.

Whiten, A. 1991: *Natural Theories of Mind: Evolution, Development and Simulation of Everyday Mindreading.* Oxford: Blackwell.

Willcutt, E. G., DeFries, J. C., Pennington, B. F., Smith, S. D., Cardon, L. R. & Olson, R. K. 2003: Genetic etiology of comorbid reading difficulties and ADHD. In R. Plomin, I. Craig, J. C. DeFries & P. McGuffin (eds), *Behavioral Genetics in the Postgenomic Era.* Washington, DC: APA.

Wilson, J. Q. & Herrnstein, R. J. 1985: *Crime and Human Nature.* New York: Simon & Schuster (from Patterson et al. 1992).

Wimmer, H. & Perner, J. 1983: Beliefs about beliefs: representations and constraining function of wrong beliefs in young children's understanding of deception. *Cognition,* 13, 103–28.

Wimmer, H., Landerl, K., Linortner, R. & Hummer P. 1991: The relationship of phonemic awareness to reading acquisition: more consequence than precondition but still important. *Cognition,* 40, 219–49.

Wing, L. 1988: The autistic continuum. In L. Wing (ed.), *Aspects of Autism: Biological Research.* London: Gaskell and Royal College of Psychiatrists, v–viii.

Wing, L. & Gould, J. 1979: Severe impairments of social interaction and associated abnormalities in children: epidemiology and classification. *Journal of Autism and Developmental Disorders,* 9, 11–30.

Wolkind, S. & Rutter, M. 1985: Children who have been 'in care' – an epidemiological study. *Journal of Child Psychology and Psychiatry*, 14, 97–105.

World Health Organisation 1992: *The International Statistical Classification of Diseases and Related Health Problems*, 10th revision (ICD-10). Geneva.

Yule, W. & Rutter, M. 1985: Reading and other learning difficulties. In M. Rutter & L. Hersov (eds), *Child and Adolescent Psychiatry: Modern Approaches*, 2nd edn. Oxford: Blackwell Scientific, 444–64.

Name Index

Subject Index